CRANLE
LIE

GNOSTICIS

Beliefs and Pract

The Sussex Library of Religious Beliefs and Practices

This series is intended for students of religion, social sciences and history, and for the interested layperson. It is concerned with the beliefs and practices of religions in their social, cultural and historical setting. These books will be of particular interest to Religious Studies teachers and students at universities, colleges, and high schools. Inspection copies available upon request.

<u>Published</u>

The Ancient Egyptians   Rosalie David

Buddhism   Merv Fowler

Gnosticism   John Glyndwr Harris

Hinduism   Jeaneane Fowler

Humanism   Jeaneane Fowler

Islam   David Norcliffe

The Jews   Alan Unterman

Sikhism   W. Owen Cole and Piara Singh Sambhi

Zoroastrianism   Peter Clark

<u>In preparation</u>
The Diversity of Christianity Today   Diane Watkins
The Doctrine of the Trinity: God in Three Persons   Martin Downes
Death and Afterlife: An Introduction to Christian Eschatology
Tony Gray
You Reap What You Sow: Causality in the Religions of the World
Jeaneane Fowler
Christian Theology: The Spiritual Tradition   John Glyndwr Harris
Jainism   Lynn Foulston
Taoism   Jeaneane Fowler

<u>Forthcoming</u>   *Bhagavad Gita (a student commentary)*
Confucianism   *The Protestant Reformation: Tradition and
Practice*   *Zen*

Gnosticism

Beliefs and Practices

John Glyndwr Harris

sussex
A C A D E M I C
P R E S S

BRIGHTON • PORTLAND

2 4 6 8 10 9 7 5 3

Published 1999 in Great Britain by
SUSSEX ACADEMIC PRESS
Box 2950
Brighton BN2 5SP

and in the United States of America by
SUSSEX ACADEMIC PRESS
5804 N.E. Hassalo St.
Portland, Oregon 97213–3644

British Library Cataloguing in Publication Data
A CIP catalogue record for this book is available from the British Library.

Library of Congress Cataloging-in-Publication Data
Harris, J. Glyndwr (John Glyndwr)
Gnosticism : beliefs and practices / John Glyndwr Harris.
p. cm. — (The Sussex library of religious beliefs and practices)
Includes bibliographical references and index.
ISBN 1–902210–07–7 (alk. paper)
1. Gnosticism. I. Title. II. Series.
BT1390.H32 1999
299'.932—dc21 98–54190
CIP

Printed by Biddles Ltd, Guildford and King's Lynn
This book is printed on acid-free paper

Contents

Contents

Preface and Acknowledgements

Rather more than fifty years ago the discovery of the Nag Hammadi library instituted a new beginning to the study of gnosticism. The discovery is one of the most extensive manuscript finds of the twentieth century. It has taken years of editing and translating into modern languages and it was not until 1977 that the first complete edition was published with a second edition in 1988. Ever since, these texts have provided the agenda for the study of gnosticism and placed research into this esoteric system of knowledge on an entirely fresh footing.

The great importance of this new evidence soon became obvious, although no one knows for certain how this collection of texts was brought together or how they were transmitted. It is clear that they belonged to Christian gnostics but were rejected by the Catholic Church as heretical. The texts are variable in quality and length and represent a broad spectrum of gnostic authors and a multiplicity of modes of thought. There are Christian and non-Christian works among them and they posed such a threat to the Church that it was bound to take a stand against them and structure its own orthodoxy more formally. The questions the gnostics posed about the nature of deity and the meaning and destiny of life are basic to Christian theology and apologetics, and the Church was forced to take action on them. If this were not so it would be impossible to understand the Christological controversies of the early Christian centuries.

There is a certain unity between the texts which is the consequence of the convergence of interest in fundamental questions of human existence in a materialistic world and the hope of deliverance. Our interest in gnosticism is historical in the sense that the issues it raises are of perennial interest, and whilst there is no one phenomenon that can be called gnosticism it continues to be of fundamental significance to the continuing search for answers to life's most intriguing questions.

The main focus of the present work is on the texts themselves although there is an attempt to set "the gnostic phenomenon" in a wide cultural context by way of providing a background to the emergence of classical gnosticism in the early centuries of the Christian era. Quotations of the texts in English have been taken from a number of translations and these are acknowledged in the notes. Quotations from the Bible are from the Revised Standard Version unless otherwise stated.

I am indebted to a number of friends with whom I have discussed the questions raised by this fascinating subject. In particular I owe a tremendous debt to Dr Jeaneane Fowler of the University of Newport for her unfailing stimulus and encouragement. Without her advocacy and infectious enthusiasm for the printed word it is unlikely that I would have embarked on this work. I also express my sincere thanks to Alun and Sallie Vaughan for their painstaking help with the preparation of the manuscript and to Alun for his professional advice and patience with its production. However, any mistakes or blemishes are entirely my own. In the later stages of the production of this book I received advice from Anthony Grahame of Sussex Academic Press and to him also I express my gratitude.

The cover pictures are details from a Christian sarcophagus from fourth-centry Arles of the handing over of the keys. The sarcophagus shows Jesus washing the disciples' feet, Jesus the good shepherd and Jesus before Pilate, as well as other scenes. The gnostics assigned a significant place to Jesus in their system but they made a sharp distinction between the orthodox interpretation of the historical Jesus of Nazareth and their own phenomenon of the heavenly Christ. The author and publisher gratefully acknowledge AKG, London, The Arts and History Picture Library, for permission to reproduce Jesus Washes St. Peter's Feet (relief), and The Good Shepherd (relief).

Jesus said, I shall choose you, one out of a thousand and they stand (exist) as a single one and they with all become one.

The Gospel of Thomas

I pray that the beginning may come for you, for this I shall be capable of salvation since they will be enlightened through me by my faith, and through another (faith) that is better than mine.

The Apocryphon of James

Possessing the seals I will descend, all the aeons I will pass through, all the secrets will I reveal, the forms of the gods will I disclose, and the hidden things of the holy way which I have called knowledge (*gnosis*) will I impart.

Speech of the Naassenes (serpent people), preserved by Hippolytus

Once upon a time, Depth thought of emitting from himself a Beginning of all, like a seed, he deposited this projected emission, as in a womb, in that Silence who is with him. Silence recovered this seed and became pregnant and bore Mind, which resembled and was equal to him who emitted him.

The Pleroma in the Valentinian System of Ptolemaeus

1

The World of Gnosticism

Insofar as the study of gnosticism has made progress in recent times it is mainly due to the discovery in 1945 of a haul of gnostic or near-gnostic texts at Nag Hammadi in Upper Egypt. Any appreciation of gnosticism since then has to take account of these writings, which were published in an English version in 1977. Yet at the same time it has to be borne in mind that the study of gnosticism is not an isolated phenomenon, as it can only be rightly understood against a background that extends far and wide beyond the beginning of the Christian era. This background is furnished with different categories and types of *gnosis* across many ancient cultures, and, what is more, it illumines the situation which brought it into existence and kept it in being. That is to say, if we were to write a history of gnosticism it would have to account for its numerous forms and manifestations, and, what is equally important, assess them as they have come down to us through the ages. But the Nag Hammadi texts are the primary source of information and exert a direct influence upon any grasp of the nature and provenance of gnosticism in the early centuries of the Christian era.

The term *gnosis* has been associated with religious knowledge and divine mystery from antiquity. Its characteristic world of thought and perception testifies to the human quest for enlightenment on the dilemmas of life in a materialistic world and the means of release from it. It testifies also to the way individuals and groups have queried and challenged prevailing views of ultimate truth and reality in their search for fuller knowledge and illumination.

In one respect gnosticism stands for progressive or alternative ideas to those currently received, and in another the characteristic feature of all its manifestations is syncretism. That is, it accommodates a variety of modes of thought and insights, from the most mysterious and pro-found to the most magical and bizarre. Therefore it manifests itself in different ways that cannot be compressed into a neat or simple definition.

To study this manifold phenomenon means that we must orientate ourselves to a changing world of sophisticated ideas, complex philosophical concepts, pseudo-scientific formulae, as well as elaborate mythological themes and involved religious expositions. At some times gnosticism may appear a coherent system of collective identity, but at other times it seems to lack a unifying core of beliefs and practices. There is not, and perhaps we should not expect there to be, an unbroken thread of consistent and changeless knowledge that links together the manifold manifestations of mysterious *gnosis* from earliest times. There is within everyone a living world of reality that thrives on new and more expansive experiences which generate fresh insights and deeper understanding. Passive acquiescence to the *status quo* would only lead to mental and spiritual stagnation.

The study of gnosticism has a long history but at no stage does it present itself as a consolidated and coherent system of thought and ideas. On the contrary, its wide range and variety makes the study more fascinating but also surrounds it with uncertainty and controversy.

The world of gnosticism may be compared to a maze of winding pathways radiating out in different directions. The pathways carry us along an inner celestial journey that is sublime and mysterious. Each step throws up fresh ideas and insights into the diversified forms of secretive and esoteric *gnosis*. Sometimes these are clothed in religious and philosophical terms, at other times they are steeped in secret occult practices, exorcisms and miracles. Celsus, neither a gnostic sympathizer nor a Christian, castigated the gnostics of the second century CE as "exorcists and sorcerers", and Irenaeus, Bishop of Lyons (*c.*170–210), a vigorous opponent of gnosticism, ridiculed the gnostics as people who produced a new gospel every day. This could only be on account of the ingenuity and the vigour with which they propagated their ideas.

At the heart of *gnosis* there is mystery, the mystery of the divine secretive purpose for the world, the unfathomable mystery that is the essence of divinity. The gnostics conceived of this mystery in metaphysical and theosophical terms, as one whose veil is only penetrated by those who are spiritually "mature" and able to receive the revealing *gnosis*. This is the "higher" knowledge that elevates the spirit through enlightenment into the nature of God and his purpose. The theme of election, prevalent in Judaism and in orthodox Christianity, flourished amongst the gnostics, who believed in an elect elite who were capable of receiving special knowledge that pointed the way to perfect fulfilment.

In the gnostic *Gospel of Thomas* the doctrine of election is expressed in the words of Jesus:

> Jesus said, I shall choose you, one out of a thousand and they stand (exist) as a single one and they with all become one.[1]

This is entirely expressive of gnostic beliefs, the context is that of Jesus fulfilling the purpose of his coming into the world. He is often described instructing his disciples to attend "to those who are mine and now and not to strangers".

Gnosis and gnosticism

Until we have some kind of definition of *gnosis* or think ourselves into the meaning of this multi-faceted term, talk about it will lack a proper frame of reference. As far as we are able we need to draw from the term what this esoteric *gnosis* really is. Gnosticism is an established part of our western culture, and, as well as engaging its religious and philosophical dimension, we have a considerable interest in it as a formidable system of thought that came near to presenting an intellectual and spiritual alternative to apostolic Christianity. It developed its own distinctive ideology by concentrating on the "higher" *gnosis* as a condition of achieving salvation. It injected such a powerful vein of opposition into orthodox Christianity that, had it prevailed beyond the fourth century, then Christian civilization in the west might have taken a different form.

Gnosis is a Greek word of Indo-European origin. It is equivalent in meaning to the English word "knowledge", but it should not be used loosely or indiscriminately of knowledge in general. *Gnosis* is not discursive, analytical or abstract knowledge but "insight" into reality that is beyond the reach of normal intellectual understanding.

Its sphere is the transcendent realm that is unpervaded by intellect alone, the realm of mystery and the otherwise "unknowable". The gnostics or "those in the know" were continually receiving new insights or new levels of mysterious *gnosis*, but not in the sense of acquiring building materials to erect a permanent structure. The perceived *gnosis* was continually enriched with fresh insights which penetrated the existing *gnosis* with further dimensions of understanding, whilst maintaining a degree of continuity. Thus each new insight stimulated progression to the ultimate goal of existence, that is, union with God, the Supreme Being, and "seeing" the reality of everything that emanates from him. Beyond this perfect insight no further *gnosis* is possible.

Those who received such privileged knowledge met together in communities or schools of gnostics, and many such flourished in the lands around the Mediterranean in the early Christian centuries. They became identifiable groups which were known by different names, such as Sethians or Valentinians.[2] Their members took up distinctive functions and positions in mystical, contemplative and magical activities, and in religion and philosophy. They were all linked with a particular way of "knowing" and a distinctive lifestyle. The practices, like the beliefs, were partisan and Christian and non-Christian elements existed side by side.

But gnostics did not set out to constitute themselves into a church or an organization or a spiritual movement. Rather they saw themselves as the facilitators of those who aspired to realize the ultimate goal of existence. They clung to powers beyond those of the intellect alone to give meaning to present existence, problematic as it is, otherwise they would forfeit the power of *gnosis*. The *gnosis* embraced knowledge of the self as having a particular purpose, as is illustrated by the gnostic *Gospel of Truth*:

> When you come to know yourselves, as you will become known, and it is thus you will realise that it is you who are the sons of the living Father. But if you will not know yourselves, you will dwell in poverty, and you are that poverty.[3]

The contrast mentioned between "knowing" and "not knowing" is characteristic of the dualism that runs through the whole of gnosticism. The self that is "mature" enough to receive knowledge of the secret of liberation from the world of evil is surrounded by a sea of "unknowing" which keeps it submerged in evil. The "higher" *gnosis* alone is the guarantee of liberation.

The term gnosticism has only been in general use since the eighteenth century. It then came into use to describe a permanent movement of the second century CE.[4] Kurt Rudolph, the author of major works on gnosticism, has reported on the conclusions of the Congress on the Origins of Gnosticism held in 1966, which proposed that the term *gnosis* should be used of "knowledge of secrets which is reserved for the elite", but that gnosticism should be used for gnostic systems of the second and third centuries. Rudolph himself takes the view that we should understand by *gnosis* and gnosticism the same thing, the former as the self-description of a religion of redemption in late antiquity, the latter as a new form of it.[5] Today the term gnosticism is used in the main to describe a religious and philosphical movement that was motivated by a passion to find an answer to the human predicament, which is compounded by evil.

The term, then, is used of a movement centred around a deep inner yearning to know the secret of deliverance. The movement is not a "sociological entity",[6] but the use of the word "movement" is intended to indicate a process of developing wider vistas of reality on the way to full salvation. There is within such a process an implicit unity or self-revealing experience that is a foretaste of that all-consuming coming union between the human and the divine. In the words of the gnostic text:

> He who has known himself already comes to knowledge concerning the depth of All.[7]

We take it then that gnosticism may be used of a form of redemptive knowledge which is expressed through a complex speculative religious and philosophical movement. Its central core is a mysterious *gnosis* conveyed to a spiritual elite who are equipped to comprehend its origin, nature and purpose.

Gnosis and faith

The designation of *gnosis* and gnosticism as forms of redemptive knowledge implies that everything we say about it is geared to the means of obtaining the goal of redemption. Whether it be the gnostic view of the cosmos and its creator, its exploration of the human predicament or its path to liberation, the goal remains constant as "perfect salvation". How can we know for certain what is beyond the reach of the intellect and ordinary experience? Does reliance on this mystic knowledge rule out faith? Has faith a role in the gnostic philosophy?

According to Basilides, a controversial gnostic teacher:

> Faith is founded on knowledge, which may be defined as reason producing faith in what is disputed [by arguing] from what is admitted.[8]

Here knowledge is the antecedent of faith, it produces trust in what is admitted. Faith is the attitude of trust which knowledge engenders, and this thought too finds expression in the gnostic text of the *Sophia of Jesus Christ*:

> Whoever thus knows the Father in pure knowledge will depart to the Father [and repose in] Unbegotten Father.[9]

Faith reaches out to this union as it is directed by knowledge. Knowledge and faith have always co-existed in the history of religion, even though they have at times been set apart. Theologians and philosophers in the early Christian centuries used a variety of language and thought forms to explain the relation between them or to distinguish between them. Neither is incidental to salvation, for faith is rooted in the knowledge of *who* we are and *what* is believed. From knowledge comes the ability to discern and discriminate, to develop hypotheses and form views, and these in turn give reason for faith. Knowledge also gives understanding of things as they are in themselves, and so engenders trust and justification in the outreach of faith.

According to the gnostic *Testimony of Truth*, those

> upon entering the faith [i.e. Christianity] do so knowing that their baptism gives hope and is the seal of truth.[10]

The issue of faith and knowledge was highly contentious within the early church. There are echoes of this in the New Testament when Christians were urged to:

> turn a deaf ear to empty and worldly chatter, and the contradictions of so-called knowledge, for many who lay claim to it have shot far wide of the truth.[11]

The knowledge in view is *gnosis*, which is here reduced to "empty and worldly chatter" and "contradictions". Rather than enriching the understanding of the faith, or being seen in the gnostic sense as an antecedent of faith and opening the mind to absolute faith, it led those who practised it "wide of the truth". The orthodox saw it as harmful and devious, the cause of sin.[12] In the context of the epistle, the author pleads for a reconciliation between "faith and knowledge" and a return to orthodoxy (faith).

The issue continued to plague the Church in the second century, as the words of Clement of Alexandria indicate:

> Faith is then, so to speak, a compendious Knowledge of the essentials, and Knowledge is the strong and more demonstrative of what is believed by faith . . . And in my view, the first *saving* change is from that heathenism to faith, as I said before, and the second from faith to knowledge.[13]

Clement expresses the orthodox view of faith as paramount and this calls for change from "heathenism" (i.e. reliance on knowledge alone) to faith.

Faith is the antecedent of knowing and the substance of hope; from faith there comes knowledge of realities, of how the universe was fashioned and came to be, the certain assurance that God exists. The reward of faith is salvation.[14]

The question was obviously devisive, for Celsus accused Christians who relied on "faith alone" of anti-intellectualism, as he taunted them cynically, "Do not inquire, only believe".[15] But did the gnostics rule out the neccessity of faith? The question whether faith apart from knowledge can mislead is one that can be asked seriously in the light of the gnostics' unprecedented adherence to knowledge as the means of arriving at truth about God and reality. The question is further aggravated by whether the aim of the Christian apologist is to enhance faith or expound and elucidate truth. That the gnostics laid claim to a source of knowledge that transcends the intellect is well established, but like so much else in religion acceptance of its ultimate truth will always need a faith element to affirm its reality. This is the inner ascent of faith that is implied in the gnostic text, *Discourse on the Eighth and Ninth*:

> Whoever sees God as he is in every respect, or who would say that he is something like *gnosis*, has sinned against him . . . because he did know God.[16]

The view that gnosticism is a system of knowledge that can be studied and assessed like any other subject is mistaken. In fact, as we have yet to see, *gnosis* is knowledge received via revelation, and the object of this knowledge is God. He is conceivable through *gnosis*, but submission to perfect communion with him is the action of faith. Knowledge and faith may be closely connected: *gnosis* as the insight of seeing beyond the horizons of the intellect alone, faith as a responsive side of submission to God, the object of transcendent knowledge. Hence the prayer for those yet to be born, in the *Apocryphon of James*:

> I pray that the beginning may come for you, for thus I shall be capable of salvation since they will be enlightened through me by my faith, and through another (faith) that is better than mine.[17]

The true gnostic

Students of gnosticism have always acknowledged the incisive influence of *gnosis* upon the understanding of truth and have paid attention to the nature of gnostic beliefs. The whole gnostic method of operation assumes that it is possible and desirable to prejudice inclination and thought in the direction of specific aims and objectives and that it is justifiable to use knowledge as a means of strengthening and confirming them. The mind is moulded, under *gnosis*, into a particular shape and maturity until it is wholly fit for the reception of ultimate truth and the confident assurance and certainty of redemption.

It is informative at this point to refer to the descriptive portrait of Clement of Alexandria (*c.*215 CE) to which the title "The True Gnostic" has been given.[18] Clement is sometimes referred to as the father of Christian gnosticism, a leading member of the famous catechetical school of Alexandria and a philosopher of mystical tendencies, who presented Christianity in the style of Greek philosophy:

> He then who has first modified his passions and trained himself for impassibility, and developed the beneficence of gnostic perfection, is here equal to the angels. Luminous already, and like the sun shining in the exercise of beneficence, he speeds by righteous knowledge through the love of God to the holy mansion.[19]

To this portrait Clement also added an "introduction to the knowledge that is according to the mystic contemplation, in which we shall advance according to the renowned and the revered Rule of the Tradition . . . so that we may be ready to listen to the transmission of the Gnostic Tradition".[20]

This portrait introduces further fundamental aspects of a special gnostic kind of philosophy. The *gnosis* that Clement expounded is knowledge of a particular kind, which, together with faith, referred to earlier, he contended to be a valid means of attaining redemption. But Origen (d. 253/4), another of the Church Fathers, who displayed some gnostic tendencies, maintained that the way of salvation through knowledge is only for philosophers, whereas for the masses it is through faith.

Gnosis and revelation

How this mysterious knowledge is acquired and why it is significant are questions we must now address. Psychology offers an explanation of *how* the mind receives knowledge in general and how knowledge assimilates mind with object, but how is knowledge beyond the reaches of the mind received? Philosophy probes the question "what is knowledge?" and explores its domain and constituency of thought, but *what* is the essence of mysterious *gnosis*? Theology expounds the meaning of knowledge and verifies and evaluates the validity of knowledge, but *why* is revealed *gnosis* significant? How knowledge is received depends largely on the individual and on individualistic characteristics. Knowledge is given to the individual from an external source, it is not self-induced. Through the reception of this revealed knowledge the individual undergoes a mental transformation which, in the colourful words of Elaine Pagels, results in developing "an unclouded mind", the outlawing of "the changing testimony of the senses" and the "misleading judgement of the imagination".[21] This reference to "the changing testimony of the senses" indicates how unreliable the senses are and how they can only give "knowledge of acquaintance" and not "knowledge of a thing in itself". We can describe such knowledge or make assertions about it, but it is not *direct* knowledge of what is intrinsically true or real. Knowledge of truth or reality transcends the knowledge the senses give.[22]

Gnosis is knowledge received from revelation. In this context revelation refers to the disclosure by God of himself through self-communication or through emanations from himself. He is the source and revealer of *gnosis* and human beings are its recipients. When the intermediary of the revelation is the world of time and space then it is "natural" revelation, but when the revelation transcends this it is "supernatural" revelation. Either way the revelation is God's prerogative alone. For example, the *Gospel of Truth* states:

> the Father reveals what is hidden of him – what is hidden of him is his son – so that through the mercies of the Father the aeons may know him, and cease labouring in search of the Father.[23]

Revelation belongs to the category of divine intervention in the natural world from the supernatural realm where God reigns supreme. Such intervention is undertaken for the sake of exercising influence within the world, most notably in a redemptive way. Its medium is a chosen spiritual agent who descends to impart the revelation. Some gnostic writings provide details of the purpose of the revelation, which in the main is confined to the gnostics' own time and place. Revelation therefore is the direct source and substance of gnosticism. This is the teaching of the leading gnostic Valentinus, who, according to Irenaeus, taught about the Supreme Being by declaring:

> there is in invisible and ineffable heights a pre-existent aeon [i.e. supreme being] . . . who is inconceivable and invisible, eternal and uncreated.[24]

This needs to be read alongside the words of Basilides:

> when the whole universe and the supramundane were finished and lacked

nothing more . . . It was necessary for the abandoned Sonship to be revealed . . . it was still necessary to illumine the formless space where we live and to reveal the mystery not known to former generations.[25]

This revelation gave knowledge of "the mystery not known to former generations", that is, knowledge of redemption. *Gnosis* is revealed knowledge given to the elect through living experience. Revelation conveyed in the realm of history shaped a particular view of history, a gnostic approach to history that differed from their protagonists. This constituted an issue of discussion between them as the gnostics cultivated a powerful and emotive view whose core was *meaning* rather than verifiable factual historical data. This salient feature of gnosticism gives the impression of people bent on expounding the meaning of history from a salvationist perspective. The revelation imparted knowledge of the *meaning* of historical events.

It is "higher" knowledge of *what* revelation is given to the world of time and space. It erased the oblivion of ignorance, or "not knowing" the inner meaning of revelation whose purpose is to reveal the secret of redemption:

> What originates in Him is the knowledge that was revealed so that the oblivion should be diminished and they might know the Father. Full oblivion came into being because they did not know the Father, therefore they attain to a knowledge of the Father, oblivion becomes, at the same time, non-existent.[26]

Gnostics believed that they were conditioned to receive revelatory knowledge. Such revelation was comprehensible only to those who were "in the know" and spiritually equipped to receive it. It could only be received in the light of certain preconceptions, especially of genuine spirituality. To those who received it the revelation confirmed and verified absolute truth, and provided knowledge of reality. The revelation came to the recipients directly so as to create in everyone who received it a sense of "individual transcendence".[27] The revelation was known only within the self, it was a special disposition of God to the individual. Spiritual contemplation and meditation were conditions for receiving the revealed knowledge;[28] providing individuals were conditioned to receive such revelation it was mediated through dialogue and dream, through vision and conversation.[29] Belief that God endows believers with spiritual revelation of his own free will has always been a feature of religious belief.

In the second century orthodox Christians looked upon the historic revelation in Christ as the touchstone by which to verify the reality of divine intervention, whereas gnostics perceived the wonder of revealed knowledge as the means of illuminating the inner meaning of the Christ-event for contemporary experience.

According to gnosticism the primal revelation was that given to Adam, with whom humanity shares the same nature,[30] and Adam, the prototype of humankind, prefigures the characteristics of all who are descended from him. In the gnostic version of the myth of *Genesis* 3, Adam is said to have received the revelation of light and to be endowed with the Spirit (*pneuma*) which brought to him the gift of insight (*gnosis*) and the means of escape from the *archons*.[31] The primal revelation carried redemptive overtures that account for "the revelation which Adam taught his son Seth".

However, the primal revelation was not the end, for divine revelation is continuous and its knowledge and redeeming impact still continue to be transmitted. The speech of the so-called Naassenes (serpent people), preserved by Hippolytus, asserts how revelation is continuous:

> Possessing the seals I will descend, all the aeons I will pass through, all the secrets will I reveal, the forms of the gods will I disclose, and the hidden things of the holy way which I have called knowledge [*gnosis*] will I impart.[32]

This continuous revelation is a thread that links the ages through the dissemination of light and *gnosis* to direct the elect to the fullness of redemption. In consecutive ages there appeared a succession of redeemer figures who descended from the higher realms to be the vehicles of this revelation. Thus one age, to the next, is endowed with the revelation of *gnosis* to illumine the way to life's destiny. The primary revelation to the earthly Adam is the progenitor of the revelations that follow until the coming of the final redeemer or "Great Adam".[33]

The gnostic texts are ambivalent about the form of the revelation of the redeemer and there is no coherent definition of this. In one sense it is natural to suppose that the way of redemption is by full submission to the way of *gnosis*, escape from ignorance and the abandonment of evil. In another sense redemption is attained through the "saving" knowledge revealed in Jesus Christ. The *Gospel of Truth* expresses this in a forthright manner:

> That this is the gospel of him whom they seek, which Jesus the Christ revealed to the Perfect, thanks to the mercies of the Father, as a hidden mystery.[34]

From this excerpt it would seem that achieving salvation is dependent on the work of the saviour. The saviour is "revealed to the Perfect", that is, the gospel reveals how he descended for the sake of bringing salvation to those able to receive it. Through his descent he conveyed the "mercies of the Father", without himself being defiled by the world (nothing is said here about his nature). As he descended directly from the Father he projected his image as "a hidden mystery" knowing that he shared his divine essence.

Elsewhere we read that the innermost reality of the Saviour is spiritual and as this is revealed it transforms the recipient:

> you saw the spirit, you became spirit, you saw Christ, you became Christ, you saw (the Father, you) shall become the Father . . . you saw yourself, and what you see you shall become.[35]

The revelation did not cease at death. At the point of death the soul leaves the body to return to God; it ascends to the place of eternal light. There it dwells with God the Father and is regaled with a continuing revelation to give perfect knowledge of the self:

> For already then (the Plasma) the power, which is light, is coming to us. For I see: I see indescribable depths: I see another mind, the one that moves the soul . . . I see myself . . . I see a fountain bubbling with life.[36]

By following the gnostic path that leads to ultimate union with God the soul is then perfected to receive God's perfect revelation. The soul, the real self purified and detached from the physical body, now realizes its innermost perfection and is able to bear the full glow of divine revelation.

Gnosis and experience

To this general account of revelatory knowledge we may add reference to experience as the condition of being "knowledge possessed". Individuals achieve awareness of *gnosis* from experience not from rational argument. The mystical experience of the impact of *gnosis* brings illumination and verifies its presence. It embraces the total self to illumine the whole so that "the depth of all things" is made luminous.[37]

According to Valentinus, experience of *gnosis* heightens awareness of truth. Neither truth transmitted through tradition or credal statement can surpass the knowledge of truth received through experience. Experiential knowledge induces understanding of self and the world, and deepens knowledge of the divine within. It stimulates and directs the inner journey to God as it kindles the spark of light within that darkness cannot extinguish. It encounters or realizes the God within, it awakens the soul to God's immanent presence, and this embraces the whole spectrum of human moods, joy and sorrow, goodness and evil, freedom and bondage.

The gnostic experience diminishes the ravages of ignorance and replaces them with the insights of genuine enlightenment.[38] Furthermore, the experience deepens conviction of realities that surpass intellectual comprehension, and affirms the reality and meaning of what is beyond ordinary knowing. The gnostic who experiences the power of *gnosis* within also acquires a deepening and direct awareness of the source of this power, that is, of God. Therefore whoever explores human experience in depth is bound to encounter divine reality.

Only on the basis of experience could the gnostic know what it really means to be "in the know"; for this reason the primacy of experience is paramount, it is more potent than hearsay or external testimony.

The intuitive experience of revealed knowledge initiated the knower into the secrets of supernatural wisdom (*Sophia*). Through experience the gnostic has a foretaste of the wisdom that abides perfectly only in God. He is the source and revealer of wisdom and the experience of this gives entry to the "higher" state of knowing and to that celestial world bathed in perpetual light. The experience of wisdom is akin to the consuming experience of God or of the gift of his Spirit or of perfectly revealed truth. Wisdom is more than an attribute of the character of God, it is the personification of himself and his purpose. To experience his wisdom is equivalent to knowing his mind, it embraces understanding of his redemptive purpose. Whoever knows this is urged:

Entrust yourself to this one who became all for your care.[39]

Theodotus (148–60), a member of the Valentinian school, described the true gnostic as one who knows intuitively or one who has genuine insight into the destiny ahead. This gives superior knowledge of the supramundane that is, according to Basilides, the progenitor of the Logos who appeared on earth to release those in darkness to the light of the "higher" realm where all is transformed by "higher" *gnosis*.[40] This appeal to experience made gnosticism attractive to others, especially to those who found formalized statements of belief remote and unintelligible. It validated faith and gave direct access to God, it made the life of God more real and visible, so that, in the words of Valentinus, "humanity itself manifests the divine life". Experience is never static, it

is continuously the recipient of fresh revelations and new insights. This
accords well with the gnostic notion of continuous revelation.

This implies that there were certain people who were capable of such
transcendent experience. Of this Basilides seemed certain:

There is the inner man, the spiritual in the psyche.[41]

It is to this that experience of *gnosis* appealed, with the consequence:

When you come to know yourselves, then you will become known.[42]

or

He who knows himself, knows the All.[43]

This moment of self-illumination is also one of knowing what a
person is redeemed from and is now becoming. The illumination-like
experience is within:

There is a light within a man of light, and it lights up the whole world. If
it does not shine he is in darkness.[44]

Darkness is a synonym for disbelief and error, ignorance and uncertainty, alienation and disillusion. But,

when knowledge drew near . . . this is the downfall [of error] and all its
emanations – error is empty, having nothing inside.[45]

For the purpose of conveying this liberating and emancipating consequence of the gnostic experience the gnostics produced a body of
redemptive mythology centred on the person and divine agent of
redemption.[46]

Experience is seen as a gateway to redemption, and in the gnostic
perception it is the indisputable basis of metaphysical knowledge and
the justification of claiming to have knowledge beyond that of the ordinary. The experience is a spur to action on behalf of one's own salvation:

If you bring forth what is within you, what you bring forth will save
you.[47]

On this account the gnostic needed to be alert to the significance of the
experience and is urged:

Open the door for yourself that you may know what is.[48]

The gnostic texts repeat many times how the experience of *gnosis* is
comprised of thoughts, desires, emotions, sentiments and a great deal
more, and how the experience frees the recipient to act in particular

ways. The actions of gnostics diversified in many directions, but it is proper to note, in general terms, the trends of behaviour of those who experienced the impact of *gnosis*:

> He who has knowledge of the truth is a free man, but the free man does not sin, for "he who sins is a slave of sin". Truth is the mother, knowledge is the father . . . knowledge of the truth makes such people arrogant, which is what the words "it makes them free" mean. It gives them a sense of superiority over the whole world. But love builds up. In fact, he who is really free through knowledge is a slave.[49]

Whilst we might emphasize how much the gnostics valued intuitive and experiential knowledge, as they undoubtedly did, this was very personal and individualistic and cannot be interpreted in a straightforward way. As it is such a personal process we cannot tell how much internal struggle or resistance the experience brought, yet the evidence is of experience as a driving force behind an intense spiritual lifestyle spent in search of the inner surety of redemption.

Gnosis and initiation

In the early Christian centuries initiation into secret knowledge and practices was widely and variously practised. There is considerable evidence that gnostics had their own secret initiation ceremonies and esoteric practices, but these varied considerably. The initiation might be conducted by an individual in the way that Valentinus confessed to having been initiated into the secret *gnosis* at the hands of Theodus, a disciple of Paul.[50] In return Valentinus offered initiation to those who had reached the stage of maturity.[51] Initiation meant induction into deeper spiritual insight of the mysterious *gnosis*. The initiates could then comprehend its teachings in a new light and have a deeper share in its secrets. Of them the *Gospel of Truth* states:

> They are the sons who appear in truth, since they exist in time and eternal life and speak of the light which is perfect and filled with a need of the Father.[52]

Initiation was not automatic and was conditional on the initiate undergoing a period of preparation. The instructor or leader (*prostates*) played a key role but needed also to exercise particular skills and be knowledgeable about the characteristics of the gnostic community involved. Preparation was a time of serious contemplation and self-discipline on the part of the initiate in order to show fitness to receive and preserve the mysterious knowledge. There was no higher hierarchic structure or rigid pattern, but there was likely to be a time of meditation, of prayer and spiritual discipline, and the sublimation of physical passions and complete concentration on the spiritual quest. There seem to have been stages in initiation, for the Naassene *Exegesis* declares:

> It is a law that those who are initiated into the lesser mysteries should like to be initiated into the great ones.[53]

But the same work speaks of "perfect gnostics" as possessing knowledge of things only they themselves know:

> This means that no-one has been a hearer of these mysteries except the perfect gnostics alone.[54]

Initiation, therefore, was not a once for all process, for to reach the state of perfection meant progression into the greater mysteries:

> One ought to terminate the lesser and be initiated into the greater and heavenly ones . . . This is the gate of heaven and the house of God, where the Good God dwells alone, where no impure man enters, no psychic, no carnal.[55]

We may assume that initiation included strange mythology, occult practices and mysteries, as was appropriate to receiving secret knowledge of redemption. The mysteries were not a theological kind but inner experiences perceived through spiritual practices and divine revelation.[56]
The *Apocalypse of Peter* refers to this experience when Jesus is reputed to have said,

> Be strong, for you are the one to whom these mysteries have been given, to know them through revelation.[57]

The experience issued in "perfect knowledge of the Perfect", that is, knowledge of God, as the initiates,

> moving in proper order, they mount up to the Father, and yield themselves to the Powers, and having themselves become powers they enter into God. God is the blissful goal of all who possess knowledge.[58]

The "blissful goal of all those who possess knowledge" through initiation is echoed elsewhere within the gnostic writings, in such expressions as "the joy of new birth", "peace and contentment from alienation", "opening the mind to truth". This was the consequence of liberation from ignorance that "drove knowledge away" and kept the soul in a "state of worthlessness" and in the "corroding power of the abyss". Apuleius declared:

> The first cup of knowledge we receive from our preceptors removes entire ignorance.

Initiation was a transforming experience; as it was performed the initiate experienced a cleansing of character, the purging of ignorance, fear and terror, a transition from darkness to light, a symbolic death and resurrection to a new being. The initiate was released from the claims and restraints of the *demiurge* and the material world. But the supreme outcome of initiation was entry into the mysteries of God:

> Now in order that they might know what exists for them, he graciously forged the initial form, in order that they may recognise who is the Father who exists for them.[59]

Along with this "higher" knowledge the initiate acquired deeper insight of self-recognition:

> I am a son from the Father – the Father who is pre-existent . . . I derive from him who is pre-existent. I came again to my own place when I came forth.[60]

A further consequence of initiation was that the initiate acquired a new spiritual authority. Its spiritual nature released the gnostic from allegiance to any temporal authority to recognize only the authority of God. The initiated were free to meet without the presence of a bishop (the temporal authority) and to discard the rulings and judgements of any hierarchy. Through initiation they acquired an inner freedom to act as they were led by the Holy Spirit.

They were their own functionaries with liberty to order their own common life, their spirituality was kindled by an inner spark of illumination that gave them authority to determine the lifestyle to be followed and the vindication of their pattern of behaviour:

> Therefore if one has knowledge, he is formative . . . Having knowledge he has the will of the one who called him, he wishes to be pleasing to him . . . He who is to have knowledge in this manner knows whence he comes from and where he is going.[61]

Different gnostic groups practised their own initiation customs but many rites were an amalgam of cults, "myths and magic". Exorcisms were practised and a sacramental meal might be shared communally as a bond of fellowship between participants and with God. A sacred drama might be enacted to depict the symbolic transfer from darkness to light, from death to resurrection and from mortality to immortality. The rite of baptism was performed as one of initiation either by complete immersion or by sprinkling, about which Valentinus in a letter to Rheginos stated:

> It is only baptism that frees us from the power of fate by *gnosis* – the knowledge of what we were, why we have come into being, what we are and at what point we have been placed in the cosmos, whither we are hastening, and from what we have been redeemed, and what is birth and rebirth.[62]

During such rites secret names, signs, different styles of greeting and secret passwords were used. At this point the gnostic school or group operated as a cult fellowship with its own pattern of worship, ceremonies and festivities. They included liturgical prayers, ritual washing, anointing with oil, and death rites.[63] The *Gospel of Philip* specifies five seals wherewith those who practised the rites were "sealed" so that they then could live spiritually as those who were initiated into divine knowledge:

> The Lord did everything in a mystery, a baptism, a chrism, a eucharist and a bridal chamber.[64]

This general account of initiation clearly shows it to be a cardinal aspect of the gnostics' practice and of the oversight and spiritual vigilance over the transmission and practice of *gnosis*. A number of the gnostic texts express intense care in preparing initiates and in performing the rites of initiation. The prime role of initiation was to absorb the initiate further into the inner and higher forms of *gnosis*, always considered to be the way to "be purified . . . from all wickedness and the involvement in evil".[65]

Presenting *gnosis*

Before leaving this excursus into the world of *gnosis* some reference should be made to the language and form of its presentation which give "shape" to the gnostic writings. Language performs its own function and words are used for a particular purpose.

The gnostics had a way with words and there is a notable vividness and vitality in some of their writings. They used language in a unique way to communicate between different schools and to interpret the insights of the mysterious *gnosis*. Yet the Valentinian gnostics were suspicious of words; they saw them as part of the "bindings" to this material world, part of the great unreality which induces sleep and intoxication. Elaine Pagels has written of the Valentinian gnostics that they:

> expressed a lot of interest in the way that we use words to talk about reality. And that when we use words . . . I'm thinking of the Gospel of Philip . . . that says that we use the word "God" or "resurrection" or "Jesus" or whatever, we're not talking about realities that these words express, but we are talking about our mental image of whatever the realities conjure up. And I think that is an effort to remind us that all of language is a purely symbolic system, especially religious language, and that it only comes to life when there is some kind of inner experience that transforms us from which our language emerges.[66]

Words like "God", "Jesus" and "resurrection" give expression to the mental image the words conjure up or the inner experience of being "knowledge possessed". The use of the words referred to is significantly influenced by the categories and insights of the mysterious *gnosis*. The gnostics did not display a consistent use of language when speaking about truth or redemption, nor were they presenting traditional beliefs in a new language. The language they used was geared to expressing the inner motive of revelatory experience and direct "knowing". This required a more discerning use of language to characterize those features of inner experience that make sense of what is authentic *gnosis* in contrast to language used to describe external events or objects. The *Gospel of Philip* seems to pour scorn on the use of religious language as if it were literal language when speaking of God, Christ, resurrection or Church.[67]

The language had to be appropriate and intelligible for its particular situation and purpose. The language of gnosticism has its own special quality; not that the gnostics set out deliberately to structure it in this way, but because they were not governed by set linguistic formulae. Their language was meant to be a disclosure of those insights and perceptions that arise from the experience of mysterious *gnosis*. In the contemporary scene of the second century, new religious (Christian) mythology was being developed alongside older existing philosophical concepts, and gnostics needed to articulate their ideas in intelligible language. Thus their language bristles with words which serve as models that do justice to what is being disclosed of gnostic insights, presuppositions and experience. For instance, they clothe the word God with mystery: he is "incomprehensible" and "inconceivable", but at the same time he is father, shepherd and judge. These may seem to be two sets of competing manifestations of God, the one abstract and metaphysical, the other picturesque and immanent and existential. They both disclose a conception of God and can be integrated. Both are rooted in experience and both use the style or model of language required to articulate the truth and reality of insight that is germane to experience.

For the purpose of articulating the disclosures of the mysterious knowledge about God, the world and human life, the gnostic writings employ a variety of literary styles, including allegory, parable, metaphor, myth, symbol and imagery.

Allegory: serves a dual purpose as an extended metaphor and the means of clarifying meaning. Narratives are to be understood symbolically and their message interpreted accordingly. The allegorical method of interpreting religious texts was in vogue in the early Christian centuries, and it may be noted how this method was often applied to the Bible rather than taking its narratives literally. They were interpreted as allegories, notably by Philo of Alexandria in the early part of the first century CE, with the result that this method greatly influenced the study of the Scriptures.

It was natural then for the gnostics to adopt this method, which combined religious and philosophical conceptions as in the rich use of allegory by the Valentinian gnostics, as in this example:

> Once upon a time, Depth thought of emitting from himself a Beginning of all, like a seed, he deposited this projected emission, as in a womb, in that Silence who is with him. Silence recovered this seed and became pregnant and bore Mind, which resembled and was equal to him who emitted him.[68]

The allegory is used to teach how the perfect pre-existent *Aeon*, who constituted the *pleroma* or invisible spiritual world, formed the seed from which emitted all that is. Underlying this method is the attempt to give symbolic expression to truths, as in the case of the well-known allegories of the good shepherd and the true vine in the New Testament.[69] The allegory conceptualizes the truth the allegorist wishes to explain, in a symbolic way or by speaking otherwise than one seems to speak. The gnostic authors adapted their allegories to convey philosophical and religious insights, to expound their ideas, and to present their major themes. The allegories were a device also for alerting attention as well as for interpreting Scripture. Thus the allegory of Eve and the serpent is presented as a vision to John the apostle of Jesus, who is bidden, "Now lift up your face that you may receive the things that I shall teach you today." It then proceeds to give a gnostic view of the role of the serpent and of the tree of good and evil in the Genesis narrative of the Garden of Eden.[70]

Much of the teaching of gnosticism is to be understood allegorically, as allegory became part of the common parlance when speaking of spiritual truths.

Parable: many of the teachings of gnosticism are given by way of parables, which are not always easily distinguishable from allegories. Like allegory, parable may also be an extended metaphor in a story form. The gnostics practised their teaching in a story-telling culture and used characteristic images of their time in order to express clearly their ideas. Either by implication or explicitly, the gnostic parables teach a message commensurate with the *gnosis* from which it sprang. Therefore their parables were used to intensify awareness of those spiritual truths that are known implicitly through experience. They also draw upon images and situations from everyday life, as in the case of this parable in the *Gospel of Philip*:

> There was a householder who had every conceivable thing, be it man or slave or cattle or dog or pig or barley or chaff or grass or meat or acorn. Now he was a sensible fellow and he knew what the food of each one was. He served the children bread . . . He served the slaves . . . meal. And he threw barley and chaff and grass to the cattle. He threw bones to the dogs, and to the pigs he threw acorns and slop. Compare the disciple of God, if he is a sensible fellow he understands what discipleship is all about. The bodily forms will not deceive him. There are many animals in the world which are in human form. When he identifies them, to the swine he will throw acorns, to the cattle he will throw barley and chaff and grass, to the dogs he will throw bones. To the slaves he will give only elementary lessons, to the children (of light) he will give the complete instruction.[71]

The prime idea of the parable is that there are many categories of people in the world, but the superior are those who are enlightened, and having received the "higher" instruction they are on the way to redemption.

Metaphor: the extant gnostic texts are pregnant with metaphor, that is, figures of speech that apply or transfer terms to objects other than in a literal way. Many extensive metaphors are encountered as words are transferred from one context to another in order to clarify meaning. The examples are too numerous to recall here, but we may observe that their variety reflects the common occurrence of metaphors in the revelatory literature of the period.

To some extent they may be said to invest the gnostic writings with commonality, but at the same time we should not minimize the significance of those that *uniquely* reflect gnostic notions and ideas. For example, "the light of the son" is a metaphor for "justice", and the "father of light" of righteousness. In the *Gospel of Philip*, Wisdom is a metaphor for the Virgin Mary ("As for Wisdom, who is called barren / she is the mother of the angels").[72] "The eye of the mind" is a metaphor for God, the "divine spark" for his presence, then "darkness", "ignorance", "flesh", "desire" are used metaphorically of evil. There are metaphors galore but we should not lose sight of the empiricism that gives them potency within the actual context.

Myth: many themes are expressed in elaborate myths. These focus on some religious truth or other which they intend to illustrate in a dramatic or highly imaginative way. They draw upon elements of the mythology of oriental mysteries as well as Judaism and Christianity. This is not to say that there exists a special gnostic mythology, but rather an extensive use of myth to describe themes that characterize gnostic teachings and conceptions.

Thus Basilides expresses his world view in a myth:

> Pistis Sophia desired to cause the thing that had no spirit to be formed into a likeness and to rule over matter and over all her forms, there appeared for the first time a ruler out of the waters, lion-like in appearance, androgynous, having great authority within him, and ignorant of when he had come into being. Now when Pistis Sophia saw him moving about in the depths of the waters she said to him, "child pass through to here".[73]

This is but one example, but there are varying interpretations of the same theme diffused throughout the gnostic texts. Thus Valentinus expressed the origin of the world in a mythical form by depicting Wisdom as the Mother of all things who brought the world out of her own suffering.[74] A number of myths are adapted from the Jewish Bible, as is the myth of the Garden of Eden in the *Apocryphon of John*,[75] and other myths that draw upon the lives of Jewish patriarchs as models of piety. The connection with the Bible is obvious but the myths are always given a gnostic slant. The themes covered are basic to all religion – especially deity, creation, nature, salvation, eschatology, and many others.

The central myth, if we might so describe it, is that the human being is set in this world, which is hostile to God, and is destined for death were it not for the divine spark within that is kindled by knowledge of redemption, which brings the individual finally to the place of inextinguishable light. Within this broad concept the mythology of gnosticism propounds such basic themes as good and evil, spirit and matter, the divine and human, the temporal and eternal. In the treatment of these themes, which are common to all apocalyptic literature, we encounter a gnostic radicalism that is a combination of cosmology, deity, anthropology, soteriology and eschatology. Hans Jonas, in his seminal work on gnostic religion, has written about how the gnostic vision of reality is conveyed through an inevitable mythology with its own personifications, hypostases, quasi-chronological narrative and consciously constructed symbols of metaphysical theory.[76]

The antecedents of gnostic mythology are clearly spread over earlier religious writings but the use of myth as a means of expressing truth as a literary form came to dominate considerable areas of the gnostic works. In these myths the authors used particular skills to convey their meaning, and at times they border on the bizarre or grotesque. Nevertheless the mythological genre of the gnostic writings invariably fulfils its purpose of transmitting revelatory knowledge, which was its primary interest and for which the myths were such effective vehicles.

Symbol: is a sign or image used in a particular way to represent an object. At the same time it communicates ideas or reveals meaning or spiritual truths. It points beyond itself not because it resembles what it represents but because there is an essential correspondence between the symbol and what it symbolizes. It is a feature of religious language, which employs symbolism regularly to convey invisible spiritual and metaphysical realities. Thus in gnosticism the diagram of ten circles circumscribed by one circle represents the world soul. The world soul does not look like a circle and yet there is a correspondence between the two that makes the circle an apt symbol of the world soul, which is called Leviathan.[77]

Symbols often express more than one meaning and are sufficiently flexible to relate to the changing character of experience. So they are open to new interpretations; for example, the cross is used as a symbol of a range of spiritual meanings, such as the passion of Christ by Valentinus, or the forgiveness of sins, by others. The remarkably rich occurrence of symbolism in the gnostic works is understandable on account of its preoccupation with mysterious knowledge of spiritual worlds within. The words of Ptolemaeus' *Letter to Flora* could apply to a whole range of gnostic writings:

> Since all these things are images and symbols, when the truth was made manifest they were translated to another meaning.[78]

Imagery: According to the *Gospel of Philip*,

> Truth did not come into the world naked, but it came in types and images. The world will not receive truth in any other way. There is rebirth and an image of rebirth. It is necessary to be reborn again through the image.[79]

An image is a pictorial symbol of some real or imaginary object. To some extent in the works of the gnostics they are narrative images which portray scenes from the Bible and the lives of its characters, or they are theological images which express the meaning of beliefs and ideas. There are examples of these especially in respect of constellations and signs and heavenly bodies. There are verbal pictorial images of life "in the worlds of light", of "being given as brides to the angels", of being "invested with loyalty", or "in the fruits of spendour", or " the courts of light", or "the house of perfection". To some extent, of course, the gnostics were obsessed with images, and they do more than just represent events, as they are intended to highlight the inner meaning and universal significance of the events. They are intended to serve as exemplars of spiritual insight into reality. Thus of the resurrection of Jesus the *Gospel of Philip* says:

> It is certainly necessary to be born again through the image. Which one? Resurrection. The image must rise again through the image. The bridal chamber and the image must enter through the image into the truth: this is the restoration.[80]

The six basic elements of the literary style of the gnostic writings have a special significance. Gnosticism attached great importance to making sure that the mysterious *gnosis* they acquired should be expressed and explored efficiently.

Such was the value they placed on its truth and message. The basic principle was that although the *gnosis* was revealed in a special way to particular persons who received experiences of illumination, the insights they received not only identified religious ideas but also pointed to a practical way of salvation of universal appeal. For the concept of *gnosis* to serve any positive purpose it needed to communicate itself in meaningful ways as well as in right and good action. This deepened conviction in the necessity to demonstrate the essence of gnosticism as essential for comprehending the meaning of human existence, God, the world and salvation.

The impression we have of the gnostics of the early Christian centuries is of their earnestness and of their complete devotion to the way set out by the secret *gnosis*. A prayer of thanksgiving expresses the spirit of elation felt through the knowledge received:

> We rejoice having been illuminated by Thy Knowledge. We rejoice that Thou hast shown us thyself. We rejoice because while we were in the body, Thou hast made us divine through Thy Knowledge.

This expresses something of what *gnosis* meant to the gnostic. We have set out some of the leading ideas of *gnosis* and their special appeal. The task ahead is to attempt to account for the appeal of this phenomenom and its relevance in the covert search for truth within the process of self-enlightenment on the meaning and destiny of human life.

Great is God, for that he has given us a mind to apprehend these things . . .
You yourself are a fragment torn from God, you have a portion of him within yourself.

Corpus Hermeticum

No-one can find fault with our universe on the ground that it is not beautiful or not the most perfect of the beings associated with the holy, nor again quarrel with the originator of its existence.

Plotinus

But mind, the Father of all, being life and light, gave birth to a Man like myself; with him he was pleased, as his own offspring, for the Man was very beautiful, bearing the image of his Father. For truly God was pleased with his own form, and he delivered his creatures to him.

Poimandres

Gnosis is interpreted not only in the final end of mankind but also in that of the cosmos for both are ordered with its cosmology.

Kurt Rudolph, Gnosis

2

Gnostic Communities: Origins and History

The origins of gnosticism are more complex than any doctrinaire theory would allow. It can be said, as a generalization, that there are no absolute origins of gnosticism. Putting it another way, it is legitimate to assert that the key to the genesis of gnosticism is in *gnosis* itself as a condition of gaining release from the traumas of existence in a hostile world. The study of its origins has deposited a number of individual interpretations, explanations and justifications, but no universally agreed conclusions. The gnostic writings are notably restrained in reference to historical origins and development. This is understandable as the gnostic quest was not to substantiate and verify historical data but to gain release from a world dominated by historical events. Hence we have to use other than the usual historical methods in the search for origins and focus instead on evidence of manifestations of "the gnostic phenomenon" expressed as mystical speculation or experience of the transcendent or self-understanding or philosophical world view.[1] In terms of its cultural context the focus has to be on eastern mysticism, Iranian dualism, Hellenistic philosophy, Jewish religion and Christian soteriology. These we shall examine more closely in the following pages.

In such an examination all that is reasonably possible is to trace elements of the "gnostic way of redemption" in human experience and behaviour. The nature of *gnosis* is such that the process of "cause" and "effect" inevitably leads not to verifiable historical data or concrete situations but to living experience of "the gnostic phenomenon", or what Hans Jonas has termed "the Gnostic Idea" or "the Gnostic Principle", that is, an experiential phenomenon that acquired "a life of its own, and unfolded abstract applications".[2] There are no absolute origins of "the gnostic tendency" (gnosticism does not have a historical founder). The ideological roots of the gnostic schools or communities of the early Christian centuries are embedded in the consciousness of knowledge or supernatural power. No period in history is independent of its predecessors, and every fresh insight into the meaning of experience and existence is a link in a sequence of such insights that stretches back to an indefinite past. They are not confined to one time or place. The principle of continuity lies not in historical happenings but in accumulating experiences of fresh insights and visions that promote a deepening comprehension of the meaning of reality and the ultimate destiny of human existence. The gnostic experience is of this order: positive, discerning and forceful, and poised to follow its insights to perfect fulfilment.

The east and *gnosis*

As an operational starting point we investigate manifestations of "the gnostic phenomenon" in eastern religions and philosophy, and ask whether elements of this may have been transmitted westwards and integrated with western cultures. It is well known that east–west communications were in operation well before the Christian era. This allowed for the influence of eastern ideas and philosophies to infiltrate into western cultures. This is the case regarding belief in reincarnation, for example, such a seminal belief of eastern religion, of which Hans Kung has written:

> It is certain that not only Orphics, Pythagoras and Empedocles, but also Philo, Plotinus and the Neo-Platonists (likewise Roman poets such as Virgil in his Aeneid) held this belief (i.e. reincarnation) thus leading to its influence in both Christian Gnosticism and Manichaeism up to the mediaeval sects (like the Cathari).[3]

The conquest of the east by Alexander the Great in the late fourth century BCE opened the way for spreading further the transcultural influences of eastern speculation. Alexander's empire assimilated eastern ideas and mythology and enabled these to spread more widely. This dispersion of religious and philosophical notions flowed freely across national boundaries to enrich the syncretism that developed in the west. Eastern religion is deeply immersed in the exercise of the spirituality that finds its fulfilment in liberation (*moksha*) and salvation (*satori*). The progress of the soul from a state of ignorance (*avijja*) to knowledge (*jñanā*) and from duality (*dwaita*) to oneness (*advaita*) is germane to the spiritual quest of the Hindu and the Buddhist. In this context it is relevant to refer to the opening paragraph of the apocryphal *Acts of Thomas* which states:

> At that season all the apostles were in Jerusalem . . . and we divided the regions of the world that everyone of us should go into the region that fell to him by lot, and into the nation where unto the Lord sent him. According to lot therefore India fell to Judas Thomas which is also the twin.[4]

According to this tradition there was a highway established in the time of the apostles that facilitated the spread of ideas across the cultural divide. Thomas, the disciple of Jesus, visited India where to this day a small Nestorian Church in the densely populated Hindu area of the far south claims him as its founder. Professor Pagels asks, could the title of the (gnostic) *Gospel of Thomas* reflect the influence of Indian tradition on gnosticism?[5] Buddhists also apparently had contact with Thomist Christians. A further tradition tells of the presence of Buddhist missionaries in Alexandria engaged in missionary work, and of Indian brahmins active in Rome where they taught what was considered to be heresy:

> they say that God is light, not like the light of light one sees, nor like the sun nor fire, but to them God is discourse, not that which finds expression in articulate sounds, but that of knowledge (*gnosis*) through which the secret mysteries of nature are perceived by the wise.[6]

Many coincidental insights transcended geographical and cultural barriers, and this makes it difficult sometimes to differentiate between mystical knowledge in one culture and that in another.

The Iranian mystic Mani in the third century CE expressed the sense of coherence in his famous designation of Buddha along with Zoroaster and Christ as "one of the apostles of light".[7] Buddha of course taught that enlightened intuition and right knowledge within, constituted the path that led to *Nibbana*, the indescribable state of bliss which is the goal of existence.

Knowledge or insight is the means of achieving the goal. It is a most coveted and desired acquisition. The Sanskrit term for this is *jñanā*, which means spiritual knowledge, that is knowledge of truth or knowledge that is pure and absolute. The Hindu religious system postulates gradations of knowledge that lead to the ultimate state of knowing which then becomes the reward of those who are fully enlightened.[8] *Jñanā* is related to the Greek word for knowledge (*gnosis*); in Indian philosophy it conveys insight into spiritual reality and also to the effects of good or evil action that determines human destiny or the progress of the soul to enlightenment. This progression takes place under the law of *Karma*, the law of cause and effect, but knowledge (*jñanā*) is instrumental in bringing about release. As such it has a redemptive import, it is a binding force between the human and the divine.[9]

This notion of the fusion of the human and the divine is another characteristic feature of eastern religion and philosophy. The integration of the human soul (*atman*) with the divine within (*Brahman*) is the highest state of being known to Hinduism.[10] It is the pivotal experience religion has to offer and intellect alone is impotent to achieve it. It is the all-encompassing experience of the divine as immanent and transcendent.[11] Even so the eastern systems are not completely consistent in this; yet we cannot overlook the fact that there is a point of cohesion in the doctrine of the progress of the soul to enlightenment.[12]

This leads to yet another feature of eastern religion which has relevance to the question of "the gnostic phenomenon", namely, syncretism. This is a well-known characteristic of eastern religion and philosophy which is inevitable in such a composite religious system as Hinduism. But the word has to be used with caution. It can be applied in a number of ways, especially when the subject is the elaborate mythology of the east. This mythology is designed, as is mythology in other cultures, to teach and expound truth in a non-literal way and in this respect the east boasts a rich and complex mythology centred in the main on a transcendent monotheism, or a pantheon of gods, an extensive dualism or a cosmic fatalism.[13] The myths are composed in the eastern style of conceptualization but the overriding intention is to convey eternal truths in illuminating ways.[14]

We have observed that the goal is complete enlightenment and personal experience of God or the ultimate. Along the path to be followed in order to achieve this there are prescribed practices and techniques.[15] Meditation is one such practice, which in both Hinduism and Buddhism is the wilful conditioning of the self, but not in an intellectual or analytical way, for seeing more clearly the nature of reality and the destiny of existence. Meditation aims to induce the state of spiritual enlightenment (*satori*)[16] and is performed for the purpose of attaining the higher reaches of knowledge, that is, to perfect the blissful union of the self with universal truth and ultimate reality. It aims to make realizable the goal of *jñanā*, as in the words of the Hindu Upanishad:

> When, to someone who knows, all things have become one with his own self, what delusion or sorrow can occur to him, he has proved the oneness.

This account of aspects of "the gnostic phenomenon" does not postulate a theory of the origins of gnosticism, but it offers hints of the occurrence and role of the special *gnosis* in eastern religion and philosophy. This phenomenon is not restricted to one time or culture. Ideas practised by eastern religions and philosophies have filtered through to enrich western culture in a variety of ways. In a narrower but pertinent sense we may say that the experience of esoteric knowledge is a feature of religion universally. It is for this reason we cannot ignore the occurrence of "the gnostic phenomenon" in the eastern experience or in its diverse systems, whose ideal is perfect enlightenment.

The Iranian experience

One such system is the ethical dualism of Persian–Iranian religion. It was once believed that the origins of gnosticism lay here,[17] although this view has been generally abandoned.[18] Nevertheless, there are some who maintain that we should not discard the Persian–Iranian background altogether,[19] and our concern in this overview is to describe why this is so.

In the mid-eighteenth century liturgical works attributed to the Persian prophet Zoroaster called *Zend Avesta* were discovered and dated to the sixth century BCE. The affinity of these texts with some early Christian writings was observed, especially with the works of Clement of Alexandria (150–215), Origen (*c.*185–254), Porphyry (232–305), Eusebius (*c.*265–340) and Augustine (354–430). The pertinent question to ask is whether there are manifestations of "the gnostic phenomenon" in these Zoroastrian texts.

The date of Zoroaster's ministry is unclear but the works depict a state of conflict in the cosmos between good and evil and light and darkness that will continue forcefully until the final victory of the good is accomplished at the end of time. The conflict is instigated by the rival deities of goodness (Ohrmazd) and evil (Ahriman). The conflict is inward as well as cosmic, human nature being a dualism of body and spirit (*gétíg* and *ménóg*). Human life accordingly is lived out against the continuous relentless struggle of inward and external conflict. The good God, Ohrmazd or Mazda, who is light and the source of light, illumines the way to final victory, blissful release and the assurance of existence after death to whoever receives or chooses the path of light. He brings them to his dominion and to abide with Mazda who makes secure the final victory:

Mazda has ordained punishment for the evil and bliss for the righteous:

Mazda teaches light and darkness, sleep and waking, morning, noon and night. Mazda the creator, brings through Good Thought, all that is good to fulfilment.[20]

This poem or Gatha describes how the immortality of the soul and its return to Mazda is accomplished. The soul is given a choice and by choosing the path of light accomplishes the way that leads to fulfilment in God. This teaching is expressed in symbolic imagery and is characteristic of Persian concepts and ideas.

The external physical realm is dominated by Satan, whilst the spiritual world is the domain of God. The dualism, however, needs to be approached with caution, as in the Zoroastrian system the origin of this dualism is the spiritual world, so that the physical world is not conceived of as being wholly evil. There is respect for the physical world and the material world need not be rejected as being totally wicked. This differs broadly from the gnostic viewpoint, and consequently the asceticism of some gnostic practices have no place in Zoroastrianism.[21]

The Zoroastrian idea of salvation is that of deliverance from the conflict between light and darkness and final participation in Mazda's moral and spiritual victory. Esoteric *gnosis* is not overtly the precondition of achieving salvation, but the role of Saoshyant, the coming world saviour who will arrive to establish the victory of good over evil for ever, is pivotal. Through his coming those who choose the path of light and virtue will be rewarded with resurrection after death. A distinct apocalyptic theme underlies the whole mythological tradition with its salvific focus on the end of the world. The Persian Saoshyant myth was known among the gnostics of the early Christian era, but, according to R. McL. Wilson, it had little in common with Christianity. However, his conclusion is that only in form and not in essence is this so, "the gnostic redeemer is not pre-Christian ... The Zoroastrian doctrine is the nearest in form, but this theory exercised but little influence on Judaism and even less on philosophy."[22]

The case is more impressive when we consider the gnostic work entitled *Song of the Pearl* and how it reflects or echoes Iranian influence.[23] The *Song of the Pearl* is a symbolic parable or story of a prince who set out in search of a pearl that had been lost. It teaches a dualism between the body ("a filthy and unclean garb I stripped off") and the soul ("my bright embroidered robe, which was decorated with glorious colours"). It makes references to the Father (King of Kings) and Mother (Queen of the East), and the Son (next in rank).[24] Emphasis on the knowledge of the self is found in this parable as it is in other gnostic writings, and has its counterpart in the concept of the self in Zoroastrian teaching.

In the *Song of the Pearl* the self is the object of redemption ("And bringing my gift and my pearl I shall appear with him before our King"), whereas the Persian concept of the metaphysical self, conveyed by the Persian word *grev*, which means self or ego, is the one who is to be redeemed.[25] The redemption of the soul at the end of life is taught in Zoroastrianism, as in gnosticism, as the goal of existence.

Some traces of Iranian religious ideas are to be found in the third-century mystic Mani (216–77 CE), whose teaching is threaded throughout with ideas taken from Persian, Jewish and Christian beliefs. This religion is one of dualism between light and darkness and a belief in a spiritual soul held bound in a material world until it is liberated by Manda d'Hayye, the saviour. It viewed nature as corrupt and redemption as achieved through the practice of virtue rather than external ritual. Manichaeism is intensely spiritual and its adherents extolled Mani as prophet and saviour. He is the messenger of light and the personification of "the *gnosis* of life", i.e. of redeeming knowledge.[26] The redeemer descends from the realm of light, as Zoroaster is thought to have done; but unlike Zoroaster he only seemed to partake of the nature of the physical world.

Allied to the Manichaeans are the Mandaeans from about 400 CE who partly shared a common identical background with Mani. According to Mandaeism redemption is not achieved by a single historical saviour, but by a series of mythological redeemers who constitute part of the process of continuous revelation following on from the primal revelation to Adam. Nevertheless, redemption is a key concept of Mandaeism, the soul is released from the body and makes its ascent to the final abode aided by divine revelation. On its way it encounters hostile forces that seek to detain it, but once having arrived at the realm of light the enlightened soul is beyond their reach.[27] It is interesting to note that in the Mandaean language, a dialect of Arabic, *Manda* means mystic knowledge or *gnosis*.

Are there distinctive elements in Zoroastrianism related to the gnostic phenomenon? Any links that there may be between Zoroastrianism and the writings of the gnostics of the early Christian centuries are exceedingly difficult to quantify. There are tenuous links in Zoroastrianism with the Jewish Bible, inter-testamental literature and with the Dead Sea Scrolls, and indeed with Mithraism, which we should not overlook, but these do not sufficiently merit hypothesizing uncritically an Iranian origin for gnosticism. Yet tenuous though the links are, they should not be completely ignored. Instead they may be added to the store of evidence that may be accumulated of the pre-Christian transcultural manifestations of "the gnostic phenomenon", but without drawing from this more inferences than the evidence justifies. In the meanwhile the words of Mani quoted by Hans Jonas may be considered as relevant in this context:

> From aeon to aeon the apostles of God did not cease to bring here the Wisdom and the Works. Thus in one age their coming [i.e. that of Wisdom and the Works] was into the countries of India through the apostle that was the Buddha, in another age, into the land of Persia, through Zoroaster, in another into the land of the west through Jesus. And after in the last age, the revelation came down to this prophethood arrived through myself, Mani, the apostle of the true God, into the land of Babel.[28]

Hellenism

In the search for pointers to manifestations of "the gnostic phenomenon" in pre-Christian times, we can observe the rapid spread and powerful impact of Hellenism. The spread and appeal of this Greek culture which followed the conquests of Alexander the Great meant that by the beginning of the Christian era the eastern lands of the Mediterranean were very largely Hellenized and a large proportion of the population had succumbed to the dynamic influence of Hellenistic culture.[29] This advance marked a turning point in the history of culture which is notable for its grandiose universalism, transcultural syncretism, expansive developments in philosophy and science, and a liberated individualism.

According to Kurt Rudolph the spread of Hellenism "became a decisive prerequisite for the genesis of *Gnosis*",[30] and Quispel is convinced that "at last the origins, development and goal of this perennial philosophy [i.e. gnosticism] has come to light".[31]

What is the ground for this? Hellenism represents a tradition in religion and philosophy from which there developed a new form of syncretism. Its more basic characteristic is universalism in which is displayed respect for and recognition of the gods of various religions, whilst Zeus, the Supreme God of the Greek pantheon, regaled with regal powers bathed in heavenly light.[32] The Greeks conceived of Zeus, the Supreme God, as the sum total of all dynamic qualities and divine attributes. This exaltation of Zeus inevitably led in the direction of monotheism as is to be gathered from the Hymn to Zeus by Cleanthes (*c.*300 BCE), which is notably monotheistic in tone. The hymn to Zeus opens:

> Thou, O Zeus are praised above all gods, many are thy names and thine is all power for ever.

A basic tenet of this monotheism is omnipotence and the soul's relation to the Supreme God. At the heart of divinity there is mystery which only the soul is capable of fathoming, since it alone shares the divine nature. Being so endowed the soul is a fit receptacle for receiving knowledge (*gnosis*) of God, and at death ascends as pure spirit to him. Possession of this *gnosis* is a condition of perfect illumination. It exemplifies a depth of self-knowledge of a spiritual or transcendent quality.

A new spirit of speculation and enquiry into religious and philosophical questions developed in a world of expanding cultural integration. Concentration on the origin of the universe and its nature was a prime interest. Plato (429–347 BCE), the most influential of Greek philosophers, taught a view of the universe as being a divine creation, displayed on two levels, the spiritual and the material. He also postulated a first cause for the creation and equated this with God, the Supreme Being.[33] The spiritual world is eternal and the material impermanent. The physical world, however, is not evil but rather is

the most beautiful of generated things.[34]

The Supreme God existed before any of the pantheon of gods[35] and as pre-existent he must be responsible for their creation. Plato also taught a positive and propitious view of creation and Plotinus (205–70 CE), a Neo-Platonist, likewise held a very favourable view of creation, as we gather from his first treatise, *On Providence*, in which he declared:

> No-one can find fault with our universe on the ground that it is not beautiful or not the most perfect of the beings associated with the holy, nor again quarrel with the originator of its existence, and certainly not because it has come into existence of necessity, not on the basis of a reflection but because the higher being brought forth its likeness according to the law of nature.[36]

There is, however, no room for divine revelation in Plato's system. The human mind he believed is equipped to find God within itself. It does not need to be enlightened by revelation from without. This view generated a wealth of mythology centred on the Platonic conception of the origin of the universe. Plato designates the *demiurge* the original creator, and distinguishes between the ideal world and the world of ideas.

Through the action of the *demiurge* there came into being the sensible world, and whilst knowledge of the *demiurge* is obscure and diffuse its function is clearly defined as the creative cause of all that is.[37] This also accounts for the order of the universe.[38] Valentinus, the gnostic teacher, used the same term (*demiurge*) of the creator but in the sense of a lesser god who is subordinate to the Supreme God. This suggests to us that Valentinus was acquainted with this Platonic theory, and we may also compare it with other gnostic writings, especially the *Apocryphon of John* and *Pistis Sophia*. The tendency of Christian writers to convey their (Christian) teaching in terms of Hellenistic philosophy is evident both in gnostic Christian texts and in orthodox Christianity.[39] The assumption was that by so doing and by extracting ideas from Greek culture and interpreting them in a new way it was possible to clothe Christian teaching in a respectable intellectual garb. The categories of Greek thought provided Christian writers with a framework for structuring their own systems of thought and doctrine.

There are elements of other-worldliness in Neo-Platonist teaching as well as a belief in the affinity of the soul with God. In an intelligible world which distinguishes between intellectual reasoning and intuition, interest in discovering what is real and what constitutes knowledge of ultimate reality is a prime concern. The question therefore arises of how to acquire this knowledge. The link that integrates intuition and intellect, religion and philosophy, is also the focal point of the synthesis between intellectual knowing and spiritual insight. The *Corpus Hermeticum* writings (from the second to fourth century CE) speak of the affinity of the soul with the godhead in such sayings as:

> Great is God, for that he has given us a mind to apprehend these things . . .
> You yourself are a fragment torn from God, you have a portion of him within yourself.[40]

The *Corpus Hermeticum,* so called on account of association with the Greek god Hermes, carries the influence of Greek philosophy and is an important witness to the nature of non-Christian gnosticism. The writings are the product of the Graeco-oriental syncretism interwoven with Platonic and Stoic philosophical concepts. They exemplify the wisdom (the proverbial wisdom of Egypt) that promotes the vision of God, rebirth and spiritual liberation.[41] The method they employ is to take disciples and instruct them through initiation which centres on questions and answers from Hermes, a god noted for mystic knowledge and who is the guide of souls to spiritual enlightenment. In this way the disciple or learner is delivered from ignorance and preoccupation with worldly thoughts and brought under the power of *nous*, the source of spiritual energy. This facilitates the ascent of the soul to the abode of the Supreme (incomprehensible) Being.[42] The *nous* is the faculty that gives insight into the affinity of the soul with God, as mentioned earlier.

Certain ideas characteristic of Hellenistic religion and philosophy are scattered throughout the gnostic writings, and to this extent they witness to their probable currency before the Christian era. But it would be an overstatement to say that they alone account for the origins of gnosticism. Gnosticism is not synonymous with Hellenistic syncretism or philosophy. Whilst there is evidence of "the gnostic phenomenon", this is not fully representative of any gnostic system, nor does it convey the essence of gnosticism to its full extent. The glimpses gained of "the gnostic phenomenon" in the thought-world of Hellenism has to be valued as indispensable evidence of how the way was prepared for the development of the separate gnostic systems of the first Christian centuries. Hellenism is a contributory factor rather than an ultimate solution to the question of the origins and provenance of gnosticism.

The Jewish dimension

Externally gnosticism in the early Christian centuries could not escape having a Jewish dimension, and internally it had significant points of contact with Jewish ideas. But Judaism is not a monolithic faith. The Jews had experienced the diaspora from their homeland to the eastern boundaries of the Roman Empire,[43] and by the turn of the era they had largely acquired a Graeco-Roman way of life and assimilated Greek modes of thought and the divergency of culture that was characteristic of the early Christian era. The extent of this assimilation and divergency is unclear, but there is evidence of syncretism, although, as in other instances, the word has to be applied with caution. The diversity within Judaism itself is illustrated by its groupings and sectarianism, as can be instanced from the Bible, from the Dead Sea Scrolls, and from the Jung Codex from Nag Hammadi. As a result of this sectarian division, along with the fact of the diaspora, the Jews developed aspects of their religion that may not have happened in any other way. But our concern is with what signs there may be of "the gnostic phenomenon" in the Judaism that was the cradle of Christianity.

In this context we must observe how Judaism had been penetrated by

Hellenistic thought to produce a synthesis of Graeco-Jewish ideas. Greek culture, religion and philosophy exerted an influence on Jewish thought and the Jews appropriated to themselves such Greek ideas as they could approve without the loss of integrity. The speculations of Greek rationalism, for instance, permeated Jewish writings,[44] and a Platonic School of Eudorus settled at Alexandria, where Philo (first century CE), a Jewish philosopher, was its most distinguished member. At Alexandria, Jews became familiar with Platonic philosophy, some of whose ideas were described earlier. These ideas included the affinity of the human soul with the deity. Philo discerned in Judaism a harmony with the best of Platonism and Stoicism, and this belief had far-reaching effects on the development of Christian theology, and is reflected also in some gnostic works.

A further point of affinity between Philo and the gnostics concerns the nature and action of God. In the thought of Philo, the Supreme God made the world, but between God and the world there are divine powers, viewed partly as attributes of God, and partly as existences in their own right. Of these the highest is the Logos, which emanates from God himself.[45]

The idea of God as transcendent is evident, and this too provides a further point of contact with the gnostic idea and with Hellenism. In the gnostic system the Supreme God is the head of the hierarchy and below him is the *demiurge*, who created the world, and below him again are the lesser powers. Here the *demiurge* is one of the lesser angels who is identified with the God of the Jews.

In Judaism God and he alone is the creator. The Supreme God (Yahweh) of the Jews and the creator are one. As in the gnostic teachings, there are intermediaries between God and the world: the gnostic emanations and the Logos and angels of Philo. There is also an implicit dualism in the thought of Philo. In his work *On Dreams* he divides those who pronounce life as "great foolery", and who call the body "a prison and a tomb", from others who "are of perfect purity and excellence, gifted with a higher and diviner temper, that they never felt any grieving after the things of earth".[46] There were Jewish schools given to speculation about the nature of human life and this led to a view of the human being as belonging to God not to earth.[47] Life on earth was thought to be the work of a lesser deity who controlled it. Those who thought in this way were the intellectual forerunners of the Kabbalists (Kabbala = Tradition), a mystical strand of Judaism wherein God is seen to be endless (Ein Sof) and ineffable, from whom there emanates powers or entities which are supposed to have had a role in the creation of the world.[48] This posits a God who is behind creation but who is not wholly identified with the totality of the created world. Such a conception borders on the gnostic notion and also preserves the distinction between good and evil and between the material and non-material.

Other aspects of Jewish thought which interact with gnosticism include the myth of Adam Qadmon, the primal man and the archetype of the human being. The myth is inspired by the biblical creation story of Adam but is couched in gnostic terms.[49] He was the man after God's image or the man of God who is endowed with the redeeming powers of *nous*, divine powers, so that the primal man is akin to God and has close affinities with a higher spiritual world. There are differing accounts in the gnostic texts of the genesis of the first man and these in different ways account for his dual nature. In general the view is of man as a compound being, a mixture of the physical and spiritual. The former is evil and holds the soul captive but it is always aspiring after release. There is a mixture in the gnostic texts of the biblical account of creation mixed with other sources. The gnostics seem to have assimilated ideas from both and account for the duality of man by including a divine element that entered into his creation at the beginning. It is this presumably that led the gnostics to assume that it is those who possess this element (or divine *nous*) who are destined for salvation. Here the divine element is one of essence not form, and this bears upon the doctrine of election. In the Ophite system the designation Son of Man denotes the son of the primal man, and the title is likely to have been used of a Jewish apocalyptic figure, as in the Book of Daniel (written around 168 BCE). The title is not all that prominent in the religion of the Jews but it is used in Christianity of Jesus, who is reported to have used the title of himself; in the Hellenistic world this divine man is identified with the Platonic man. In respect of the Ophite designation R. McL. Wilson states:

> As Ophitism seems in many respects to be pre-Christian we have a clear example of the assimilation of Christian elements into an earlier and primarily alien scheme.[50]

The figure of *Sophia* (wisdom) is prominent in both Judaism and gnosticism. In the Jewish religion wisdom functions as an assistant to God in the creation of the world,[51] and in gnosticism wisdom is a female being who is also called the Holy Spirit, and represents the maternal element in the Christian Trinity of Father, Son and Holy Spirit. She is also the creator who enlightens human beings. She is depicted too as the benefactor of Adam and Eve who assisted in the conception of their children Seth and Norea.[52] In the Valentinian gnostic system the fall and restoration of *Sophia* is described and developed as part of its doctrine of redemption. The links between the Jewish concept and that of the gnostics is that in Judaism wisdom refers to the creative power of God and is expressive of his purpose. In gnosticism there are traces of Jewish influence in *Poimandres* which draws upon Jewish stories of creation. For example:

> But mind, the Father of all, being life and light, gave birth to a Man like myself; with him he was pleased, as his own offspring, for the Man was very beautiful, bearing the image of his Father. For truly God was pleased with his own form, and he delivered his creatures to him (of Gen. 1: 26–28). Having observed the creation made by the *demiurge* in the fire, man himself desired to create, and permission was granted by the Father. So, entering the creative space, where he received all power, he observed things created by his sister, and the Governors were pleased with him, and each gave him a share in his own region.[53]

These themes are some of the basic insights that contribute to the view of *gnosis* as a phenomenon that extends to many religious systems, including that of Judaism. They also come into prominence in some gnostic writings, notably the *Apocryphon of John*, which combines the myth of human creation from a Jewish source with gnostic conceptions. Since the Nag Hammadi texts have become available the case for the Jewish–gnostic connection has been strengthened and some scholars are inclined to trace the origins of gnosticism to a Judaistic source. There are certain features in gnosticism which substantiate this influence, but although there does seem to have been adaptation of Jewish ideas by the gnostics, this is not the only primary factor for determining the precise origins of gnosticism. There is evidence, moreover, that Jewish ideas were interpreted in a gnostic sense, and much clear evidence of the adoption of Jewish teaching. However, the point to be observed is that not *all* that is characteristic of gnosticism can be traced to this source, although it has to be said that in the case of Judaism it exerted an indisputable influence that provides us with a standard for measuring the extent to which external factors contributed to the making of gnosticism.

Apocalyptic writings

The Jewish apocalyptic writings that have survived from around the beginning of the Christian era give us yet another source of investigation of "the gnostic phenomenon", especially into those aspects that relate to the human predicament treated by Jewish apocalyptic writings. The word "apocalyptic" is notoriously difficult to define.[54]

In general terms it covers notions of the primordial condition of the human being, the continuous conflict between temporal and non-temporal forces, the final outcome of the struggle between hostile forces and the rule of God, and the ultimate complete consummation of all things in God.[55]

The ambivalence in the teaching of the apocalyptists from the second century BCE onward is reflected in its negative and fatalistic tone, its anti-cosmic stance on the one hand, but on the other hand, despite its weird world of fantasy and extravagant and esoteric ideas, it offered hope of release to the hard-pressed. It taught a world view of the whole creation in the grip of *archons* and demons and the approaching end of the present age (*aeon*). Its message proclaimed the final redemption through God's intervention, catastrophic though that would be. It made knowledge of this final event available to the righteous and the wise. Such knowledge only comes from God himself; it is his revealed wisdom and in essence therefore it is redemptive. The righteous alone are fit to receive this superior knowledge, as is demonstrated in the gnostic teachings of Silvanus whose separation of the *"pneumatic"* (spiritual) from the *"sarkitos"* (physical) ensures that the former are on the way to receiving the essential knowledge of redemption.[56]

A further point of interest is the apocalyptic teaching on the estrangement felt by the righteous in the world. They are aliens in the physical world. The apocalyptists were deeply conscious of the gulf between matter and spirit and the persistent craving for spiritual liberation. This is achievable through the exercises of virtue and self-discipline. The outlook of this dualistic thinking manifested itself in a special kind of spirituality whose focus is on "other-worldliness". The division drawn between this world and the world beyond, between the restrictions and the passing associations of this world and the delights and joys of the heavenly world, is ever an appealing element in apocalyptic literature.

This dualism, which is a notable feature of the apocalyptic, is sensitively expressed in *The Wisdom of Solomon*,[57] and finds a counterpart in the gnostic text the *Gospel of Philip* where contrast is drawn between this world of darkness and night and that of perfect day and holy night.[58] Reference here to *The Wisdom of Solomon* reinforces the earlier observation of the confluence between Judaism and gnosticism.[59] In this work Wisdom is portrayed as the spouse of God and his representative at the creation, who then arises like a mist to be a pure effluence from God's glory and a flawless mirror of his active power.[60] Wisdom is the Holy Spirit and the emanation of eternal light, helper of people to a knowledge of God who then grants them the gift of immortality.[61] Wisdom is equated with the law[62] and this is equivalent too to knowledge of redemption. Likewise in the gnostic texts knowledge of the law is given a role as one of the redemptive factors, and by virtue of its status of being equated with mysterious *gnosis*[63] it plays a key role in the process. On the other hand, error and malevolence operate against knowledge of God's plan, as we gather from this excerpt:

> So they argued, and very wrong they were, blinded by their own malevolence, they did not understand God's secret plan.[64]

Other aspects of apocalypticism that bear upon the subject of this enquiry include the idea of salvation. Its origin is beyond this world and its outcome of course is also beyond it. When the redemptive process is complete then the world as it is will come to an end and will pass away, it will be no more the sphere of operation. Then the *eschaton* (consummation) is complete, transcendent, supramundane, supernatural and totally perfect in its outcome.

In this respect apocalyptic teaching is radical and daring, and all-embracing. For the world to be redeemed it has to come to an end, all preoccupation with its operation will cease, all travail within it will end, existence within it will terminate. All that is will cease to be.[65]

Against this background we can estimate the origin of some basic gnostic teaching. It assimilated some typical apocalyptic ideas, especially the separation of God and the world, the dualism within the world, world-renouncing tendencies, and the apocalyptic termination. Gnosticism adopted these various strands of apocalypticism and interweaved them into its own systems. The combination is not just a matter of assimilation as gnosticism ensured that its systems bore the distinctive imprint of its own unique insights. The type of thought represented by the apocalyptic appealed to the gnostics, and there is a case for saying that it took root of this soil, but this applies only to the more congenial of its ideas rather than assuming it to be in its entirety an offshoot of Jewish apocalypticism.

Gnosticism and the Dead Sea Scrolls

The discovery of the Dead Sea Scrolls in 1947 in the Qumrân region of Jordan has been hailed as the major archaeological discovery of ancient manuscripts relating to a devout religious Jewish sect and their Bible. These manuscripts emanated from a sect of pietist Jews who settled in the Jordanian desert in the second century BCE and remained there until the Roman–Jewish war of 68–70 CE. The manuscripts are confidently dated from the second century BCE to the first century CE,[66] and they have been perused by many scholars to see whether there may be any points of affinity with the gnostic texts of Nag Hammadi. The evidence is inconclusive as not all the scrolls have yet been published, but there are certain terms and concepts that merit being considered briefly.

One such term obviously is *gnosis*. The word occurs in the sectarian scrolls in respect of knowledge of a particular kind which the sect members received and cultivated. It is not abstract or intellectual knowledge. Rather it is knowledge given to the initiated for the study of God's law and commitment to God's covenant. Knowledge here is of a theological kind that comes from divine revelation; its special features include sacred knowledge of creation, prophecy and divine law, and especially eschatological knowledge. Knowledge of redemption is only given to the spiritual. Emphasis on practical knowledge among the Qumrân covenanters is akin in places to knowledge expounded in the Wisdom literature of the Jewish Bible, that is, knowledge that finds its source in the fear of God, in obedience to his laws and awareness of his purpose, knowledge which will be unfolded at the end of time in all its fullness. God is addressed as the "fountain of all knowledge" and the "wellspring of knowledge" who has "opened the heart of Thy servant to knowledge".[67]

However, the special conception of *gnosis* in the gnostic writings, which conditions the individual's progress to liberation, is not of the same order as that of the Dead Sea Scrolls. The Essenes and the gnostics shared a common cultural milieu but this does not mean that they held all religious and philosophical concepts in common.

An additional feature of the scrolls is dualism between good and evil, light and darkness, truth and falsehood. In the scrolls the spirits of light and darkness are identified respectively with the spirits of truth and falsehood. In the Qumrân text the *Community Rule* the dualism is portrayed as follows:

> He has created man to govern the world and has appointed for him two spirits in which to walk until the time of his visitation, the spirits of truth and falsehood. Those born of truth spring from a fountain of light, and those born of falsehood spring from a source of darkness.[68]

We observe here that these spirits emanate from God who has created "two spirits". This brings them into subjection to God, the creator. The two cosmic spirits of light and darkness rule in the world at the order of the creator God, and are under his control. Their design is determined by God, whose power over the world is supreme. The evil in the world is ruled by the devil, and this struggles against the children of God (one of the Qumrân scrolls is entitled *The War of the Sons of Light against the Sons of Darkness*).[69] There is a powerful element of predestination in the teaching. The children of light have knowledge which causes them to discomfort the forces of darkness through the power of God which strengthens their hearts. God is not a philosophical concept but a living person whose presence is felt and is active at every turn.[70]

This is not as radical as the dualism of gnosticism where the creator is hostile to man and the evil of human existence is so much damned. The fundamental conception of dualism among the gnostics is that of spirit and matter but in the scrolls it is that of belief and unbelief, life and death. Such terms are used in the scrolls in a figurative sense and have an eschatological rather than a cosmological connotation. Accordingly, it is only the "Sons of Light" who will enter the light of eternity.[71] The revelation of God's will is communicated to whoever he wills.

Along with these features we may add the strong community association of the Qumrân covenanters, its rules and hierarchical structure, admission to the community by swearing of an oath of loyalty to the law of Moses, the ritual practices and customs observed (especially baptism), ritual washing, cultic meals, communal ownership of property, asceticism and celibacy. These largely differ from the gnostic position although there are some minor points of convergence. The Essenes have been classed as pre-Christian gnostics,[72] but this is difficult to accept in the light of the evidence at present available. The existence of a pre-Christian gnosticism may be granted but it did not have all the characteristic features of the gnosticism of the early Christian centuries.

The proper conclusion is to accept that there is refreshing evidence of elements of "the gnostic phenomenon" amongst the sect of the Dead Sea Scrolls,[73] but the absence from the scrolls of anything approaching the gnostic myth of the divine redeemer or the conception of the soul being imprisoned in a world of materialism, makes a conclusion that goes beyond the words of Miller Burrows precarious:

> On the whole, it seems unnecessary and only confusing to apply the term Gnosticism to the form in which such ideas appear in the Dead Sea Scrolls.[74]

At the same time, as G. R. Driver observed, the connection of the Dead Sea Scrolls with the gnostic sect of Mandaeans and the Therapeuts receives a fresh significance, as they breathed the same spiritual atmosphere and shared a common set of ideas derived from Judaism, apocalypticism, Iranian beliefs, dualism, Egyptian gnosticism, Oriental religions and Greek philosophies. Driver comments, "Each group took what it wanted from this common stock, adapted it to its own purposes, and in so doing transmuted it", but he also warns, "Once again, however, resemblances few or many do not by any means prove identity." This view seems sustainable in the light of present knowledge.[75]

Gnosticism in the early Christian centuries

The flowering of gnosticism coincided with the emergence and early growth of Christianity. The *gnosis* that had always transmitted special knowledge of redemption was at the heart of gnostic aspiration. This now assumed a new dimension as it claimed special revelation for Jesus Christ. It assimilated this into the essence of Christian experience and taught it as the condition of universal redemption. The gnostic interpretation infiltrated the early Christian Church, and communities of gnostics became active in its propagation from Antioch to Egypt and as far as Rome. Notable gnostic teachers spread its message and schools of gnosticism became dynamic centres of action. The variety of forms produced different emphases, but the differences were only a matter of degree. On the basic principle of divine *gnosis* as the key to salvation there was unanimity.[76]

Certain of the Christian gnostics are notable for their ability and skill in communication and propaganda. They operated against the background of developing Christian thought and theology, and they pioneered a new religious language and imagery free from ecclesiology that was effective in projecting a distinctive gnostic view of the person, work and significance of the redeemer.

This radical reinterpretation of Christian redemption was undertaken alongside that of orthodoxy with fervour and a sense of spiritual adventure. The Catholic Church saw it as a dangerous alternative to the Christian message preached by the first apostles and opposed its infiltration into mainstream Christianity, since it uprooted the historic foundations of Christianity. The Church responded to the challenge with vigour and positive action. It was its response to the threat of gnosticism that partly accounts for the steps taken by the Church to form a canon of Christian Scripture, an authentic Christian Creed, and to establish a threefold ministry.[77]

By the end of the second century the Church had become more institutionalized and structured in its ministry and worship. The pressures of an alternative gnostic Christianity made a crucial contribution to this process of institutionalization.

The inevitable tension between the gnostics and the apostolic church, as it struggled to establish itself in a pluralist world, developed into a hostility that threatened to divide the Church. The quality of relationships between members of gnostic circles, their life together as a community centred on special knowledge and enlightenment that no others had, whose spiritual fellowship was infused with a holistic sense of spiritual purpose, and whose spiritual unity was engendered by *gnosis*, coupled with their vision of a heavenly church and their direct access to Christ, and the depth of insight into the secret of redemption, proved attractive to other members of the Church and other seekers after truth. This disconcerted the orthodox church, which believed itself to be the sole defender of traditional apostolic belief and the custodian of the faith entrusted to it by Christ himself. Irenaeus was particularly venomous in his condemnation of the gnostics who deviated from "the Church, meaning the faithful who are from everywhere . . . since it is that tradition that is from the Apostles . . . having founded and established the Church" and that tradition was now opposed by "evil-minded men" (Valentinus and Marcion are named) and those who are "the first-born of Satan" and "who perverted the truth".[78]

It is not easy to convey the depth of the spiritual and intellectual ferment that the propagation of "the gnostic phenomenon" caused. The clash of ideas and interpretation of the person of Christ fanned the flames of conflict and made the meeting of minds between the orthodox and their detractors more impossible. Apart from the internal struggle within the Church between orthodoxy and heresy, in the wider world numerous systems of thought and idealism competed to win the souls and allegiance of people. In an age of spiritual hunger and uncertainty, the religious and philosophical stances of the gnostics appealed greatly to those who were capable of receiving mysterious *gnosis*, and gnostic views of reality and redemption captured the imagination of the educated classes. The gnostics interpreted the new age of Christianity as the *aeon* of spiritual illumination through *gnosis*, whereas orthodox Christians regarded it as the *kairos* which had arrived with the appearance of the historical Jesus to inaugurate God's kingdom.[79] This difference in the understanding of time in respect of God's action in the advent of Jesus proved contentious.[80] It extended to the perception of eschatology, which the gnostics related to the deliverance of the whole cosmos. As Rudolph remarks:

> *Gnosis* is interpreted not only in the final end of mankind but also in that of the cosmos for both are ordered with its cosmology.[81]

On the other hand, the eschatology orthodox Christians espoused was linked to the hope of the early inauguration of the messianic age, and many Christians awaited expectantly the imminent return of Christ to establish his kingdom.[82]

The strongest link between the diverse currents of thought that flowed from the variant gnostic and non-gnostic interpretations of Christian revelation was salvation. Both orthodox and gnostic Christians had their sights on the certain hope of redemption, but on the means of attaining this they profoundly differed.[83] The gnostics viewed salvation as being wholly other-worldly, and so renounced the world for the evil that it is, and taught a complete separation of soul and body and of spirit and matter as all that is material and physical is evil. Redemption is wholly spiritual.

The complex ideas which emerged from *gnosis* have to be viewed against its background of the early Christian struggle for identity. Leading churchmen looked upon gnosticism as a distraction that was disruptive of Christian unity; its appeal, mostly to the sensibilities of educated people, was divisive. Gnostics projected their teaching, as though it came direct from heaven, with intellectual vigour and positive and creative purpose, to ensure it had particular appeal to the educated classes.[84] We should not overlook the fact that it had also had a wider following. The gnostics were a force to be reckoned with in the prevalent multicultural world of the second century CE. Some of those who were converted to the Christian faith came from a Hellenistic background and had been brought up in the attitudes and fashion of a Hellenistic lifestyle. Many of these individuals came into contact with the gnostics and they found gnostic ideas and ideals congenial. The Christian Church had not only to contend with the inevitable impact of a religious and cultural pluralism, but it also had to struggle against the unwelcome intrusions of gnostic inducements to faith and salvation. The roots of gnostic spirituality penetrated so deeply the soul of orthodox Christian belief that it could not easily be uprooted. The upshot of this was dissension, as we shall demonstrate later.[85] The Church could not shake off completely the powerful impact of the appeal of extraordinary spiritual knowledge given to some as the means of knowing in a direct and immediate way the inner heart of God's redemption. The Church from that day to this has never been mono-lithic in theology or uniformly orthodox in belief, but the tension this roused in the early church shook it to its very foundation.

This emphasis on the primacy and sufficiency of spiritual knowledge turned the gnostics away from preoccupation with ecclesiasticism, permanent organization and structuring. The *Gospel of Truth* shows an aversion to ecclesiasticism.[86] The gnostics avoided truck with any form of church hierarchy and discounted the necessity of organized ministry as an encumbrance. They believed in the Church as the bearer of the gospel (good news), but the true church was not identified by its external forms and structure. On this the gnostics were not completely at one and they disputed among themselves the question of churchmanship. Some followers of Valentinus, for example, identified themselves with the Church while others dissented. The point at issue was whether the true church was an *invisible* community and whether orthodox believers should be included or not. There was the "spiritual church", to which only truly enlightened Christians belonged, among whom Pagels includes eastern Valentinians, Theodotus, and Tertullian in his later years; but on the other side were Ptolemy and Heracleon and western Valentinians.

Behind this division is a deeper issue of who and who is not fit to belong to the Church. There were gnostics and non-gnostics in the Church but who were the *true* church? The gnostics claimed special knowledge from God that they could impart only to those who were able to receive it. Could those who received the true mystical knowl-edge and those who did not both be assured of salvation? What distinguished gnostics from non-gnostics was their level of under-standing of divine redemption. Those who received *gnosis* were those who were united with Christ, but did Christ then reject the non-gnostic? Who were and were not fit for redemption? The debate was fierce and it is notable that the gnostic work *Interpretation of Knowledge* advocates reconciliation between the parties.

The need for reconciliation was imperative if the Church was to be at ease with itself. This did not happen and tension continued as Christian gnostics persisted in teaching a doctrine of salvation through Christ who revealed to them direct knowledge of this. By embracing a thorough-going dualism of matter and spirit, how could gnostic Christians accept with impunity the incarnation of Jesus? That God who is wholly spiritual could incarnate himself in flesh was unthinkable. Wherein then lay the foundation of Christian belief? In the human Jesus of history or the Christ of faith? The orthodox church taught the physical death and resurrection of Jesus as a means of salvation. But could God suffer, asked the gnostics, and be killed, and could a physical body be raised? In elucidating these questions gnostic Christians and others parted ways, and harmony was not achieved. The Church was alert and sensitive to the danger of gnostic views being accepted and replacing orthodoxy but it could not accommodate such heretical ideas, but neither could the gnostics settle to the orthodox insistence on a form of Christian belief grounded wholly in a historical perception of the person, death and resurrection of Jesus Christ. The Christian gnostics were intent on formulating a Christian gnostic theology of Jesus that would convey Christian truth in an acceptable orthodox view of him as a historical person and acceptable to all who genuinely sought salvation. They did not reject the record of the life of Jesus, but in their formulation of Christianity they interpreted it in existential terms. This enabled them to shed enlightenment on Christian truth in terms and catagories suited and intelligible to the culture of the time. This illumination and special insight enabled them, so they believed, to propound a meaningful and creditable system of Christian belief. The Church saw the problem this caused as immense and one that had to be resolved. The gnostics saw the solution as the condition of a progressive Christian commitment. Neither could evade the challenge, both were entrenched in elucidating the meaning, verifiability and truth claims of Christianity from its own perspective.

Why did gnosticism disappear?

In the event it was the Church that prevailed and by the end of the fourth century the gnostics were no longer a threat. The Church grew more powerful and structured after the conversion of Constantine (306–37) and it is likely that gnosticism, which was not notable for its organization, no longer competed with the existing Church system. For it to have survived as a threatening movement would require greater structuring and closer attention to organization. Insofar as this did not happen the gnostics contributed to their own decline. They did not mobilize themselves to develop a constitution that would make for permanence. They could not sacrifice the freedom of spiritual knowledge nor compromise their spiritual message for more structured and authoritarian forms of Christianity. Their spirit of individualism and care for individual experience and thinking about matters of faith forbade them from becoming immersed in rigid organization and ecclesiastical structure. They never cultivated or coveted hierarchical support or distilled their beliefs into authoritative creeds or liturgies.

The gnostics embraced what they saw as a religion of perfection wherein the believer had access to spiritual insight and growth independent of any external imposition. Possession of this insight (*gnosis*) was the secret of their solidarity and cohesion, and they did not feel the need of an ecclesiastical structure to make this possible.

What the gnostics sought to offer the Church was an inspired Christianity, a perception of Christian faith that was immediate and pure, not bound by organization or dependent on an ecclesiastical hierarchy. They claimed to know Christ and this was sufficient; it was the secret of progression to genuine Christian maturity, and this knowledge constituted the true church. From this angle they defended the necessity of the Church as a community of enlightened Christians who shared immediate experience of Christ received through divinely inspired spiritual knowledge. Such qualitative criteria differentiated between essential and non-essential elements in determining the nature of the Church. No external rite could make a true church; no conformity to external authority could take the place of spiritual conformity to the spirit within; no sacrifice, not even martyrdom, could be more meritorious than the spiritual sacrifice of renouncing evil; no set of doctrines could take the place of the true *gnosis* of Jesus Christ. This offered hope to the world of new life in Christ. On these principles gnosticism made its stand; it was uncompromising. Yet its appeal diminished after the Edict of Constantine in 311 CE, but "the gnostic phenomenon" did not disappear and there are signs of its influence in the history of Christianity up to the present. Wherever questions about the origins, nature, meaning and destiny of human life have been explored in earnest the insights of *gnosis* have continued to agitate the mind, and its influence has been felt by philosophers and poets, religionists and artists throughout the centuries.

In respect of Christianity, the impact of gnostic ideas continued to rumble on and the theology of the Jesus of history and the Christ of faith continues to be discussed. The question "who is the real Jesus?" continues to be explored. So also is the question "what is the Church?" Many gnostics viewed the true Church as an invisible community of kindred souls who imbibed the spirit of Christ and recognized one another in him. They believed that they were called to this spiritual fellowship through the direct gift of the divine *gnosis* and that the spirit of Christ met their spirit. They lived life as the Spirit directed. Many aspects of this teaching are still met amongst Christians and practising churchmen.

By the seventh century the physical presence of gnosticism had very largely disappeared from the Mediterranean world. The appeal of the gnostic schools was on the wane after the fourth century, and with the possible exception of Manichaeism, its public image was greatly diminished. As we saw above, there were elements in gnosticism, such as its anti-cosmic attitude and other aspects of its teaching, which would undoubtedly have been rejected by many. But it was the way the Church mobilized its life after the time of Constantine that made it more difficult for gnostics to penetrate the wall of authoritarianism in creed and ministry with which the Church surrounded itself. The conversion of Constantine was a momentous event for the Church, and the Council of Nicaea invested the bishop with the power of veto over appointments and other matters. It became more difficult for "subversive" elements to penetrate the more authoritarian structures of the Church.

Nevertheless, the characteristic ideas of gnosticism about God, the world, human life and salvation have never been far below the surface of theological and philosophical enquiry. The questions that were the core of gnostic predilections are too deeply embedded in the human psyche to be ignored. They cannot be eradicated by canon law, episcopal decree or ecclesiastic pronouncement. The visible communities may have vanished but the issues that preoccupied the gnostics at the height of their influence have not, as Elaine Pagels contends:

> the concerns of gnostic Christians survived only as a suppressed current, like a river driven underground. Such currents resurfaced throughout the Middle Ages in various forms of heresy, then with the Reformation, Christian tradition again took on new and diverse forms.[87]

It is as difficult to trace the line of development onward from the early Christian centuries as it was to trace the line of development before the Christian era. But it is possible to highlight a selective number of examples which have manifested aspects of "the gnostic phenomenon" in a recognizable way from one age to the other. Not all the examples bear the marks of pure gnosticism, but they serve to illustrate the fact that "the gnostic phenomenon" did not disappear altogether.

Bogomil

Bogomil lived in Bulgaria in the tenth century where he served as a priest.[88] His fame is that he is the chief architect of a powerful gnostic opposition to the Church of his day. He and his followers, Bogomils, were attracted to elements of Manichaeism and the dualism between good and evil. The Bogomils were reasonably well organized into three groups – "the perfect", "the hearers" and "the believers". The first group was the heart of the Bogomil movement and they were strictly ascetic. They were led by elders, apostles and teachers. They renounced wealth and this gave them freedom to denounce the opulence of the Byzantine Church. They also opposed war as evil and were hostile towards civil authorities.

In matters of belief the Bogomils embraced categories that are reminiscent of earlier gnosticism, notably belief in the devil as the creator of the material world and humankind. The name given the creator of the physical world is Satanael, but the creator of the soul is the Lord God. The Bogomils believed that the Good God had two sons, Satanael and Christ. Satanael rebelled and became the opponent of the good and the leader of evil. The visible world is the work of the evil power, which holds it in bondage. The soul is held captive in the body but is capable of being redeemed by the action of the Logos. The material body is evil and the struggle to get free from it goes on all the time. The achievement of release is assisted by virtuous practices, repentance, love and goodness. The body of Jesus was unreal and his humanity only an appearance, but the Logos was present in it to make real the genuine spiritual nature and origin of Christ.

As well as holding this docetic view of the person of Jesus, the Bogomils rejected the Old Testament and looked for redemption and return to heaven by receiving knowledge of the redeeming God. Then the soul was free to return to him.

The Bogomils, the name means "beloved of God", rejected many of the ordinances of the Church, including the sacraments and the cult; they also regarded relics and icons as the creation of Satan. However, they practised the laying on of hands, and baptism by the Holy Spirit, and used the Lord's prayer and confession. The movement flourished until the seventeenth century and its influence continued on in Catharism, which we refer to next.

Cathars

The Cathars were a group of "the pure ones" who operated in the twelfth century in southern France and northern Italy where they were also known as Albigensians. They founded their own church, which had many points of affinity with gnosticism. The Cathars were devoted to living a life of purity in the illumination of a spiritual light which shone from God. They made a strict distinction between those who were truly enlightened as the elect and others who were non-supporters, hearers. They professed belief in cosmological and anthropological dualism and the spiritual nature of Christ and viewed his flesh as a perversion. In respect of redemption the Cathars viewed the visible church as irrelevant and they preached a message of unpolluted spirituality. Tobias Churton records this description by Gerard Zuchetto of this unalloyed spirituality:

> the Cathar *parfaite* (a woman who had passed through the Cathar "baptism of fire" or spiritual baptism, the Consolamentum) may have been a romantic subject for the enamoured troubadour. The *parfaite* was chaste, was good, was spiritually pure and her heart was fixed on the divine world.[89]

Those who received *consolamentum* were enrolled in the ranks of the elect, were released from the grip of the devil, and followed the Cathar ethic of anti-nominianism, vegetarianism and asceticism. At the same time the Roman Church dismissed the *gnosis* of the Cathars, and accused them of licentious behaviour and sexual laxity. In return Cathars denounced the Church of Rome as a false and counterfeit creation of the devil which led people away from the true knowledge of the nature and means of Christian redemption. This evil God must be rejected. In place of the hierarchic organization and sacraments of the Church the Cathars proclaimed a message of simple spirituality and believed in the baptism of the Spirit and the laying on of hands. They taught an anthropological dualism and expressed this and other beliefs in a mythical style in epic poems and chronicles. The souls of angelic beings had been embedded in human bodies from where they yearned for release into the realm of the wholly spiritual. They declared that:

> Matter was inherently evil, the action of the devil, the work of God was the universe of souls and the path of salvation was their release from sinful flesh. It followed that the Catholic doctrine of the incarnation of Christ was a monstrous perversion, and the crucifixion, an illusion, since the Saviour could not have been contaminated by participation in the material world.[90]

As in the case of the early Christian gnostics, the Church saw the Cathars as a threat. The Cathars insisted that they were the true Church, true Christians who had passed through the "baptism of fire" as the rite of being "consoled" (*consolamentum*) – a rite of liberation that could be administered on the deathbed to any who believed in the good God as the source of goodness and the goal of existence as union with him. The Church opposed the Cathars by the rigour of its own teaching and by the Inquisition. Some recent knowledge of Catharism has come to light from the discovery in Florence of the *Book of the Two Principles* and *The Questions of John*, which tells of an encounter between Jesus and the apostle John when the apostle questioned Jesus about the origin of the world. The work of God centres on the universe of souls and the means of release from the traumas of the flesh to the pure realm of the spirit.

Jacob Boehme (1575–1624)

During the Middle Ages Christianity underwent many changes, and a number of Christian mystics displayed an interest in gnostic or near-gnostic ideas. Jacob Boehme was a Protestant mystic and theologian. He was born into a Lutheran family in an age when the doctrines and procedures of the Protestant Reformation had raised public awareness of the controversy that surrounded fundamental theological and ecclesiological issues and practices. Boehme settled in the city of Gorlitz and associated himself with a number of religious groups. He took an active part in the religious controversies and shared a wide range of religious interests.

Boehme became deeply involved with the question of theodicy and the origin and nature of Christian salvation. He was also keenly interested in the nature and development of Christian spirituality, and this led him to the centre of the religious turmoil and controversies of the age. He wrote his major work, *The Aurora*, in 1612, as a kind of compendium of theology, philosophy and astrology.[91] The book is notable for its strong mystical element and Boehme's own particular theological insights. His mystical experience led to a strongly individualist approach to religion, especially concerning theodicy and the problem of evil in a world created by a good and loving God. The *Aurora* did not find favour with the Protestant pastor of Gorlitz and it was confiscated. Boehme was banned from writing other books.[92]

For a period Boehme accepted the ban, but after a notable visionary experience he resumed his theological activity and writing. He developed a doctrine of creation which he linked closely with the biblical account in the Book of Genesis. His exposition has a distinct philosophical flavour, and is related also to views on predestination, a subject widely discussed in the early seventeenth century.

His teaching on creation and salvation is conveyed in a work called *The Great Mystery*. Briefly his thesis began with "the nothing", which, as a single unified will, wills "a something". In this act of willing the Son is produced and through him the "nothing" discovers the "something" within itself. The "willing" proceeds from the Son as Holy Spirit to the contemplation of itself as wisdom (*Sophia*). He deals also with the various possibilities present in the Son or the Word for whose creation he is responsible. These possibilities are fire and light, which are fused and reflect in themselves the being of the universe. These are manifested through properties that are present in all being.[93]

These properties are categorized into principles, one of which represents fire. While searching for the fire or light, Lucifer refused to accept the light principle within himself and fell. The temporal creation came into existence at this moment. Adam stood at its height embracing the elements of fire and light, male and female. Adam chose to know the principles and fell, and male and female were then divided. They entered into a state of intemperate and self-destructive existence until eventually God revealed the light element in Christ. In him humankind was able to live in harmony with the virgin Sophia.[94]

Boehme's views of light and fire, the properties and principles which are linked with his doctrine of creation and human life, express the same fundamental concerns as are found in the earlier gnostic systems. His view of salvation as the ultimate harmony of life with Christ echoes the gnostic contemplation of a final state of redemptive union with God. Boehme's ideas received attention in a number of European countries and exerted an influence on poets as well as theologians and philosophers, especially Platonists. He wrote a number of substantial works, made a scholarly study of gnosticism and pioneered the study of the philosophy of religion. His original thinking inspired such notable leaders of thought as Schelling, Schleiermacher and Hegel.

Goethe's Faust

The classical drama *Faust*, created over many years by a German lawyer from Frankfurt, Johann Wolfgang von Goethe (1749–1832), has affinity in a number of places with key gnostic ideas. *Faust* is one of the greatest classics of the human spirit, a timeless drama of the spiritual quest of humankind in which Faust takes the role of representative man. The main themes of the drama focus on the ceaseless human conflict and rebellion against imposed authority and custom, and the struggle to attain ultimate freedom and blessedness. The framework of the drama is Christian and the action is set in heaven and hell. The battlefield is the human soul where the struggle for answers to ultimate questions of life and death is waged relentlessly. A recurrent theme is the futility and meaninglessness of submission to external forces and values, which holds the soul in bondage, rather than submission to subjective values of freedom and knowledge of reality. In this relentless struggle the soul is empowered by the flow of spiritual energy within, which braces and strengthens the soul with vitality to sustain it through the merciless, remorseless and savage conflict. This conflict is the devising of Mephistopheles whose devilish wranglings are intended to keep the soul in endless captivity. The struggle exerts all the powers of the senses, the emotions and the imagination. No one is able to escape the hazards of this inner conflict, an inescapable component of all human experience.[95]

The drama, therefore, mirrors the life of the soul and Goethe seems to visualize himself as the soul of Faust in the throes of this dramatic and inevitable conflagration of which Faust is representative of every man. Of himself Goethe said:

> When I need a God for my personal nature as a moral and spiritual man – He always exists for me. The heavenly and earthly things are such an inward realm that it can be grasped only by the collective intelligencies of all beings.

Of this it has been said:

> This book will display in a slowly moving panorama the landscapes of his soul.

The tone of Goethe's work is Christian and Christianity is described as the myth of ultimate truth. Many biblical themes are included and there are many quotations from the Bible. The story portrays a German necromancer who made a pact with the devil, who in return offered knowledge, wealth and magical powers for his service. The soul of the magician is carried off to hell to experience its torments, doom and damnation. The conflict is between God and the devil, between good and evil, between freedom and captivity.

In the course of the drama Helena (a reborn Helen of Troy), the Mother of all, descends to the lower regions where the angels and powers who created the world are gathered. Also Simon Magus is introduced as one who was accompanied by Helena on his journeys as a prophet and miracle worker. Helena is the chief conception of his mind and through her at the beginning he had the idea of creating angels and archangels. Helena, knowing what the father willed, descended to the lower regions and powers that created the world. Hans Jonas has concluded that this involvement of Simon Magus in Goethe's drama distinguishes him from the Simon Magus of the Book of Acts and other gnostic writings. Simon Magus travelled under the name Faustus (= the favoured one) and Jonas says of him:

> Surely few of the admirers of Marlowe's and Goethe's plays have an inkling that their hero is a descendant of a gnostic sectory, and that the beautiful Helena called up by his art was once the fallen Thought of God through whose raising mankind was to be saved.[96]

Faust's pursuit of knowledge ushers the drama to its climax, and the hero's liberation and reconciliation to God. The salvation is complete and the striving soul of humanity has achieved its apotheosis. The interest in Goethe's masterpiece for the student of gnosticism is its realism and spiritual penetration. The inner conflict is true to human experience without exception – no one has escaped its trauma. The inwardness of the conflict is a binding factor between all human beings, hence the view of Faust as representative man. The inner conflict is resolved through divine intervention. The final outcome of the conflict between God and the devil is the liberation of the soul. Faust emerges victorious and his redemption is complete. Conflict ceases and gives way to the harmony of the soul with God.

William Blake (1757–1827)

The poet and social visionary William Blake has been called the most representative gnostic of the Anglo-Saxon world. His work was inspired by the mystic Jacob Boehme and many of his poems display the insights and spirit of gnosticism. Tobias Churton has written:

> Blake was gifted with an exceptionally strong visionary faculty . . . Vision means to see, really see, not "with the eye", the "vegetable eye", but through it. To see reality is vision. It is the universal counterpart of "intellect" *nous*. The mind is creative of reality – the mind is not a blank screen.

The individual can share in the vision of the eternal form of humanity – humanity itself. Individuals share the source in the divine being.[97]

What justifies us regarding Blake's work as relevant to the subject of gnosticism? He was a Christian, yet his Christian beliefs fitted neither Protestant or Roman Catholic orthodoxy. He believed deeply in the spiritual world and in the reality of the spiritual in every person. Human beings inherit a spiritual universe which is alive with divine presence. It is the abode of the personal God who gives it its unity, and for those who discover truth then "everything would appear to man, as it is, infinite" (*Marriage of Heaven and Hell*).[98]

Blake denied that matter was the source of what exists or that creation is only materialistic or mechanical. He was aware of the duality of spirit and matter, and of the contradictory forces that pervade all things. The creator God (Urizem) is inferior to the Supreme God, he is the fallen God even though he was given birth by the Supreme God. Blake was a man of the world, a social visionary who also had a political message. Yet he was concerned with the inner significance of events, and in this respect reflected the concerns of the early gnostics. He stressed the priority of vision as the means of discovering truth and the superiority of vision to intellect. It is probable that Blake knew the gnostic work *Pistis Sophia*, which was discovered in Egypt in 1785 and tells of the vision of Christ's disciples on the Mount of Olives after the resurrection. But there are traces also of the *Hermetica* literature in his writings and familiarity with Hellenistic ideas, the works of Plato and the Neo-Platonists.

Many of the images and concepts found in his poetry come from the Bible. Whilst the visionary aspect of his works is the most protrusive there are various levels of vision, and vision reaches its ultimate in moments of inspiration. He was aware of the contradictory forces that pervade everything, such as light and darkness, but to see the contradiction is itself a method of perception, as "without contraries is no progression":

> from these contraries spring what the religious call Good and Evil. Good
> is the passive and obeys reason. Evil is the active springing from energy.
> Good is Heaven. Evil is Hell.[99]

The contrast between good and evil operates in a profound way to influence thought and perception. They are linked together and account for the paradox of life which requires a response in action. Life is an endless struggle between negative and positive forces, that is expressed in Blake's imagery, as the Spectre (the negative) and the Emanation (positive). The latter is the divine potentiality in all things, the holy that lives in everything:

> My Spectre round me night and day
> like a wild beast guards my way.
> My Emanation far within
> weeps incessantly for my sin.[100]

The struggle is waged between conventional religion and its liturgy and ritual and the truly spiritual. The good is the attainment of the positive Emanation, the self-discovery that is the essence of genuine salvation.

Reason alone is unable to attain this ideal. On its own, reason creates severance from the spiritual source of reality. It contrasts with faith and rejects the elation of inspiration and the power of the holy that is within. Reason without vision distorts the divine image within. It may distort, but reason can never efface the divine image, or the creative energy that is the precious gift of imagination. Therefore he taunts the deists and materialists:

> Mock on, mock on, Voltaire, Rousseau,
> Mock on, mock on, 'tis all in vain
> you throw the sand against the wind,
> and the wind blows it back again . . . [101]

There is a positive emphasis on the significance of experience in the works of Blake. The loss of innocence has to be retrieved and experience alone is able to achieve this. Human life is impoverished and immersed in recurring dilemma because of the refusal to learn from experience. This causes the loss of innocence and produces a state of bondage from which the human being needs to be released so as to enjoy the freedom of love. In the well-known *Songs of Innocence and Experience* Blake portrays the struggle engendered by the contrary states of existence that the inner spirit experiences. These songs are resonant with images of contradiction, such as the image of the soul as the sick rose, or the fire that can cleanse or destroy, or the Tyger, and the fear and uncertainty of love as a poisoned tree. The images are not easy to interpret, but the use of images and symbols to convey meaning and thought is reminiscent of some gnostic writings. The difficulty of being precise about the meaning of the symbolism is as characteristic of Blake as of the gnostics. What is the image of the rose, we may well ask in this poem:

THE SICK ROSE

O Rose thou art sick.
The invisible worm,
That flies in the night
In the howling storm:

Has found out thy bed
Of crimson joy:
And his dark secret love
Does thy life destroy.[102]

The visionary Blake held tenaciously to the reality of the spiritual world. His insistence on the claims of vision over intellect is paralleled by the gnostic claims of knowledge over blind faith. Blake's preoccupation with the internal significance of events and the primacy of experience finds its counterpart in gnostic presuppositions. His social and political vision, which might have been sullied by the events of his age, did not lead him to abandon his vision of restoration and the wholeness of life. The experience of innocence lost with the ensuing contradictions this caused still kept alive the hope of reconciliation. Blake saw the potentialities for reconciliation and harmony in the body and in the soul. He affirms the possibility of people finding fulfilment and hence salvation.

Carl Gustav Jung (1875–1961)

Jung's interest in gnosticism was known before the discovery of the Nag Hammadi texts. The eminent psychiatrist secured the acquisition of a number of texts for the Bollinger Institute in Geneva, which were then grouped together to form the Jung Codex.[103] Jung's thesis is that human beings are naturally religious, and his interest in and fascination with religion was profound, particularly so in respect of its symbolism. He undertook an interpretation of gnostic symbols as he portrayed the nature of the self under a number of symbols. In his work the *Psychology of the Unconscious* (1916) he advanced the theory that religion arises from a tendency to regression, to the attitude of infantile reliance on parents. He identified within the unconscious the properties of thought, emotion, sensation and intuition. Thought and emotion were classified as rational, and sensation and intuition as irrational. Every individual experiences these modes of functioning, rational or irrational. Each possesses a natural religious action. Deeply embedded within the collective unconscious, deeper than personal consciousness, are primordial images or types that impinge on human behaviour. These archetypes are primordial images of an infinite variety and manifest themselves through personal experience. They are the equivalent of religious dogmas.[104] However, in Jung's view, the long tradition of interpreting religious symbolism has not satisfied spiritual needs, but in the case of the gnostics they had devised signals that were essential for achieving spiritual growth. There is much practical importance in this use of symbols for understanding the meaning and purpose of life.

Everyone has an interest in discovering the meaning and purpose of existence, and for this reason their archetype image of God has to be invoked. The archetype *image* is to be distinguished from the archetype itself. Human beings need to relate to God and gain insight into the ultimate meaning of life through embarking on a variety of experiences. Through experience, insight can be gained into the meaning of life, and be the means of achieving satisfaction and wholesomeness. The source of understanding the meaning of life is not revelation from a divine source but rather from what lies within the psyche.

The idea that religion is necessary for salvation is therefore to be rejected. Salvation is not dependent solely on faith (Jung spoke of this notion as childishness), nor indeed on the salvific religion of Christianity.[105]

Jung differed from the gnostics in the matter of creation. He could not accept an anti-cosmic view of the created order. He was deeply respectful of evil. He viewed the God of the Old Testament as harsh and jealous, but he rejected the gnostic view of the Supreme God, who was unknowable, as an alternative to the God of the Old Testament. Jung conceived of the existence of God in a symbolic sense and maintained that the cosmos could only be transformed from within humanity and not by any external forces. In this way Jung conceived of the end of the world (eschatology) as the psychological counterpart of the spiritual development of humankind in its entirety. This perceives the end of the world as a fundamental wholeness or completeness.

The relevant aspects of Jung's teaching to gnostic doctrine are both implicit and explicit. Both convey a view of eschatological wholeness, both teach the need to relate to God in order to achieve the ideal, although Jung only consented to his existence in a symbolic sense. Jung was not interested in a dogmatic or coherent theology, but he expressed his feelings for gnostic thought in the following terms:

> We have in Gnosticism what was lacking in the centuries that followed; a

belief in the efficacy of individual revelation and individual knowledge. This belief was rooted in the proud feelings of man's affinities with the gods.[106]

In this review we have pointed to the incidence of "the gnostic phenomenon" in different cultures and periods of time. In some there are parallels between one strand and another, in others there are purely individual strands with no parallels. Yet the belief that the authentic truths about human existence and its destiny are accessible to humankind through the possession of special *gnosis* is a thread that runs unbroken from the beginning to this moment. The achievement of one's destiny is the supreme human achievement. It is still, as it has always been, the preoccupation of religion and philosophy. It cannot be isolated or restricted to one age or culture, and evidence of it in different cultures, whether this is due to deliberate borrowing or because of its special features, is an enrichment to our appreciation of one of the most potent forces that have shaped human destiny. Parallels and non-parallels apart, *gnosis* in its many permutations is the priceless treasure that helps to unfold the mystery that is at the heart of all genuine human experience.

Beware let no-one lead you astray, saying,
"Lo here" or "Lo there"
For the Son of Man is within you.
Follow after him.

The Gospel of Mary

John, for the men below I am crucified in Jerusalem and pierced
with lances and with reeds and given to drink of vinegar and gall.

Acts of John

If the spirit descends upon them, it is quite sure that they will attain
salvation.

The Apocryphon of John

Glory to thee Wise Word!
Glory to thee, thou hidden one who hast many forms!

Song of the Pearl

3

Gnosticism and its Literature

As in any study of this kind a key factor is the volume of available resources. Prior to the recovery of the Nag Hammadi texts the primary sources for the study of gnosticism were meagre, diffuse and variable, and the secondary sources were mainly the works of the Church Fathers who were either prejudicial or overtly hostile. However, the situation has changed since 1945 when the Nag Hammadi documents were discovered, but there are valuable materials other than the Nag Hammadi texts that inform about the progress of "the gnostic phenomenon".

This literature covers what has been termed "a large and somewhat amorphous group of religious systems".[1] Not all of it is gnostic in the strictest sense and some exudes only the spirit of gnosticism, but it does nevertheless offer important insights into this "amorphous group of religious systems" and informs about its development and outreach. In fact, the first source we mention is only gnostic in "tone" rather than being pure gnostic in substance. This is a gnostic-type Coptic manuscript which has been available since 1769. It dates from the early Christian centuries and originated in Upper Egypt. Its main interest is in the conversation it reports between Jesus and his disciples. It sheds light on the range of disciples, who include women as well as men, and, significantly, it provides insight into the nature of the person of Jesus which reflects the views reminiscent of the gnostics of the early Christian centuries.

More substantial and extensive is the so-called Berlin Coptic Codex, which was discovered near Achmin in Egypt in 1896. The codex comprises three gnostic texts of considerable interest and importance. One of these is an incomplete copy of the *Gospel of Mary*, which is also part of the Nag Hammadi collection. Although it is only a fragmentary copy it has attracted considerable attention on account of information it contains about the account of the disciples together and Mary comforting them with the assurance of the continuing presence of Christ with them, and the words of Jesus are recorded:

> Beware let no-one lead you astray, saying,
> "Lo here" or "Lo there"
> For the Son of Man is within you.
> Follow after him.

Mary is portrayed as being specially favoured by Jesus and as having received special knowledge of the divine world from him. The other texts in this codex are the *Apocryphon of John*, which is also one of those recovered at Nag Hammadi; this also sheds light on the attitude of the gnostic to the world as a transient dwelling and tells how the soul upon whom the Spirit descends will attain salvation:

> If the spirit descends upon them, it is quite sure that they will attain salvation.

The third gnostic text of the codex is the *Sophia of Jesus Christ*, again among the Nag Hammadi documents, which is set in a revelationary context centred on the redemptive mission of Jesus Christ, the "first begotten". Also within the codex is an apocryphal work, the *Acts of Peter*, which is only of marginal interest to gnosticism. It does, however, reflect aspects of gnostic teaching, especially the injunction to keep the mind focused on the reality within, and to turn away from the allurement of this impermanent world. The Berlin Codex is believed to date from the third century CE.[2]

The Church Fathers

The works of the Church Fathers, emanating from the second century and later, constitute an indispensable source of information about gnostic views and practices. The substantial writings of Justin Martyr (*c.*100–165), Irenaeus (*c.*130–200), Clement of Alexandria (*c.*150–215), Hippolytus (*c.*230 CE), Epiphanus (*c.*315–402), Origen (*c.*185–255) and Eusebius (*c.*265–340) are extensive mines of information, and wherever it is possible to penetrate the polemics and prejudices it enables us to piece together a reasonably coherent picture of "the gnostic phenomenon" through the eyes of its critics. They treated the gnostic menace to the Church, as they saw it, vigorously and without restraint. Their method of presentation suited their motive and purpose; their writings are biased and polemical but invaluable for information on "the gnostic phenomenon". They all viewed it with alarm, although some of the Fathers are less vituperative than others. Irenaeus was particularly hostile and extreme in his condemnation of gnosticism. He despised it as a cause of schism, as being unsound in doctrine, self-assured and conceited. Those who practised it he denounced as heretics who acted for self-gain and vanity.[3] Clement of Alexandria assumed a more philosophical stance by examining analytically the heretical *gnosis* in relation to the true *gnosis*, by setting out the "tenets of notable heresies" and "the answers that must be made to them . . . by way of introduction to the knowledge that is according to the mystic contemplation, in which we will advance according to the renowned and revered Rule of the Tradition, so that we may be ready to listen to the transmission of the Gnostic Tradition".[4] Origen, the famous Christian teacher and theologian, produced something like an exposition of Christian *gnosis*, but his method also ranged over a wide field of Greek and eastern learning, as well as spiritual and secular subjects.[5]

In a broad sense the Church Fathers complied with the affirmation of Irenaeus when he stated that "by knowledge of the truth we mean the teaching of the Apostles". So they built their systems of Christian doctrine on the foundation of apostolic doctrine and tradition. They made numerous references to biblical texts, which they interpreted in order to authenticate and justify their critical attitude to the impositions of gnosticism. They were alarmed, if not fearful, at the consequences of the gnostic doctrines, were these to prevail. They gave a picture of a fundamentally incompatible rift between their strict adherence to apostolic tradition and the more liberal stance of the gnostics. They were fully committed to the Church as an authoritarian and institutionalized community. The rule of faith delivered once and for all time to the apostles they contended is unassailable.

The Church Fathers not only based their exposition on the essence of apostolic teaching but also found support from non-canonized works currently in circulation. They made direct attacks on individual gnostics, as for instance Tertullian's attack on the determinism taught by the gnostic Valentinus, and on those heretics who stated that nature cannot be changed.[6] According to the Fathers the Church had to be catholic in doctrine and uniform in governance, consistent in ministry and worship. Justin Martyr offers a forthright view of heathenism, but also of Christ the true teacher as against teaching that is false. Irenaeus, to whom further references will be made, wrote works against the gnostics, and stressed the pre-eminence of the Catholic Church in all matters of faith and doctrine. Clement of Alexandria wrote about the preparation of the world for the coming of Christ and his own conception of the Christian character in the light of gnostic behaviour. Hippolytus was a disciple of Irenaeus and he followed his master in opposition to the gnostics, especially to the way they believed without judgement in the faith. Origen taught the spiritual meaning of Scripture and replied to gnostics who denied the resurrection of Jesus. The learned Eusebius found a basis for authority in the scriptures and reported on measures taken to establish orthodoxy in conformity with this authority.

Of lesser significance is a work from the second century called the *Odes of Solomon*, a collection of hymns in Syriac which has been called the song book or the prayer book of a Syrian Christian community of gnostics. It was written either in Greek or Aramaic, and a collection of the odes has also been found in Egypt. There is a Coptic version which comprises five complete odes. In all there are forty-two odes, a Syriac manuscript containing all but two of them was discovered in 1909. Their language is figurative but their interest for us is the link they have with the gnostic doctrines prevalent in the east in that period. The odes were composed in praise of the Lord, the Word and the Master. They express mystical truths in ecstatic poetry and literary images that are very reminiscent of the Jewish Wisdom literature. The odes express awareness of the presence of God and the soul in colourful metaphors, which describe consciousness of the inner spirituality that God inspires and will bring to perfect fruition:

> The Lord is upon my head like a wreath,
> and I shall not leave him:
> The wreath of truth has been plaited for me,
> and it has let my branches bud within me.
>
> For it is not a withered wreath that does not bud:
> For thou art alive upon my head,
> and thou hast budded upon me.
> The fruits are full and perfect:
> they are full of thy salvation.[7]

The odes highlight the deficiency of knowledge that is untested by experience, and of the Word being sent into this realm of darkness in order to bring illumination to those who are genuinely able to receive it. The mystic touch is manifested in a Master whose essence is divine love, and those who know him are accounted, "Blessed are those who have understood everything through him."[8] A feature of particular interest in the odes is the view of redemption, where Christ, after his own deliverance, delivers his own people from the captivity of the world.[9]

Apocryphal works

Whilst referring to works from the second century we should include the apocryphal *Acts of Thomas*, which contains the famous *Song of the Pearl*.[10] In the *Acts* there are numerous references to the indwelling Spirit, to the self-sufficient God who is known by reference to his attributes, and to Jesus being identified with Wisdom:

> Glory to thee Wise Word!
> Glory to thee, thou hidden one who hast many forms![11]

The authorship of the *Acts of Thomas* is unknown, but some of its tales and mystic discourses breathe the atmosphere of gnosticism. It appears to be a brief history of the apostle Judas Thomas, but it also includes prayers and invocations of anointing ceremonies, as were practised amongst gnostics.[12] The *Song of the Pearl*, as we saw, has affinities with Iranian ideas, it reflects late Valentinian doctrine and the dualism between the body and soul is described as a filthy and clean garb. It is a good example of gnostic poetry in a parabolic and symbolic form.

An older work of an apocryphal kind, reputed to date from the middle of the first Christian century, is the *Acts of John*, whose main interest lies in the account it gives, ostensibly from experience, of a gnostic kind of Christology. It contains a whole range of gnostic-like sayings of the mysteries taught to the disciples of Jesus in secret. It also tells stories from the canonical gospels but with clearly mystical elements added – for example, the story of the transfiguration, or the account of the summoning of the disciples by the Sea of Galilee. In these narratives the view of the person of Jesus is docetic, that is, his physical body is a mere semblance, the only reality is the spiritual or the divine. This is evidently the case in the account given of the crucifixion. In the *Acts of John*, Jesus, having risen from the physical body, interprets to John the "cross of light" whilst the crucifixion is in progress. Jesus says to John:

> John, for the men below I am crucified in Jerusalem and pierced with lances and with reeds and given to drink of vinegar and gall.[13]

Pagels designates the *Acts of John* one of the most famous gnostic texts prior to the discoveries of Nag Hammadi, notable for its revelation of Jesus as a spiritual being who adapted himself to human perception.[14]

Mandaean literature

Another source of information is the Mandaean literature, which has been known in Europe since the sixteenth century but whose actual date is difficult to establish. The Mandaean script was in use in the second century CE and the Mandaean texts probably come from this period. They are of particular interest in this context on account of affinities with ancient Middle Eastern religion and with Judaism. There are three extant writings from this body of literature that have survived, namely, the *Ginza* (the Great Book), a *Book of John* and a *Book of the Zodiac*.

The *Ginza* is a detailed account of the beginning of the universe. It is compiled in two main parts with mythical, theological and moral tractates and liturgical hymns devoted to the ascent of the soul. The *Book of John* tells of the activities of John the Baptist for whom the Mandaeans had great respect. They gave him allegiance as one of the saviours of the past. The book includes examples of his teaching. A number of discourses, sayings, stories and allegories are attributed to John the Baptist, which are also echoed in the teaching of Jesus. The *Book of the Zodiac* is a collection of magical and astrological texts which contain horoscopes used by priests.[15]

This body of literature belongs to an independent strand of gnosticism with a purely philosophical orientation. The word Manda (Aramaic *manda*) means knowledge and is equivalent to the Greek *gnosis*. As well as their wealth of imagery, these writings are of particular interest to the study of gnostic philosophy, especially as the Mandaeans, who originated from the lowland of Persia, claimed to possess and act upon mysterious knowledge of divine origin. They considered themselves to be an elect group, the "plantation of the pious". They espoused a dualistic philosophy and taught the way of salvation through esoteric knowledge whose source is the divine being. The release of the soul from evil forces is effected through the work of the messenger of light. The *Ginza* reads:

> He opened the doors for me and came,
> he split the firmament and revealed himself.
> He opened the doors and came,
> he opened the gates before me and drove the Seven from my path.
> He clothed me with radiance
> and wrapped me with light.
> He gave me a wreath of radiance to me
> and my form shone forth more than all the worlds.[16]

On its ascent to the heavenly spheres the soul is hampered by evil *archons* but it is assisted in its progress by the two mythical saviours, Silmai and Nidbai, as

> The two delegates of Manda-d-Hiia [lit. Knowledge of Life]
> who rule over the great Jordan of life,
> for they baptised with the great baptism of Light.[17]

Baptism is a magical process which ensures purification and immortality. Along with baptism various other rites were practised, including marriage, masses for the dead and acts of consecration. The Mandaeans, who have survived in small numbers to this day, invested a great interest in their own culture, and, according to Rudolph, we are here dealing with a heretical Jewish sect which "like other comparable groups of late Jewish religious history, stood in opposition to official Judaism and was widely open to non-Jewish influences, above all Iranian and gnostic".[18]

Manichaean literature

Whilst we are considering sources for the study of gnosticism other than the Nag Hammadi documents, we must include the religion of Mani. He came from Babylon and saw himself as "Apostle of Light". The religion he founded, after his first supernatural vision in about 240 CE, is one of the many sects classified as gnostic. It was an amalgam of Buddhist, Zoroastrian, Jewish, Christian and gnostic thought which spread to the west and Rome. Here it was influential and for ten years Saint Augustine was a follower. It is a dualistic religious movement which is known from papyri discovered in Egypt in 1930 of gnostic writings by Mani, including *Kephalaia* (chapters), a psalm book, homilies, poems and theology. Mani taught an eternal dualism between good and evil that brought the world into being and that will continue to the end of time. *Gnosis* is here equivalent to religious truth, and salvation is achieved through acquiring knowledge of a spiritual kind. Inner illumination that accompanies the gift of *gnosis* reveals how the soul, which shares the nature of God, has fallen into captivity to the physical world from whence it can be eventually released only by means of *nous*, the spirit or intelligence within. The release is described in Manichaean literature as "the seduction of the demons", that is, reference to the cosmic conflict between light (God and the messenger of light) and darkness (the devil and the *archons*). They were originally separate but particles of light were stolen by the demons for the purpose of constructing the earth and all inanimate things contained in it. The human soul is entangled with evil matter and passes through three stages: the separation of light and darkness or spirit and matter, the amalgamation of the substances, and a final stage when the separation is made complete. This is the point of death, when the righteous soul returns to paradise to be with God forever. In Manichaeism knowledge of oneself is equivalent to seeing the soul as of the nature of God and its final abode as in the transcendent world. In this way Mani expounded the existence of evil in the world and offered a remedy for overcoming it. He viewed revelation of the true function of human life within the cosmic process as a "Messenger of Light" sent to promote salvation.

Mani founded an alternative Christian Church. He acknowledged Jesus as a true prophet and "manifestation of the glory (*Kavod*) of God". At first he was embodied in Adam to whom came the divine message to free the imprisoned light, then he revealed himself to the Jewish patriarchs, and ultimately in the Messiah Jesus. A Manichaean–Christian psalmist describes how Jesus, the life-giving master, raises from the dead the imprisoned souls:

> Blessed and praised be Jesus, the vivifier,
> the New Aeon, the true raiser of the dead.
> Who is indeed the mother giving life
> to those who have died from the wounds
> and lesions of greed and lusts.
> And the healer of those who have become unconscious
> through the illness of the body of death.[19]

The Manichaean Church followed the pattern of much that was common to religious groups of the time, but it differentiated between believers who were "hearers" and the "elect". The latter lived a life of purity and asceticism. The clergy were held as paragons of virtue. Mani esteemed Christianity as the model for right belief and action. He referred to himself as an "apostle of Jesus Christ", but, as we observed earlier, he viewed Jesus as one with other founders of religion who are also the revealers of the way of redemption. Mani designated himself as a universal prophet along with others like him and claimed that with him their line came to an end. He was the last of the prophets. Salvation is obtained through virtue not sacraments.

Hermetic literature

In this context we need to include also the Hermetic literature from the second to the third centuries CE. It is not entirely gnostic and does not reflect the spirit of gnosticism throughout. Its background is the proverbial wisdom and mythology of Egypt, but it also bears marks of the Hellenistic philosophy and the Platonic School of Eudorus of Alexandria. For our purpose the most important branch of this literature is the tractates of *Poimandres* and *Asclepius*, which have been known since the sixteenth century. The literature is called Hermetic after the Greek Hermes, a mythical god with winged feet who communicated between heaven and earth, but who also has affinity with the Egyptian god Thoth, the father of all wisdom and knowledge. The Hermetic texts are of a philosophical character and present the religion of paganism in a good light, and so far as traces of gnosticism go they show that it was more than just a Christian heresy.[20]

The philosophy of the Hermetic literature, which shows signs of Hellenistic influence, provides important evidence of the spread of Greek culture and ideas, but it also has a strong mystic character. It is thoroughly syncretistic, identifies the Greek Hermes and the Egyptian Thoth, and displays knowledge of Jewish religion, and also of pagan and Christian writings. The Hermetic book *Asclepius* is represented in the Nag Hammadi texts. Asclepius, the Greek god of healing, has a Greek name and he engages in dialogue with Hermes, who is also called Hermes Trismegistos, that is, Thrice Greatest Hermes, on philosophical themes. In one of the dialogues Hermes declares that "The world is the image of God", that is, that God is omnipresent and that through his presence in the natural world it is possible to communicate with him. The world as the image of God is the sphere wherein the mind of God is projected. Within this pantheism the human mind is illumined as it receives divine revelations. Consequently the soul is prepared for its ascent through the spheres to its final destination of union with the deity.

The first tractate in the Hermetic collection, the *Poimandres* (shepherd of men), has a Hellenistic flavour but it also draws upon Jewish sources. For instance, it adapts the creation story in Genesis, but expresses this in the form of a vision of the Father God from whom emanates the Son of God. This emanation accounts for the origin of the elements, sets the spheres in motion, and from this there then emerge the irrational beasts and, finally, the creation of the first human life. The words of the *Poimandres* affirm that:

God the Father, from whom men came, is light and life. If you therefore learn that he consists of life and light and that you derive from him, you will again attain to life.[21]

The Bruce Codex and Codex Askew

To the foregoing we need to add the Bruce Codex (Codex Brucianus) discovered in Egypt and published in 1891, but originating from the third century CE, which contains *"The Two Books of Jeu"*, or more properly, the *"Book of the Great Word (logos)"*. The main feature of this work is the revelation of the risen Jesus and knowledge of the spiritual world. After his resurrection Jesus appeared to his disciples to reveal the higher *gnosis*, and, especially, cosmogony. The God of Truth figures as an emanation and Jeu praises him as the Supreme God who Jesus calls Father. The God of Truth evolved out of sixty emanations all called Jeu, and all received signs and seals. There in the eternal realm of God the soul enters into the mystery of divine knowledge and "the great seal" of the "Great Name", the Word "which is king over the Treasury of Light":

> Again you will go into their interior to the rank of the five Trees of the Treasury of the Light, which are the (eternal) Trees. They will give to you their mystery and their Great Seal and the Great Name of the Treasury of Light, which is King over the Treasury of Light.[22]

Another part in the Bruce Codex is the *United Text*, which introduces the supreme, unknowable Mother who dwells in the "twelfth deep", the highest region, but she is also the eternal and ineffable Father as well as the "Creative Word" who is Jesus Christ. Thus there is offered a portrait of

> This characterless one in which all are characters,
> which is blessed forever.
> This is the eternal Father . . .
> The Creative Word became a power of God,
> and Lord and Saviour and Christ
> and King and Good and Father and Mother.[23]

The Bruce Codex is undoubtedly gnostic in character, and so is the Codex Askew, which has been housed in the British Museum since its recovery in 1778 in Upper Egypt. It is important as the home of the *Pistis Sophia* (Faith Wisdom), which reports conversations between Jesus and his male and female disciples. The name is given to the revealer of a gnostic vision. The subject is the fall and redemption of a heavenly being, Pistis Sophia. Within this there is an account of the revelation of the spiritual Jesus to his disciples. The scene is the Mount of Olives where Jesus remained teaching his disciples and giving his final revelation before his return to the Father and the realm of light. Through this revelation he gave them knowledge of what he had done and how he had ascended through the *aeons*, and found Pistis Sophia in the thirteenth *aeon* where she was at the mercy of demonic forces. Her only action is to sing a dreary hymn – Jesus reveals himself as the author of salvation, and reveals his place in the universe. All other mysteries are eliminated by him and the disciples are authorized to teach the mystery of light. For this purpose they must renounce the world and be free from the pressure of matter. The soul is freed from the body at death to fly upward through the spheres to heaven.

The work is said by some to be uninspiring and its thought degenerate, but its tone is gnostic and is most likely to have been associated with the gnostic school of the Valentinians. It is dated in the early second century and is translated from Greek originals. Other works in this codex are *Extracts from the Books of the Saviour* and *The Book of the Great Logos*. These works include developed views of the mysteries of the aeonic regions, and the instructions of Jesus about how the soul advances through these regions having first received knowledge of mysterious numbers and seals as the means of entrance into the kingdom of light.

The foregoing catalogue of works gives some indication of the variety of literary sources which in one way or another are related to elucidation of "the gnostic phenomenon". They also display the diversity of the literature that accumulated in the early Christian centuries in the field of religion and philosophic speculation.

Yet they are only a fraction of the works that were produced in an age that avidly sought after answers to ultimate questions of meaning and purpose, and about the nature and destiny of life. The age was one of spiritual unrest and animated by a desire for answers to the paradox and enigma of existence. The picture we have is far from complete, but the intense interest in these topics is fully confirmed by the Nag Hammadi gnostic and near-gnostic texts discovered in Upper Egypt in 1945.

The Nag Hammadi texts

What are the Nag Hammadi texts?

The first glimpse the outside world had of these texts was an incomplete and poorly preserved Coptic papyrus codex which was the complete content of an ancient library near Nag Hammadi in Upper Egypt. It emerged that the total find consisted of thirteen codices, eleven bound in leather, one (Codex xii) very thin, and one (Codex xiii) containing only pages slipped into another codex. Altogether some forty previously unknown documents were recovered, together with copies of several that were already in existence, as we have earlier indicated. The codices mentioned were in their original bindings; in the case of Codex xiii only eight leaves were found inside the cover of Codex xi. The total length of the codices is over a thousand pages, but only some are complete, many are in varying stages of disintegration. The Nag Hammadi texts constitute the largest early collection of its kind and provide fresh evidence of the book formula in use in the early centuries of the Christian era. Prior to the development of the codex only rolls such as the Torah Scrolls or the Dead Sea Scrolls were current.

For a complete list of the works of the Nag Hammadi library the reader should refer to one of the catalogues that are available.[24] For the present purpose it will help to get a perspective on the contents by classifying the works into five categories and giving examples of each.

- **Gospels** – works which have "gospel" as their title, for example, the *Gospel of Thomas*, the *Gospel of Philip*, the *Gospel of Mary*, the *Gospel of Truth* and the *Gospel of the Egyptians*.

  The names do not identify the authors nor do they resemble the New Testament characters of the same name. By using these names the writers may have wished to be known as Christians, although their opponents criticized this as a way of misleading the faithful.[25] The nature of the gospels will be considered in chapter 6.

- **Apocryphal** works – the *Apocryphon of James*, the *Apocryphon of John*, the *Apocalypse of Paul*, the *Apocalypse of Peter*, the *Apocalypse of Adam*.
- **Apostolic Titles** – i.e. works which carry the names of apostles in their titles, the *Prayer of the Apostle Paul*, the *Acts of Peter*, the *Letter of Peter to Philip*, the *Book of Thomas the Contender*, the *Twelve Apostles*.

- **Jewish associations** – the *Paraphrase of Shem*, the *Second Treatise of the Great Seth*, the *Three Steels of Seth*, *Melchizedek*. Obviously there is a strong Jewish influence in these works.

   The occurrence of the name Shem, the true son of Adam and Eve (*Genesis* 4: 25) has posed the question whether, as he is described as being full of light, the gnostics might have traced the origins of their community to him.

- **Miscellaneous** – works which name the subject rather than a personal name in their title, for example, the *Treatise on the Resurrection*, the *Tripartite Tractate*, the *Dialogue of the Saviour*, the *Concept of our Great Power*, *Authoritative Teaching*, the *Testimony of Truth*.

The discovery of the Nag Hammadi texts ranks as one of the twentieth century's two most remarkable discoveries of ancient documents relating to the beginnings of Christianity. The other is the chance discovery of the Dead Sea Scrolls in 1947. Both discoveries happened accidentally and were made by Arab peasants, one in Egypt and the other in Jordan. Each heralded a major readjustment in our knowledge of the background to the origins of Christianity and the turbulent period of its earliest beginnings. Links between the Nag Hammadi Codices and the Dead Sea Scrolls are a matter of continuing investigation, and lie outside the purpose of this study.[26] The Scrolls provide invaluable new light on the earliest forms and transmission of the text of the Jewish Bible, which was taken over by the Christian Church, and which belonged to a pietistic sect, probably Essenes, who lived in the Judaean wilderness around the beginning of the Christian era; whereas the gnostic texts are the production of a group of expositions whose theories threatened to disrupt the early Christian movement in a way that the sect of the Dead Sea Scrolls did not.

The exact details of the discovery of the gnostic library are rather confused, but from the broad picture that has been pieced together, it seems that two Arabs from the ál-Sammán clan, Abú and Muhammad, out searching for bird lime (*sabakah*) near the town of Nag Hammadi (the ancient Chenoboskion), to the north of Luxor and the high cliff of Jabal-al Tarif, in Upper Egypt, accidentally hit upon a jar containing the codices. The jars were taken to al-Qasr and disposed of to friends and acquaintances. They passed through a number of hands and eventually turned up in Cairo where they were purchased by the curator of the Coptic Museum, Togo Mina, for two hundred and fifty pounds.

It is impossible to say whether this was the total find or whether any of the documents were lost or destroyed.[27] Only gradually did news of the discovery spread, but once it was known orientalists, religious historians, antiquarians, archaeologists and others registered an interest. In 1966 the extant works were handed over to an international team for translation and publication, but it was not until 1977, and after "a persistent curse of political road blocks, litigation and worst of all, scholarly jealousies and firstmanship",[28] that the contents of the Nag Hammadi library were published in facsimile.

Concealment

The question "why were these documents concealed in the cave at Nag Hammadi where they have been hidden for around sixteen hundred years?" admits more than one explanation. The time of their concealment is likely to have been the fourth century, a time when the Catholic Church's attitude to what it regarded as heretical works was hardening. The Church was suspicious of works that did not conform in substance to the orthodox interpretation of the faith, and was especially wary of apocryphal works. Leaders of the Church set about hunting out heretical works and confiscated them, believing that this served "the need and advantage of the Church".[29] Those who produced them were accused of just compiling them "into order for themselves", and therefore they placed themselves in the firing line of opposition and risked eventually being excommunicated. Their authors and guardians may have hidden them for safe-keeping from the heresy hunters, in much the same way as the Qumrân covenanters had buried their precious scrolls in jars for safe-keeping in a time of persecution.[30]

Nearby where the Nag Hammadi texts were discovered there was a monastery headed by Pachomius (c.290–346), which would of course have had its own collection of sacred writings. At this time monasticism was much respected and supported by the Christian community, and orthodox Christians revered the monastic order as the heartbeat of true Christian faith and practice. Heretical Christian literature existed alongside that which the Church judged to be orthodox, and the long route to the formation of the Christian canon is evidence of the tension this caused. It could have been that the Nag Hammadi works formed part of the library of Pachomius and that his monks were responsible for depositing them surreptitiously when it became unsafe for the monastery to house condemned writings. Kurt Rudolph goes a step further and states:

Since the fragments of letters in addition mention a "Father Pachom", presbyters and monks, we can infer a monastic environment. Perhaps the writings derive from the library of the monastery and were singled out and buried because of their heretical character in the course of some purging operation, or perhaps more probably they were brought to safety by interested parties and adherents.[31]

Date

A key question for evaluating these works is their date. The authors of many of them are completely unknown to us but they shared a common purpose of teaching a view of truth and salvation they believed needed to be heard. Behind the written documents there was a period of oral transmission of esoteric *gnosis*, as may be gathered from some of the comments of the Church Fathers. There are no clues as to when the Nag Hammadi collection was compiled but external evidence places the *terminus ad quem* no later than the middle of the fourth century CE.

The internal evidence of language and style, the quality of the Coptic translation and the reconstruction of the Greek originals, as well as the subject content and comparison with other works of the first three Christian centuries, all need to be investigated in any detailed examination of the date. Each document will need to be subjected to the minutest critical analysis before a precise date can be absolutely affirmed. The crucial question so far as the origins of Christianity are concerned is whether any of the documents are earlier than the birth of Jesus, whether any are contemporary with the canonical gospels, and which are later, and if so, how much later. There is evidence that some Nag Hammadi documents come from the first century. Their language, thought forms, conceptions and the images they give of the Church can be paralleled with those current in the apostolic age.[32]

It is conjectured, but is probably unlikely, whether any of the gnostic works are earlier than the age of the apostles. Some forms of gnosticism are rudimentary and not fully developed, and this presumes an early date, probably the first century CE. In this connection those works that contain the sayings Jesus is reputed to have spoken are particularly informative. They are illuminating insofar as they present his sayings in somewhat different form from what has been called "the original state of transcendence central to the very beginnings of Christianity".[33] We must therefore ask, "Could any of the sayings of Jesus reported in the canonical gospels have been drawn from gnostic sources?" This would presume an early date for the gnostic writings, at least as being contemporary with the canonical gospels.

Some Nag Hammadi codices are known to have been in circulation in the second century CE, as can be gathered from the writings of Irenaeus and the Church Fathers. Some of the content and thought of gnostic teachers is dealt with by way of response in the works of Irenaeus, so they must have been in existence at the time. In fact the evidence points clearly to the existence of a series of gnostic works in the first two Christian centuries which display less developed forms of gnosticism when compared with those of the following century. Taking the gnostic works from Nag Hammadi as a whole we can trace a development or progression of thought from the first to the third and fourth centuries. They are the works of some of the keenest minds of the age whose teaching developed into a highly sophisticated system of impressive magnitude. But by the middle of the fourth century gnosticism was on the wane. By then the library of texts had been compiled and circulated as the reading matter of a gnostic community that was destined for oblivion in its present form.[34]

Evaluation

The discovery and subsequent publication of the Nag Hammadi codices naturally aroused considerable interest but its significance was not at first recognized by everyone.[35] But here was information that was unique and now available for public consumption. One of its best-known texts, the *Gospel of Thomas*, states emphatically, and enthusiastically, the words of Jesus:

> I shall give you what no eye hath seen and what no ear has heard and what no hand has touched and what has never occurred to the human mind.[36]

This is also the gnostic author's perspective on his work; its uniqueness and impact are clearly relayed and commended. Other authors would no doubt have felt the same about the value of their works. In our own day Hans Jonas has written enthusiastically of the significance of this discovery:

> A priori, and quite apart from questions of doctrine, it is obvious that so large an accretion of original writings will afford us much more full-blooded, full-bodied experience of the ultimate flavour of gnostic literary utterance, a more ultimate view of the unity and manner of self commu-

nication of the gnostic mind, than any doxographic excerpts or rendering of doctrinal substance can convey.[37]

At an elementary level we can say that these books inform us about the literary interests and the reading habits of the gnostics and how well documented their teaching is. We gather from them information about the way they saw things and how their minds functioned. The works convey the genuine spirit of gnosticism and its independent and liberal functioning. They tell how the devotees of gnostic knowledge branched out in a number of directions as its champions claimed fresh insights with which to embrace truth and reality. They did so with vigour and without restriction other than the constraints imposed by the mysterious *gnosis* itself. The *gnosis* assimilated a variety of fresh ideas as it progressed, yet kept itself immune from the pressures of a disorientated and degenerate culture. It operated a spiritual and intellectual freedom that refused to be submerged in an authoritative and higher hierarchic system or to succumb to the method of discerning truth only on the basis of external or objective criteria.

These works are a mirror through which we are able to see how the gnostics projected themselves; we hear them speaking for themselves without having to rely on the words of others about them, which are more often than not antagonistic. They inform directly of the gnostics' grasp, evaluation and response to the perennial questions of human existence from birth to death and beyond. There is hardly any question about the origin, nature and destiny of life that is not raised and examined in these works. As primary sources they are indispensable for knowledge of how the gnostics acquired the secret of salvation and how they conceived of the figure of the redeemer. This is in places notably different from that portrayed in some other contemporary writings.

The works are also a valuable mine of information about the struggle of the early church to purge itself of the influence of a devious and dangerous alternative to orthodox faith that impeded its progress and threatened to disrupt its internal unity. These texts also expound major theological themes including the nature of God and man, the person of Jesus, crucifixion, resurrection, salvation and eschatology. They also include an interpretation of the sayings and teaching of Jesus, and provide information on the attitude of gnostics to the major Christian rites of baptism, the eucharist and anointing. From them too we learn about the moral lifestyle of the gnostic Christians.

The Christological spectrum of these works gives rise to the crucial question of how far the anti-gnostic prejudices of the Church Fathers can be said to be justified. Does this prejudice call for re-evaluation in the light of the evidence of the Nag Hammadi texts? Whilst the Church Fathers had a case against the gnostics, does it now seem likely that the gulf between them may not have been as great as was once thought? According to Pheme Perkins:

> The pluralism of second-century Christianity shows that gnostic expressions of Christianity are closer to those of orthodox Christians than they – with the hindsight of later Christological controversies – appear to be.[38]

The Nag Hammadi library is not a complete compendium of gnostic religion and philosophy, but its works are assured of a central and undisputed place in any investigation into the origins and growth of early Christianity and what precisely constitutes orthodoxy. This concrete body of knowledge is by now an established base from which to judge the extent of the unity of Christian doctrine and practice in the early church, and what headway it needed to make in order to achieve complete uniformity in faith and practice.

Censorship and tolerance

The codices of the Nag Hammadi* collection represent a variety of gnostic systems of thought and theory. Some have a distinctly Christian content and purpose, some reflect Jewish or even pagan influence, and some are not gnostic at all. Relating the texts to the philosophical, religious and cultural background of the time makes us aware of the acute problems which faced the Church on its progress to orthodoxy and uniformity in doctrine and practice. Those who produced the gnostic works believed they were inspired and given a vision which carried them beyond the natural world of time and space. They claimed to have a preview of the eternal world where normal conventions of thought and belief were no longer operable. The works they compiled were divinely inspired; their authors believed they originated through the insights of experience and the revelation of divine _gnosis_. This affirmed the confidence of gnostics in their beliefs but at the same time they posed a challenge to the Church which it had to answer.

With the victory of the Catholic Church in the fourth century the influence of the gnostic writings diminished without further additions. Were the gnostic works barred or confiscated? The first ecumenical

*See pp. 203–5 for indexes of the Nag Hammadi collection.

council at Nicaea in 325 is a landmark in the history of the Christian Church,[39] but it also had consequences in respect of gnosticism. It produced the Apostles' Creed and agreed an authoritative canon of Christian scriptures.[40] Bishop Athanasius (c.295–373) was present, and in a festal letter to Theodore, head of the monastery of Tabinnisi, he expanded on those books which were in current circulation. He divided them between books that had been handed down and which were "credited as divine", and were the "fountains of salvation", to which no one should add or take away anything, and "apocryphal books", which existed alongside the divinely inspired scriptures, but which by their subtlety were leading the simple astray. They only favoured the personal views of their authors. The works which Athanasius said should be rejected were those which mislead the faithful even "by the similarity of their names with the true books".

The spread of heretical literature obviously agitated Athanasius and was an issue he felt he must tackle. What we need to know is which books he had in mind, where did he get them from, and why did he wish to purge the Church of them? There was a tide of subversive literature flowing against the Church and Athanasius adopted a firm policy of stemming it by authorizing only those books that "proclaimed the doctrine of godliness". Athanasius exercised an ecclesiastical censorship in the matter of the spread of heresy through the written word. The spiritual ferment their spread caused hindered the progress of the Church in establishing a uniform code of belief and practice based on apostolic authority.

Behind the establishment and exercise of episcopal authority we may also deduce the increasing prominence and agitation of the intellectual and visionary gnostic in Church circles and the menace this would cause the Church if it were not stemmed. Irenaeus took a hand in this by denouncing and wishing to impose a kind of ecclesiastical embargo on "the views of those who are now teaching heresy". He could not endure being silent and not making known "how absurd and inconsistent with the truth are their statements". He wished to remove all heretical writings from the hands of believers. The defence of orthodoxy also preoccupied the mind of Hegisippus who wanted to keep pristine pure "the true doctrine of sound faith received from apostolic tradition".[41]

Others of the Church Fathers – such as Clement of Alexandria, Origen and Tertullian – knew of the existence of books of a gnostic kind, but not all the Fathers displayed an equal degree of antipathy to the gnostic writings. Origen, for instance, seems to have had contact with students of heretical persuasion, for Eusebius (d. 339), the church historian, reports that "a great many heretics and not a few of the most distinguished philosophers" came to study under Origen.[42] It would seem that there was a degree of tolerance towards heretics, and this may have been more than patient impassive endurance if the words of C. H. Dodd are accepted:

> There is a sense in which orthodox Christian theologians like Clement of Alexandria and Origen, on the one hand, and Hellenistic Jews like Philo, and pagan writers like the Hermetists, on the other, should be called Gnostics.[43]

We have observed that certain works deposited in the cave at Nag Hammadi were known as early as the first and second centuries when they were in circulation. Can we be sure that *all* the gnostic works in existence were gathered together and deposited at Nag Hammadi? If they were not, did their owners select which works were and which were not to be hidden away? Was there then an expurgation of gnostic works rather than a complete withdrawal of all those in existence? Only time and further discovery can answer this question.

I desire to learn the things that really exist and to understand their nature and to know God. This I desire to hear. And he replied to me, keep in mind the things you desire and learn, and I will teach you.

Tractate 1 Poimandres

The soul of Adam (man) came into being by means of a Breath. The partner of his soul is the Spirit.

The Gospel of Philip

I am the light that is above the all.
I am the All.
The All came forth from Me and the All attained to Me.

The Gospel of Thomas

Just as gold placed in mud cannot harm the world, so we cannot damage or lose our spiritual nature, even if we engage in various material actions.

The Gospel of Philip

4

Beliefs and Practices

———

The Teachings of Silvanus is among the most informative documents of the Nag Hammadi library. Silvanus is mentioned in the New Testament as a most worthy apostle (*2 Corinthians* 1: 19), and we conclude from the gnostic texts that the author Silvanus was an able teacher with a commitment to the education of the mind as "the guiding principle" for attaining genuine knowledge. The *Teachings* range widely over a number of matters, but of particular interest for our present purpose are his words addressed to his son on the subject of education and teaching:

> My son accept the education and the teaching. Do not flee from the education and the teaching, but when you are taught, accept it with joy. And if you are educated in any matter, do what is good. You will plait a crown of education by your guiding principle. Put on the holy teaching like a robe.[1]

It is unlikely that we should infer from the definite article that "the" education or "the" teaching implies that there existed an authoritative or approved collection of religious teaching which Silvanus was urging on his son. Rather than a body of doctrine cast in a solid mould the likelihood is that the teaching referred to was individualist and particular to Silvanus himself. Nevertheless, he urged it upon his son as that which leads away from "the forgetfulness which fills you with darkness". The state of darkness is likened to sleep and forgetfulness, but being enlightened is to be in a state of *gnosis*. The teaching was "a saving grace" to be received with joy, and guidance for life. The education therefore was to be accepted as a guiding principle for living the life of the gnostic. In the absence of an authorized or approved version of gnostic teachings and beliefs we are obliged to single out individual examples from the amorphous collection of gnostic writings and identify, wherever possible, a common thread that moulds them together. The case would be different were we to be dealing with an authoritative statement, such as the Apostles' Creed, authorized by ecclesiastical authority, compiled according to agreed consensus, consented to with formal agreement, and interpreted according to approved criteria. How different it is when we come to consider gnostic beliefs and practices:

> The characteristic of gnosticism in all its forms . . . is blending together elements of every sort . . . There is in consequence no one uniform set of ideas that may be singled out as gnostic, rather it is a type of thought which manifests itself in different ways in different groups.[2]

Gnostic beliefs were not standardized or officially sanctioned so that it is difficult to be pedantic in defining their precise status. The nature of the beliefs is determined by the special kind of *gnosis* with which they are associated. Insofar as the beliefs of gnosticism can be given shape or pattern it is due to the possession of special knowledge which the gnostics elevated into a creditable system of belief with redemptive implications.

Their beliefs ranged comprehensively over a wide spectrum of religion and philosophy, so that, outside the New Testament, they are the major source of knowledge about how Christian claims and ideas were being viewed and interpreted in the early centuries of Christianity. To communicate and expound their beliefs intelligently became a matter of priority as the Church closed ranks against heretical teaching and the circulation of subversive literature. Some of the sharpest minds of the age expounded the basic philosophy of gnosticism not only in speculative abstract terms but also for the sake of promoting beliefs and practices for a salvific purpose. They have been designated as early "salvationists" with a passion for imparting knowledge of the Father:

> Just as man's ignorance is dissolved of itself when he comes to knowledge (of the Father), as darkness dissolves when light appears, so also the deficiency dissolves in the perfection. From this time on the external "form" is no longer visible, but it will be dissolved in union with the oneness.[3]

According to this tractate, the *Gospel of Truth*, knowledge of God replaces oblivion; as oblivion vanishes so knowledge of God becomes known. This is the true secret of salvation.

Deity

In *Tractate 1* (*Poimandres*) from the Hermetic literature[4] there is an account of a conversation between the author and Poimandres in which Poimandres asked him what he wished to hear. He replied,

> I desire to learn the things that really exist and to understand their nature and to know God. This I desire to hear. And he replied to me, keep in mind the things you desire and learn, and I will teach you.[5]

This desire to understand God would be echoed universally among the gnostics. No previous age had produced a view of God comparable to that of Christianity but the Church's interpretation of this view was not completely consistent with gnostic perception. They did not feel bound by stereotyped imagery in the presentation of God; instead they aimed to develop their own symbols and criteria for understanding and interpreting his nature and purpose.

The teaching which Poimandres offered in the above tractate is one strand in a complicated complex of ideas. The problem of identification and analogy faces anyone who probes the gnostic conception of God. How did the gnostics approach the question of identifying God? Did they make sense of the being of God? What contribution did they make to the interpretation of the character and action of the God of Christianity?

We begin this brief examination of the gnostic conception of God with a view attributed to the gnostic Basilides (130–60 CE), who is reputed to have declared that in the beginning there was only the godhead.[6] The godhead is an utterly incomprehensible reality, impenetrable, unfathomable and inaccessible. According to Valentinus the godhead is:

> perfect and pre-existent . . . dwelling in invisible and unnameable heights, this is the pre-beginning and forefather and depth. It is uncontainable and invisible, eternal and ungenerated, is quiet and deep solitude for infinite *aeons* . . . with it was thought, which is also called peace and silence.[7]

The concept of godhead is beyond the capacity of intellect or rational argument to prove. It is a characteristic of gnostic thought that it aimed to penetrate and expound even though its mystery must remain forever unfathomable. It perceived of the godhead acting of its own volition to give knowledge of itself, and then proceeded to develop appropriate symbols and analogies to make this comprehensible. The eternal and invisible godhead released energies from within its own orbit in the form of emanations, the first of which was the Supreme God. So God came to be. The process of emanation is important in gnostic teaching of both deity and the nature of reality. The God who thus came to be remained unknown and could only be spoken of in negative terms. He was enthroned above the world and beyond the reaches of pure reason. All knowledge of him was unattainable and hidden from everyone except those who were the recipients of special *gnosis*.

Before it was possible to penetrate the depth of divine being or postulate anything about him, further emanations were necessary. These emanations were forthcoming and the gnostics related them to the category of experience. Only those who received the mysterious *gnosis* were capable of discerning the nature of the divine emanations. They proceeded from God in pairs of emanations which established that he is the source of all that is, and at the same time that he chose to declare those attributes that distinguish him from any other being humans can conceive of. The basic premise fundamental to gnosticism is that God is supreme and pre-existent. The gnostic work *Allogenes* states:

> Since he is not one of those that exist but is another thing; he is superior to all superlatives even in comparison to both what is properly his and not his. He neither participates in age nor does he participate in time. He doesn't receive anything from anyone else. He is not diminishable, nor does he diminish anything, nor is he undiminishable. But he is self comprehending, as something unknowable that he exceeds those who excel in unknowability.[8]

According to the *Gospel of Truth* "all the emanations of the Father are *pleromas* and the root of all his emanations is the one who made the all grow up in himself".[9] The idea of the Supreme God incorporates a *pleroma* (fullness), that is, an assembly of angels, heavenly beings, principalities, powers and abstractions. It consisted of thirty *aeons*, all under the control of the Supreme God, the head of the spiritual world, the Lord of the universe and the highest being of all. This supra-transcendent being who incorporated the *pleroma* contained within himself the totality of all inhabitants of the divine sphere.

He rules supreme as the head, possessing the monopoly of divine power, dwelling in "ineffable heights" as a "pre-existent powerful *aeon*, whom they also call Pre-beginning, Forefather and Primal Ground (*bythos*) that is inaccessible and invisible, eternal and uncreated (or unbegotten), and that he existed in great peace and stillness in unending spaces (*aeons*)", according to Valentinus.[10]

On account of his pro-active nature there proceeded from him *aeons* or worlds which bear different names, including an *Ogdoad*, which is named primal depth, as head of the whole system, and thought (*ennoia*),[11] and from this pair the world species emerged up to the last *aeon.* All these are emanations from the Supreme God, says the gnostic *Tripartite Tractate*, the offspring of his pro-active nature, who is the cause of their establishment.[12] He holds the monopoly of power and brought into being a series of intermediaries between God and the world. From that world where God dwells in the *Monad* (Source or Good), which is unknowable or unknown, "dwelling in the heights above the regions below", there emerged a series of *aeons* who became imprisoned in a visible world of evil through the fallen element of the *pleroma.* As we shall see, it was in order to rescue this fallen element that Christ came into the world. He comprised the *true gnosis* that had the power to redeem those who were capable of receiving redemption. He alone could know the Father directly, as to all other *aeons* he remains incomprehensible.

This briefly is how the gnostics expounded the question of the internal coherence of belief in God. It offers a view of how God, who is believed to be transcendent and beyond the universe, can be known. His existence makes understanding the world intelligible, otherwise the world would not be intelligible to the finite mind. He is the most perfect being possible and nothing can surpass or harm him. His attributes are characterized as:

> Father of All (Ennoia) of the light dwelling in the heights above the regions below. Light dwelling in the heights, Voice of Truth, upright Nous, untouchable Logos, the ineffable Voice, incomprehensible Father.[13]

Although Norea has made use of these descriptions, no one name does God justice:

> Not one of the names that are conceived or spoken, seen or grasped, not one of them applies to Him, even though they are exceedingly glorious, magnifying and honoured.[14]

God does not approximate to any human ideas about him, and the impossibility of encapsulating God in human terms is a firm tenet of gnostic belief:

> My son, do not dare to say a word about the one
> and do not confine the God of all to mental images.[15]

God is represented in gnostic thought as all that he can be, as both transcendent and immanent. He is changeless and timeless, a being whose essence is all that he is, omnipotent and all-sufficient, boundless and beyond change.

To this extent there is a tendency to remove God from the known world and from those ancient religious, philosophical and mythological traditions that sought to contain him. The "otherness" of God could not be so contained. *The Teachings of Silvanus* states:

> Consider these things about God: He is in every place; on the other hand He is in no place. With respect to His Power to be sure, He is in every place, but with respect to divinity he is in no place. So, then, it is possible to know God a little. With respect to his Power, it is true, he fills every place, but in the exultation of His divinity nothing contains Him. Everything is in God, but God is not in anything.

In this context the word "alien", used as a predicate of the Supreme God in order to highlight the circumstances in which God is alienated from the world, is particularly relevant.[16] By his very nature God is alien to the world and stands in complete antithesis to it. No image could make his "otherness" more plain than that of alienation, and this applies to the totality of his being.

Whilst this is so, the *Apocryphon of John* takes us along the route of depicting God as one who lies within all and is the essence of all:

> He (God) is pure and immeasurable . . .
> He is an aeon-giving Aeon . . .
> He is life-giving life . . .
> He gives the immeasurable, incomprehensible Light.[17]

To this metaphysical description of God as being here and everywhere we add how the Hermetic writings present a view of God *within*. He does not exist alongside the world governing it from without, but he exists within. The principle that God exists within is what gives the world meaning and the means to be. This becomes comprehensible to those who possess *nous*, that is, spiritual life energy, "the *nous* was the faculty of gnostic perception".[18] *Nous* is the product of *ennoia* (thought) and *charis* (grace) and has a redemptive function. In the gnostic text *The Emergence of the Soul*, *nous* is the first emanation as the world comes into existence. As it does so the soul is caught in captivity.[19]

There are echoes of the "God within" in other gnostic texts, especially The *Gospel of Philip*, which makes the starting point in the search for God within the self or in the ability to identify oneself.[20] God lies deep within human nature as well as outside. The I–Thou relationship is a real stimulus and absolves us from the error of confining the notion of deity to external identity alone. The "God within" is the source of the spiritual potential wherein his Spirit is felt, the Spirit that is identified with the breath of God that gave life to the first man (*Genesis* 2: 7; Job 34: 16):

> The soul of Adam (man) came into being by means of a Breath. The partner of his soul is the Spirit.[21]

The spirit within is of the same nature as the Spirit of God – God's incorruptible presence within and everywhere.[22] This counteracts the idea of God as wholly other, which was referred to above. The view equates knowledge of self with knowledge of God, or makes the self identical with the divine.

This brief glance at leading gnostic views of deity leaves a number of questions unanswered. There is an ambivalence in the gnostic teachings. In some cases the view that God is unknowable is contested, in other instances there are signs of blending of ideas from more than one religious tradition, and even, arguably, of some pre-Christian ideas. The concept of God is not wholly consistent throughout the gnostic works. On the one hand, God is incomprehensible and self-sufficient, he lacks nothing and he wants nothing; yet, on the other hand, he acts in creation and shows love and compassion, and passionately requires responses from those he cares for. Yet the gnostics were all convinced theists and monotheists. There is no evidence of the abandoning of belief in deity because of contradictory views of God and his actions.

The gnostics never consciously seemed to conceive of God as *only* male. From many sources there is evidence of God as female as well. Many different images of God are encountered throughout the gnostic texts, some of which are expressly in terms of maleness (Father, King, Lord), but there are remarkably impressive word pictures of the divine that portray God as beyond male and female. God is also known as male *and* female. In other religious systems, especially the oriental, Egyptian, Greek and Roman, the idea of the female goddess was very strong and the cults associated with this were widely popular. The prevalent ideas in Judaism were essentially male and these spilled over into Christianity where they were given a Christian orientation. It is noteworthy, however, that Clement of Alexandria characterized God in feminine as well as masculine terms:

> The Lord is everything to the child, both father and mother.[23]

In the case of gnosticism there are many examples in the texts of female qualities in association with male qualities to give a picture of a God who combines both male and female characteristics. God is one being who is a *dyad* of feminine and masculine feelings. The *Apocalypse of John* says:

The One to be praised, the father–mother, the one rich in mercy, takes form in her [its] seed . . . The mother once descended before me. But there are the things which she effected in the world, she raised up her seed.[24]

The female qualities surface into prominence when these meet the purposes of the moment. In an account of the human death of Jesus, the *Gospel of Truth* goes on to say:

The Word of the Father goes forth unto the all . . . purifying it, bringing it back unto the Father, unto the Mother, Jesus of the infiniteness of gentleness.[25]

References to the divine Mother and her qualities abound, especially when the conditions merit the expression of mainly "feminine" feelings and characteristics, as at the crucifixion of Jesus. Jesus spoke to John:

He said to me, John, John, why do you doubt, why are you afraid? I am the one who will be with you always. I am the Father, I am the Mother, I am the Son.[26]

The Valentinian gnostics represented the female aspect of God in their works. Wisdom (*Sophia*) is portrayed as the divine Mother. She is the power by which the creation was conceived. She conceives in her womb and produces new life. She is spoken of as Mother Wisdom, and the Spirit, and is set forth as sister power, as both Mother and Virgin, portrayed in the *Gospel of Philip* as the consort of the heavenly Father:

The Holy Spirit, who is called Life, the Mother of All. And she named it Ialdabaoth. This is the first Archon.[27]

Manichaeism also used the image of the Mother of Life of the divine being, no doubt under the influence of eastern teaching and concepts. The Orphites taught the female aspect of deity, as Father, Son and Mother. The triad expressed every aspect of deity but the essence was the same. Gnosticism conveys a picture of God that uses sexual symbolism in a specific way. God is presented as both male and female. At times the Father is at the centre of the picture – perfect, profound and absolutely good. There is in God the Father no error. At times the Mother is at the centre of the picture, graceful, loving, tender and creative. God is *not* now father and *then* mother for both maleness and femininity are conjoined. But the deity is a trinity not a duality, Father, Mother and Son are co-existent. The term for Spirit (*ruach*) is feminine and the second person (Mother) is equivalent to this.

Christology

In those gnostic systems which give prominence to the redeemer and his mission the agent of redemption is Jesus Christ, the redeemer of orthodox Christianity. The information is spread over a number of gnostic systems and there are similarities and differences between them; sometimes the stress is on the human Jesus or on the transcendent Christ, or on the difference between Jesus and Christ, or the union of both. The *Gospel of Philip* provides a useful insight into this trend:

> Jesus is a private (personal) name, Christ is a public name (epithet). For this reason "Jesus" is not particular to any language, rather he is always called by the name "Jesus". But the word for Christ in Syriac is Messiah, and in Greek it is Christos, and probably all the others have it according to the particular language of each. The Nazarene is he who reveals what is hidden.

And:

> The Apostles before us used to employ the terms "Jesus the Nazarean Messiah", which means "Jesus, the Nazarean", the Christ (anointed one). The last name is Christ, the first one is Jesus, the middle name is the Nazarene. Messiah has two meanings, "Christ (anointed one)" and the "measured". Jesus in Hebrew means "the redemption". Nazarene means "the truth", thus the Nazarene means "the truth".[28]

We gather from this excerpt how the gnostics adopted the figure of Jesus Christ as an essential element in their scheme of redemption. By the second century there had evolved a comprehensive scheme of Christian salvation with Jesus Christ as its centre point, but the scheme also raises many intricate questions. The uniqueness of Christian redemption never seems to have been in doubt, but whilst the gnostics forged literary, didactic and catechetical patterns to interpret this, they also differed from the formulae of orthodoxy. The Jesus Christ of gnosticism is both like and unlike the Jesus Christ of apostolic Christianity. They tended to use words and images of their own rather than repeat slavishly those that had been handed down.

To some gnostics Jesus was an enigma, as this passage illustrates:

> Compare me to someone and tell me whom I am like: Simon Peter replied that he was like "a righteous angel", and Matthew that he was "like a philosopher". But Thomas replied: "Master my mouth is wholly incapable of saying who you are like".[29]

The words of Thomas are echoed elsewhere and this leads us to ask what is the real origin of Jesus Christ? Is Jesus purely human or wholly divine? Could he be simultaneously human *and* divine? How does the appearance of Jesus on earth relate to God's eternal purpose?

The historical presence of Jesus was never in doubt. The gnostics accepted the traditional view of the Church of his appearance as a historical being. They asserted his pre-existence as *Monogenes* with the Supreme God, who in the gnostic system of Valentinus is unknown to the higher *aeons*, apart from *Monogenes*. He produced a consort (*syzygy*) in the person of Jesus Christ who descended to reveal God for the purpose of restoring the fallen souls to himself. In this system the revelation through *Monogenes* (only begotten) is parallel to that of The *Gospel of John* 1: 18. He existed from primal times where he belonged in the fullness of the *pleroma*:

> Unbegotten, incorporeal and without form.

He descended to earth as a divine being, the "only begotten" of the primal Father, therefore his essence was unique to himself and higher than that of any other being. His sonship to God was of a "functional" character, as is implied in the *Sophia of Jesus Christ*:

> I am come from the first, who was sent that I might reveal to you what was from the beginning. I am come to lead them (mankind) "out of their" blindness, that I may show all the (true) God who is over all.[30]

Cerinthus, a contemporary of Polycarp, the Christian martyr of the second century, and a pioneer of Christian gnosticism, taught that Jesus was born of Mary and Joseph, and that Christ descended on him in the form of a dove at his baptism, and then withdrew from him before his suffering and crucifixion. His pupil Carpocrates, a founder of one of the gnostic sects with connections with the famous catechetical school of Alexandria, followed his teacher in declaring that "Jesus was begotten by Joseph, and having come into existence as other men became more righteous than the rest."[31]

He did, however, go a step further and teach that believers were able to share the same power and become Christ's equals. The *Gospel of Thomas* taught a similar view, through engaging in redemptive activities the redeemed became as Christ, the redeemer. They became bonded together and partook of the same nature:

> He who will drink from my mouth will become as I am.

The redeemer is not external to the redeemed or inferior to them.

These examples show that certain of the gnostics rejected the virgin birth of Jesus. They may have found the idea of God fathering a human child grotesque, and many dissented from the doctrine of a virgin birth. The *Gospel of Philip* is adamant that those who held such a view are in error,[32] and, according to Hippolytus, Elchasai and Apelles also rejected the virgin birth of Jesus.[33] So did the mystic Mani. All these seemed to have been less interested in the external form of the advent of Jesus into the world than they were in inward aspects of the significance of his advent and mission. As in the case of Cerinthus, who concentrated more on his righteousness, prudence and wisdom, they were more intrigued by the meaning of his ministry than the method of his arrival. However, the gnostics were not all of one mind in this. Saturninus, as we saw earlier, spoke of Jesus the redeemer as "unbegotten, incorporeal and without form".[34] He also asserted that Jesus appeared only "as a man in semblance". Likewise, the Sethian Ophites held the view that:

> Jesus was generated from the virgin through the working of God . . . he was wiser and purer and more righteous than all other men; Christ combined with Sophia descended unto him and thus Jesus became Christ.[35]

Whoever expects a definitive answer to the vexed question of the virgin birth of Jesus in gnosticism will be disappointed. The gnostics did not agree about *how* the pre-existent and sinless Jesus entered the world. Nor did they use the virgin birth as a valid explanation of the two natures of Jesus. Nor do the gnostic texts supply an easy answer to the divine–human person of Jesus in whom divinity and humanity function simultaneously. They do, however, recognize the role of Jesus in history and the significance of his earthly existence. He appeared on earth to perform a predetermined function. This included his works and his teaching.

The works he performed related to the purposes of God and were under his command and power. Two illustrations will make this plain:

> When Christ descended unto Jesus he began to work miracles and to heal and to proclaim the unknown Father and to confess himself openly as the son of the first man.[36]

In *Eznik's Résumé of Marcionite Doctrine* it is noted:

> God grieved for those fallen into the fire and tormented. He sent his son to go to save them and to take the likeness of his slave and to be fashioned in the form of a man among the sons of the law. Heal, he said, these lepers

and raise their dead, open the eyes of their blind and work among them the greatest healings freely.[37]

He also performed the role of teacher. This is the substance of the *Gospel of Thomas*, and of other works as well. In this capacity he brought *gnosis* to those who were capable of receiving it. *Gnosis* thus imparted gave knowledge of self, and insight into its meaning, and knowledge of the destiny ahead. The teaching enlightened the self, so much is this the case that the *Gospel of Thomas* declares:

There is light in the son of light, and it lights up the whole world.[38]

As the teacher and messenger of light, Jesus acts as the extension of the heavenly light or the light *nous*. He is credited with teaching:

I am the light that is above the all,
I am the All,
The All came forth from Me and the All attained to Me.[39]

We shall deal with the work of Jesus Christ as redeemer later,[40] but now we must probe further into the gnostic presentation of his person. Here the crucial question is: was he genuinely human or was he wholly divine, or a mixture of humanity and divinity? These were matters of acute theological debate and the gnostics could not avoid being involved. The way to reconcile the human and divine qualities in Jesus proved difficult and how to explain his sinlessness if he were only human was puzzling. Some gnostics rejected the reality of his humanity altogether, but others did not wish to destroy his humanity completely, otherwise how could human beings relate to him? His nature proved enigmatic and a paradox to the gnostic theologians.

There is a strong gnostic body of opinion that his physical body is not real. It is a phantom. Saturninus described his body as only a semblance – "He appeared as a man in semblance."[41] He appeared only as a man in semblance in order to be free of the physical body of evil. He descended from the world beyond to appear on earth as a spiritual being, and in typical gnostic style the *Gospel of Thomas* expresses the abhorrance of the physical:

If the flesh came into being because of the spirit, it is a wonder. But if spirit came into being because of the body, it is a wonder of wonders. Indeed, I am amazed at how this great wealth has made its home in this poverty.[42]

This gnostic perception of Jesus was of him as the Son of God and the luminous Logos. His origin was heavenly and immaterial, but his presence changed the outlook, as the *Poimandres* states:

> And the luminous Logos which came out of the mind is the Son of God. "How so"? I asked. "Understand it this way," he replied. "That which in you sees and hears is the Logos of the Lord and your Mind is God the Father".[43]

This version of the gnostic Christ is an aspect of docetism, that is, belief that the body of Jesus was not real, or, in gnostic terminology, he assumed a human (phantom) body to give a vision of one who appeared on earth to kindle the divine spark within the human being that illumines the way of redemption. The appearance of Jesus on earth affirms the significance of his historic mission as the deliverer, but not as a perfectly human being. The gnostic perception of the nature of Jesus is inseparable from the conception of his work as redeemer. All accounts of Jesus as redeemer in the early church tell of his crucifixion. Justin Martyr in the *Apology* he addressed to the Emperor Antoninus Pius makes this plain:

> In saying that the Lord, who is the first offspring of God, was born for us without sexual union, as Jesus Christ our Teacher and that he was crucified and died, and after rising again, ascended into heaven, we introduce nothing new . . .

How did the gnostics view the crucifixion of Jesus? The most radical and astounding feature of the gnostic interpretation of the crucifixion is that it was not Jesus who was crucified "it was another".[44] It was not Jesus of Nazareth or the Christ who was crucified but a substitute:

> He whom we saw being glad and laughing above the cross is the living Jesus. But he into whose hands and feet they are driving the nails in the fleshy part, which is the substitute. They put to shame that which remained in his likeness.[45]

Nevertheless the crucifixion was a public event that was openly witnessed, and the *Apocalypse of Peter* provides a vivid description of Jesus who is said to have been a spectator at his own crucifixion. According to the *Second Treatise of the Great Seth* the substitute is named as Simon, who bore the cross and on whom the crown of thorns was placed, whilst Jesus was an onlooker.[46] This Simon is the Simon of Cyrene of the canonical gospels who, according to Basilides was transfigured into the likeness of Jesus and crucified in his stead. The manner of the crucifixion is described in the *Gospel of Truth*:

He was nailed to a tree. He nailed the decree of the Father to the cross.
Oh what a great and glorious teaching! He humbled himself even to death
even though eternal life clothed him. After he had laid aside these perish-
able ways he clothed himself with incorruptibility which no-one can take
from him.[47]

His death was a humiliation, "He humbled himself over to death
though eternal life clothed him." To the gnostic authors it was unthinkable that a divine person should suffer the agony of death on a cross. The
real Christ could not have been crucified. The explanation that someone
else acted as a substitute is one gnostic explanation of the crucifixion,
another is that Christ left Jesus before the crucifixion. Still the gnostics
viewed the suffering and death of the crucifixion as inevitable. Jesus was
vulnerable to suffering and his suffering was for the sake of others:

> So for their sake, he became manifest in an involuntary suffering . . .
> Not only did he take upon himself the death of those he intended to serve,
> but also he accepted their smallness.[48]

The crucifixion is presented as a struggle or conflict between the
archons and God. The body was under the control of the *archons*, as was
the whole of the material world. Their attempt to destroy the redeemer
was outmanoeuvred for they were ignorant of the redeemer's certain
return to the divine realm from which he had descended. He was certain
to be released from the body for the divine spirit within him could not
be killed. This assured him that he was free to ascend to God.

He transcended suffering and death, for death could not hold him in
captivity. The words attributed to Jesus in the *Second Treatise of the
Great Seth* refer to his victory over death:

> from my death which they think happened, happened to them in their
> error and blindness, since they nailed their men unto their death. It was
> another upon whom they placed the crown of thorns. But I was rejoicing
> in the height over all the wealth of the archons and the offspring of their
> error, of their empty glory. And I was laughing at their ignorance.[49]

The *Gospel of Truth* explains the victory of the crucifixion in
metaphorical terms as new fruit on a tree, the symbol of new life:

> he became the fruit of the knowledge (*gnosis*) of the Father, which,
> however, did not become destructive because it was eaten, but gave to
> those who ate it cause to become glad in their discovery.[50]

The gnostic Valentinus offers a more expansive version of the crucifixion, although not radically different from other texts. His followers linked this with the person of Jesus who was born of Mary and who at his baptism received Christ in the form of a dove. This endowed him with the property of the redeemer.

As the redeemer he was beyond suffering otherwise he would be defeated, and the thought of Christ the redeemer as conquerable was unthinkable. Therefore when he appeared before the Roman judge, Pontius Pilate, the Christ withdrew from him. But the person to whom Mary had given birth did not suffer either:

> But the seed which was from the Mother also did not experience passion, for it too was impassible because it was spiritual and invisible, even to the Demiurge. What suffered was the psychic Christ, the one constructed from the constitution of the universe, in a mysterious fashion, as that through him the Mother might set forth the model of the Christ above, when he was extended on the cross and had shaped the essential form Achamoth.[51]

After the crucifixion and burial, the third day he rose from the tomb. So taught the orthodox church. Without the resurrection Christianity would have died with the crucifixion. The Church saw this as a turning point in the history of religion. Nothing like it had been experienced previously. It caused Christians to have a new awareness of the presence of Christ although he would not be physically visible. But this belief had to be intelligently communicated to believers and non-believers. What line did the gnostics take on the resurrection of Jesus? Like much else there is some diversity on this, but in general the gnostics understood the resurrection in symbolic terms and interpreted it in the light of its cosmic significance. We know that the "orthodox" account of the resurrected Christ is ambiguous and can be interpreted in different ways. After his resurrection he appeared as someone who was recognized by his physical features as when he showed his hands and side to Thomas,[52] when he shared a meal with Cleopas and his companion in Emmaus,[53] or when he ate with the disciples on the lakeside of Galilee.[54] On the other hand, he appeared as an incorporeal being who was not recognized by Mary Magdalene in the garden[55] or by the two travellers on the Emmaus Road,[56] or when he stood at the lakeside.[57] However, the gnostics are consistent in rejecting the idea of a physical resurrection. It was repugnant to them; the concept that a dead body could be restored to life was unthinkable.

Salvation ensured the liberation of the spirit from the captivity of the physical body. How then could the Saviour remain bound to a physical

form? Yet his spiritual presence continued to be felt, so much so that it
is possible to experience the resurrection as a present reality:

> While we are in this world it is fitting for us to acquire the resurrection
> so that when we strip off the flesh we may be found in rest.[58]

Jesus ascended inwardly to the higher regions during his lifetime and
then died. The same gospel says that

> Those who say that the Lord died first and then rose up are in error, for
> he rose up first and then died.

The importance of encountering Christ in the present mattered
greatly to the gnostics. The risen Christ continued to be experienced by
those equipped with the special *gnosis*. According to the sect of Sethian
Ophites, Jesus remained in the world after his resurrection to teach the
great mysteries of his presence and redemption before his return to
heaven. Mary Magdalene, according to the New Testament the first to
witness the resurrection, received a vision of the risen Christ and
enquired what this meant, Mary asked:

> How does he who sees the vision see it? Through the soul, or through the
> spirit?[59]

The answer given is that the vision is perceived through the mind.
"Lord", retorted Mary, "the mind that sees the vision, does it see
through the soul or through the spirit?" The Saviour answered, "it sees
neither through the soul nor through the spirit, but the mind which is
between the two which sees the vision".[60]

The experience of the resurrected Christ is on a spiritual level. It
happens in the present so that the spiritual experience is vivid and individualistic. Its personal character carried implications for achieving
insight into the divine mysteries and perceiving the effluence of the
divine glory. The restoration of the Son of Man to life gave assurance to
the believer of eternal life. The resurrection brought liberation to the
spirit from its captivity in a material body. The act of crucifixion which
destroyed the body and released the spirit through resurrection is one
act; in the light of this teaching the gnostics acquired the conviction
expressed in the *Letter of Peter to Philip* after personal experience of
Christ and of his continuing presence:

> a great light appeared, so that the mountain shone from the sight of him
> who had appeared. And a voice called out to them saying, "Listen . . . I
> am Jesus Christ, who is with you forever".[61]

Varying conceptions of the nature of Christ, some docetic and others anti-docetic, are to be found throughout the writings of the gnostics, as in other early Christian literature. The gnostics engaged this vexed question of the real Jesus as did others, for how to reconcile the two natures in Jesus Christ had plagued the Church from the beginning. Gnosticism did not resolve this dilemma, yet gnostics seemed able to live in creative tension with it. Silvanus wrote that even when Christ is comprehended he is in his nature incomprehensible. And the *Apocryphal Acts of John* testifies:

> Another glory, also, would I tell you my brethren: namely that sometimes when I take hold of him I would meet with a material and solid body, but again at other times, when I touched him, the substance was immaterial as if it existed not at all.[62]

There is a mysterious blending of the human and divine, the comprehensible and the incomprehensible, in the person of Jesus Christ, and gnostic Christology has to be understood against this background.

Anthropology

The understanding of human life in the religion and philosophy of gnosticism is highlighted by a recently discovered saying from an Armenian collection, attributed to Hermes Trismegistos from the second to third century CE:

> He who knows himself, knows the All.[63]

Knowledge of self is basic to the gnostic philosophy of life. Complete knowledge of the essential self is a prime condition of salvation. This knowledge is akin to knowledge of God and is a foundation stone of the gnostic "doctrine of the God man".[64]

> "So while you are accompanying me", says the gnostic text, "though we are uncomprehending, you have (in fact) come to know, and you will be called "the one who knows himself." So he who has not known himself has known nothing, but he who has known himself has at the same time achieved knowledge about the depth of all."[65]

The origin of man is explained reasonably comprehensively by the gnostic writings. It has to be said though that gnosticism lacks a uniform doctrine of the creation of man, and there are elements of similarity and difference from the account in the *Book of Genesis*. According to the

Poimandres, after the creation of the world, the first man was brought forth. His origin is with God and his creation, that is, Adam Qadmon, the primal man, is told from the perspective of the serpent who figures in the *Genesis* narrative, as we have already seen. The body of Adam was constituted by the elements and was equipped with a divine spirit and exalted above all other creatures. Thus he became the prototype of humanity, so that in him there existed divine and human attributes. The existence of the God–man is a cherished gnostic idea, and in the view of Hans Jonas:

> This (according to one branch of the Valentinians) is the great and hidden secret, that the name of the power that is above all things, the fore beginning of everything is Afar.[66]

Such is the stature of man and so exalted did the gnostics portray him that Plotinus castigated them for "thinking very well of themselves, and very ill of the universe".[67] However, the understanding of the real self and of the divine within is the bond of union between God and man. Thus man is identified. He bears the Father's image and has dominion over all his creation, including the *demiurge*. Saturninus designated this as the image of the higher being; man is the creation of a group of seven angels who, being the Father's creations, exalted themselves and said, "Let us make man after the image and after the likeness".[68] According to the Sethian Ophites, the first *archon*, Ialdabaoth, and the whole *aeonic* group saw in the water the appearance of the image, and they said to one another, "Let us make a man, after the image and after the appearance of God".[69]

The likeness is one of life and light and his dominion is accorded the unique power to create life. This desire to create brought him to the lower world and the sphere of the *demiurge*. Man is then brought into contact with nature but he does not belong to the natural world but to a higher heavenly world. Man is a compound being whose life is dominated by the planets or the powers that govern them.

This compound being comprises a *carnal* nature, which is incapable of receiving the divine *gnosis*, a *psychic* component, which is capable of receiving knowledge of salvation, and a *pneumatic* component in which resides the divine spirit. The spiritual element is that which unites with the spirit of Jesus and achieves salvation. Thus the spirit within assures man that he belongs with God.

The goal of liberation is achieved through the action of the divine spirit within the individual soul. In this way the individual soul is consummated within the universal or the totality of souls. In its redeemed state the soul (*pneuma*) is awakened from sleep, the state of darkness as ignorance, to the state of liberation through possessing divine *gnosis*. Gnosticism therefore accounts for the dual nature of man by asserting the presence of a divine element which has entered the physical body. Within this the soul is imprisoned and escape (salvation) is only achieved through the power of mystic *gnosis*. The gnostic myth of the primal man accounts for the soul or divine element within, but his fall into matter has made him the captive of evil. Man as a physical being is without knowledge of his true nature; he is at the mercy of carnal impulses, and must be awakened to his true glory. For this purpose God breathes into him his own spirit and points him to the path of his true destiny.

Whilst there are some variations in the gnostic views, they all share a common view of man as a duality, a captive in the world, however this is expressed, whether as the work of the *demiurge*, or as the creation of a higher being, or as possessing a divine element through the action of the divine spirit. Life at the present is dominated by the powers that govern the planets and man's role is to ascend above them to the higher world which is his true abode. The gnostic exposition of these contrasting elements can be seen from these two excerpts, the first of which describes how man was fashioned from clay:

> And having seen that the world was beautiful, the God of the law thought to make man upon it. And descending to earth into Hyle, he said, "give me this clay and I will give spirit from myself and let us make man in our image". When Hyle had given him of her earth, he shaped it, breathed spirit into it, and Adam became a living soul and for that cause he was named Adam because he was made of clay.[70]

And this gives further insight into how the first man was endowed with the spirit and given power over the first *aeon*:

> And the Invisible Spirit gave him an invincible, intelligible power. Then man said, "I glorify and praise the Invisible Spirit, for because of thee all things came into existence, and all things aspire to thee. But I promise Thee and the Self born with the Aeons, the Three, – the Father and the Mother and the Son, the perfect Power".[71]

The three constituents mentioned above (carnal, psychic and *pneumatic*), combined in the primal man, are the product of cosmic forces that gave form to the physical body and endowed it with the primatic substance. Whichever of these elements predominates determines man's destiny, either to be kept subjected to the power of the world or to be liberated. The *pneuma* (soul) is the product either of the breath breathed into the carnal being or of the divine spirit. The concept of them as a psychosomatic whole is replaced by a duality, of a carnal nature and an immortal soul. The soul belongs to the divine, to the "beyond", to the realm of peripheral light. This makes man a unit of vital power or a being of moral substance. The term soul (*pneuma*) admits of a wide range of meaning, but it stands here for that vital principle within that dominates in the form of consciousness. Philo distinguished between two aspects of the soul, a rational and an irrational. According to him the irrational is the part of the soul that is evil.[72] Man is already a spiritual being here and now; he lives in the spiritual realm where he really belongs. Spiritual qualities are the essence of his true self but these can only be spiritually discerned.

This gives proof of his spirituality, it can only be really known from within. The material or the physical body has no part in this, for it is evil and is destined to perish. The soul (*pneuma*), however, shares in the disciplining of the physical along with the psychic, and thus it determines whether the body is an organ of good or evil. The Valentinian *System of Ptolemaeus* expounds the three elements – the material, the psychic and the spiritual – and quotes the words of the Apostle Paul in so doing:

> as is the earthly man, so are the earthly men . . .
> the psychic man does not accept the things of the spirit . . .
> and the spiritual man judges everything.
> The psychic man does not accept the things of the spirit spoken in regard to the *demiurge*, who, since he is psychic, did not know the mother, since she is spiritual, or her seed, or the Aeons of the Pleroma.[73]

This interpretation of the nature of man poses critical questions, especially in respect of the fact of evil. The existence of evil is both undeniable and puzzling. The gnostic view of the creation, with its hierarchy of realms, and of man as a being with a distinct identity who is subject to the pressures of evil forces, posed a severe problem. In the world there are powers that operate to influence human life in an evil and destructive way. The world is evil because matter is evil. Whilst he is held captive to his physical body, man is subject to the hostile forces that govern the material world. His own physical body is the root of evil. Evil cannot be laid at the feet of God, the Creator. How then could its prevalence be explained? In the works of the early gnostics the concept of the chief ruler (*archon*) of the world is given as an explanation. This was identified with the *demiurge*, the inferior god who created the world.[74] He was responsible for evil and keeps man in subjection to it. In a work entitled

Baruch by Justin there is an illuminating discourse on the cause of evil
and a description of the wish of the Father in respect of evil:

> Lord, let me destroy the universe which I have made, for my spirit is
> imprisoned among men and I wish to take it back.

Then the Lord said to him:

> "Nothing that comes from me can be evil", you and Eden made the
> universe from material satisfaction . . . Under the control of the Good,
> however, Elohim no longer descended to Eden. This Eden commanded
> Babel (Aphrodite) to festive adulteries and divorces among men, so that
> just as she herself was separated from Elohim, so the spirit of Elohim in
> men might be grieved and tormented and experience the same sufferings
> as did the abandoned Eden.[75]

The gnostics expanded the use of the Greek term for evil (*Kakia*) to
include torment, grief, sickness and suffering. There is an emotional element in it, aptly described in the *Gospel of Truth* as man lost in a fog or
haunted by frightening nightmares or experiencing anguish and horror.
As a result, "error became strong and worked on its hylic substance
vainly, because it did not know the truth".[76] According to Irenaeus the
Valentinians looked upon all evil (materialism) as suffering, terror, pain
and confusion, so the word literally means "not knowing where to go".[77]
These experiences happened within the physical world and require an
explanation and, more urgently, a way of release.

The gnostics proffered an answer in terms of knowledge of the
destiny of man, which is linked with the elimination of evil. In the event
the answer to the dilemma is to eradicate the discord within the self for
this then inaugurates the inward and upward personal spiritual journey
to the place of rest. The answer given by Hermes Trismegistos to his son
when questioned about the inward journey to salvation expresses the
matter as follows:

> Abolish the senses of the body and the birth of the deity will take place.
> Cleanse yourself from the irrational afflictions of matter . . . Do I have
> these executioners within me, my father? . . . Not a few my child, indeed
> they are fearful and many . . . I am unaware of them my Father . . . This
> ignorance, my child, is the first affliction; the second is grief . . . [78]

Free from the pressures that keep the soul bound the soul returns to
its proper place to be with:

> the God of Truth, the Father of All, the Holy Spirit, the invincible one,
> He who is over All.[79]

In conclusion it may be said that evil resides in the body, which is but a semblance as opposed to reality, in the impermanent as opposed to the eternal, thus breaching an infinite gulf between evil and good. *Gnosis* has a redemptive function of delivering man from this stranglehold of evil until his soul is completely illumined with the celestial light of truth.

Cosmology

The gnostics were obsessed with understanding how the world came to be, what is its substance, has it a purpose, how can its order be explained and its destiny identified. These questions involved them in lengthy and complicated speculations and theories. The first and most obvious point to consider is the gnostic view of the process that brought the world into being, and how the gnostics conceived of the creator and ruler of the world as other than the Supreme God. He is called the *demiurge* and to him the gnostics attributed the creation of the natural world and all its components.

In the Valentinian *System of Ptolemaeus* the *demiurge* (architect) is described as an angel, like God, whose abode is the seventh heaven of the heavens that surround the earth. Above this is the eighth heaven, the abode of the Supreme God, who is completely remote from the world. These seven heavens are cosmic spheres enclosed in concentric circles. Within them dwell the *archons* exercising their role and authority to keep the spheres under their control. The angel of the lowest sphere (the *demiurge*) is designated as the creator of the world. He is the chief of the hierarchy of *archons* (the *Hebdomad*) through whom Achamoth, the Mother (*Ogdoad*) acted, so that "the Mother was the cause of his creating; so he wanted to bring him forth as the head and beginning of her own nature and as lord of the whole operation".[80] Behind the *demiurge* there is a coterie of subordinate powers (*archons*) who were his collaborators. The world is therefore the creation of lesser powers beneath the Supreme God, the purpose being, in the gnostic sense, the separating of God from material evil and establishing a spatial distance between him and the material world.

The lesser *archons*, being directed by the *demiurge* whose creation includes psychic as well as material things, keep the material world in the power of evil and thus the *demiurge* is conceived of as a hostile being. The *demiurge* and the *archons* constitute an anti-divine force against the Supreme God and the spiritual forces. They represent the demonic forces that hold people captive. From within the sphere of the eighth heaven the *demiurge* exercises dominion over the material world. Towards the end of the second century Celsus produced a diagram, attributed to the gnostic Ophites, of the universe and named the ruling *archon* as "the accursed god of the Jews, who makes rain and thunder. He is the Demiurge of this world, the god of Moses described in his creation narrative."[81]

In this creation myth the process shown is that of downward descent from the Supreme God. Beyond the heavenly spheres (given the names of planets) is the ultimate realm of the Supreme God, the *pleroma* and its graduated world of *aeons*. It is from this that the complicated process of the creation of the world is described, and this that makes way for creation to be effected. The physical world is the lowest or outermost region of creation. There are numerous references in the gnostic texts to *aeons*, the *pleroma* and the All, which taken together make up the sum of the gnostic view, namely that nothing happens except that the Supreme God has knowledge of it. The whole of creation is known to God, for he is totally aware of all that exists:

> This is the manifestation of the Father and his revelation to his Aeons. He revealed that of him which is hidden and explained it. For who is it that exists if it is not the Father himself. All the spaces are his emanations.[82]

The Sethian gnostics called the creator "Ialdabaoth", a name derived from mystical Judaism.[83] His status is inferior to that of the Supreme God as we infer from the *Gospel of Philip*, but he achieved the status of creator of the *archons* and of the natural world:

> Ialdabaoth, becoming arrogant in spirit, brashed himself over all those who were below him, and explained, "I am father and God, and above me there is no-one", his mother, hearing his speech thus cried out to him, "Do not lie, Ialdabaoth, for the father of all, the primal Anthropos is above you, and so is Anthropos, the son of Anthropos."[84]

Before the beginning of time there existed the primal *aeon*. Within this was the source of all being, the depth of the origin of all that came into being. Having existed for innumerable *aeons* the primordial source brought forth from himself "the beginning of all things". From this there emanated a pair of beings, one masculine and the other feminine. These brought forth others until the divine being reached its fullness, and last of all his feminine counterpart, Wisdom (*Sophia*). Wisdom dwelt in the intermediate region between the Supreme God and the *demiurge*. However, Wisdom acted contrary to her nature. One theory is that Sophia found a *demiurge*, a pale representation of the eternal archetypes and whose purpose was inferior to that of the Supreme God. But he brought into being the cosmos and all its creatures. In the Valentinian myth of creation the world is explained as having originated when Wisdom, the mother of all being, brought it forth out of her sufferings. The four elements – earth, air, fire and water – were created from her experience:

> Thus the earth rose from her confusion, water from her terror, air from her consolidation of her grief, while fire . . . was inherent in all these themes . . . as ignorance lay concealed in these three sufferings.[85]

According to Irenaeus, she did not achieve her purpose, and so encountered the Power that sustains and preserves all things, called "the Limit", by whom she was restored and supported. Thus she was brought back to herself and became convinced that God (the Father) was incomprehensible.[86] Thus the Father, wanting to save others from the suffering of Wisdom, revealed to the other *aeons* that all things come from him. Power became the chief aspect of cosmos and the laws of the world those that thwart human freedom.[87]

Fate is dispensed by the planets, bound to the rigid and hostile laws of the cosmos. Fear, confusion, grief, ignorance and suffering keep the human being in servitude in a universe that is contrary to spirit and to life. In this universe some divine sparks became separated and trapped in matter, and some human beings received the divine spark and others did not. Life in the world is under the power of hostile or alien forces, which seek to exercise power for their own ends.

The *Apocryphon of John* provides information on the way the gnostics drew freely upon the narratives of the *Book of Genesis* when accounting for the consequences of evil in the world. It relates how Ialdabaoth, the creator of the *archons*, held the descendants of Cain and Abel in a state of captivity, and how he sought to destroy the world and how Noah and his neighbours escaped:

> Not only Noah, but the people of the generation which does not waver, went to a place and covered themselves with a cloud of light. And he recognized the authority from above, together with those who were with him in the light which was his own then, for the darkness was poured out over everything in the earth.[88]

The sense of alienation intensified the yearning for release to the soul's ultimate home. This alienation created a spirit of deep pessimism and a greater desire to transcend it and advance to a state of freedom in the realm of mystical enlightenment. In this struggle the *archons* seek to keep man in the state of ignorance of the divine spark within. They encourage the lustful gratification of carnal appetites and passions of the physical body.

Gnostic cosmogony is noted for its elaborate cosmologies with multi-storeyed heavens and spheres which are the seeds of *archons* and demonic forces, and its presentation of the Supreme God as spatially and purposefully distant from them all. This complicated account is probably an amalgam of more than one cosmogony, and has blended various theories of the origin and nature of the cosmos. Some gnostics offer a free interpretation of the creation narratives of the Book of Genesis, and to construct a consistent gnostic theory is difficult. On the one hand, there are echoes of an evolutionary view of the origin of creation, and on the other, views of the creation as the work of an inferior god (*demiurge*) subordinate to the Supreme God but hostile to humankind. The myths are not to be interpreted in a literal way: the task is to penetrate the inner meaning the myth enshrines and seek to comprehend the truth. The creator god is not external to the creation but he keeps the natural world under his control. The material holds captive the divine spark that had fallen from the *pleroma* (whether the fall is explained as that of Sophia or of the *demiurge*) and the key to release is the mysterious *gnosis*. The divine spark within, once it is kindled, directs the progress to the ideal of complete fulfilment.

Soteriology

The goal of gnostic striving is the release of the soul from the servitude of the material world. This release is not from sin but from ignorance. Redemption is the prerogative of divine intervention aimed at release of the soul from the limitations of mundane existence and an assurance of return to the realm of perpetual light. The vehicle of the intervention is the saviour who descends through the various spheres to reach the lower regions of earth.

By outwitting the *demiurge* and the *archons* (also called "gate-keepers") who oppose his advent at every stage, the saviour descends and then awakens the spirit from the slumber of ignorance and endows it with the power of redemptive *gnosis*. This equips the soul with the necessary knowledge required to transcend the obstructing barriers that would keep it in captivity. At the point of physical death the soul ascends through the spheres until it reaches the realm beyond the world, where it is reunited with God in his own abode.

Before this blissful state can be realized there are numerous steps to be undertaken. The gnostic is first initiated into the true way of salvation. As we have observed earlier, this ensures that the initiate is equipped with the means of overriding and overcoming the powers of evil that hold the soul back from progressing to the goal of salvation. It also creates awareness of the spheres that have to be passed through on the way to full enlightenment. Then, according the *Gospel of Truth*:

> The end will come where all that is spiritual is shaped and perfected in knowledge. All that is spiritual means the spiritual men who have perfect knowledge about God and have been initiated into the mysteries of Achamoth . . . we (Spirituals) shall certainly be saved not by conduct but simply because we are by nature spiritual.[89]

The spiritual nature of salvation is clear but it is not earned by human effort alone. No one is saved solely on account of personal endeavour. Divine intervention is necessary to achieve this. This includes, as we saw earlier, primal and continuing revelation.[90] The revelation was perfected in the saviour Jesus Christ. He appeared on earth as the redeemer figure and through his spiritual presence continues to make himself known. He is known to the believer personally as the redeemer, and his continuing presence authenticates the experience of redemption. This liberates the soul from the corruptive powers of the material world and opens the way to the blissful fulfilment of perfect redemption. The continuing experience of the presence of the redeemer is the bedrock of the gnostic concept of redemption.

There are variations in the way this is portrayed. Among the Naassenes, for example, the heavenly mother is related to the redeemer Christ as an *aeon*. Also his redemptive work is associated with *Sophia* (wisdom), which may be viewed as a concession to the Jewish concept of wisdom.[91] The Valentinians also developed the redemptive role of Christ in relation to Sophia. Wisdom is here a prototype and symbol of the saviour.[92] Christ is said to have been born the son of Sophia (the mother) but in order to avoid the suffering of the world, Christ is brought forth with the assistance of all the *aeons*. His work as redeemer is to offer guidance to the end so that souls might find escape from the evil that originates in the world. The destination of the soul is outside the boundaries of history and beyond the world in the realm of God,

> the Father, the perfect one, the one who made all things.[93]

Knowledge of the redeemer matters as much as knowledge of the path of redemption. Knowledge of the redeemer originates with knowledge of the self in its relation to God:

> This therefore is the true testimony: when a man knows himself and God who is over the truth, he will be saved.[94]

The *Apocryphon of James* links this knowledge with the work of Jesus Christ as saviour, especially his crucifixion:

> The Lord arrived and said, "Verily I say to you, none will be saved unless they believe in my cross. But those who here believed in my cross, theirs is the Kingdom of God."[95]

But not all gnostics subscribe equally to the doctrine that redemption is only attained through the death of Jesus Christ. In the Valentinian *System of Ptolemaeus* the means of redemption is effected through the coming of the saviour to the psychic element that lies between the material and spiritual components of the human being.[96] He brings with him the light of revelation and redemption. As Ptolemaeus says:

> And the saviour came to this psychic element, since it has free will, in order to save it. He assured the primary elements of these beings which he was going to save . . . The end will come when all that is spiritual is shaped and perfected in knowledge.[97]

The saviour is portrayed as the figure of light who illumines the soul, and as the illuminator he is also the one who saves. Light has a soteriological function, and sprinkled throughout the gnostic texts are other abstract entities, such as *Sophia*, *nous*, *logos* and *epinoia*, all of which have redemptive overtones. All relate to the ministry of the saviour; apart from his action, salvation is unachieved. Jesus became the emanation from the world of pure light to shed the light, that is, the knowledge of salvation. This answers the question of what makes possible the escape from the dilemmas of the world to perfect spiritual freedom. Only those who are spiritual will participate in salvation, for the remainder are incapable of receiving it, and in return the purely spiritual will no longer participate in the debilitating ways of the world. Redemption is wholly spiritual in character. This cannot be valued too highly or emphasized too strongly, for:

> Just as gold placed in mud cannot harm the world, so we cannot damage or lose our spiritual nature, even if we engage in various material actions.[98]

However, with regard to salvation there are similarities and differences from the orthodox Christian conception. Jesus is a wholly spiritual being and his humanity is downrated. Redemption through death on a cross is unthinkable, for God cannot suffer, and the necessity of a historical saviour in order to attain redemption is not germane to the gnostic system. The outreach of salvation as freedom from sin, in orthodox teaching, gives way in the gnostic system to freedom from ignorance. Redemption is the release of the spirit within, which is held captive by being bound to a physical body.

It is the spirit and not the body that is saved, that is, that which needs release is what is held captive. Redemption is not of a whole being, body, mind and spirit, but of the spiritual component alone. The spiritual self is as alien in the world of matter as is the holy transcendent God. Redemption is promoted through the soul's knowledge of its divine origin and its need for liberation. Coupled with knowledge of the transcendent God, who cannot be known in the world apart from revelation, the soul savours the prospect of redemption. This is accomplished by the divine saviour, who existed from the beginning, and now opens the way out of the world for the soul's ascent to the abode of God. Aided and equipped with *gnosis* the soul ascends until it reaches God above and beyond the world.

Eschatology

In one of the Hermetic writings there is recorded a discourse delivered by Hermes Trismegistos to his son in which the son questions his father:

> Tell me, my father, will this body which is composed of this power ever perish?

To which Hermes replies,

> The perceptible body of nature is far removed from the body which comes from real birth. For the one is perishable, the other is not, the one is mortal, the other is not![99]

In considering the gnostic doctrine of the last things (eschatology) we see how closely connected this is with its cosmology and soteriology. The doctrine concerns the fate of the cosmos as well as the final destination of the human soul. We noted above how at the point of death the soul is released to traverse the spheres until it reaches God beyond the world. This is its true home to which the soul is directed at death, or, in gnostic terms, on "the day of escape". The fate of the soul begins to be realized at the point of death, but this does not rule out the final consummation of the cosmos in the end of time. The end of the world is the restoration of what it was at the beginning. The gnostic work the *Three Steles of Seth* describes the path of the soul to its final place of rest where Christ sits at the "Right hand of the father Ialdabaoth in order to receive to himself the souls of those who have known them, after they have put off the worldly flesh".[100]

But before this Christ had prepared the way by travelling this path himself and remained for eighteen months after his resurrection to teach these things to his disciples before he "was taken up into heaven". On this journey heavenward the soul needed help to transcend the barriers of the way, the seven demons who surround the body, and this help is described in symbols and signs, magical and cultic formulae, and death ceremonies. The soul is sustained on its journey by angels of light who inhabit countless worlds of light, and there are accounts of how the soul has to travel.[101] The Mandaean literature depicts how the soul traverses the infernal regions for forty-two days as it is sustained by the prayers and rites of the community on earth. In this context the ascent (*masiqta*) is viewed as a kind of Mass for the dead.

The route of the ascent passes through the celestial spheres of the planets and the creatures of the zodiac where only the purely spiritual are allowed to pass through. All others have to suffer purgatory. The soul has also to face Abathur or Keeper of the Scales, and the "measurement" of the piety of the soul determines its entry into eternal light or, in Mandaean terms, to be with the "Lord of Greatness" or "Mighty Spirit" or "King of Light".[102] Reference above to purgatory refers to the place of punishment for the sinful or the ignorant. Here the "King of Darkness" or "Lord of Darkness", who is described as a giant, a monster or dragon, reigns supreme.[103] This is the fate of those who do not attain knowledge. Their punishment is to undergo a process of purification and their final fate will be decided when the world comes to an end. The possibility of a second death and confinement to permanent darkness is very real. Souls can be confined to purgatory for ever. The doctrine of universal redemption is non-existent:

> For he who is ignorant until the end is a creature of oblivion, and he will be scattered along with it.[104]

Punishment stations are described in vivid images, reminiscent of the biblical narrative of the Red Sea in the book of Exodus, and the Ocean of the End, reminiscent of the biblical Book of Revelation. Here the evil are subjected to torture and to unjust judgement by sorcerers and witches, on the principle of the unjust being meted injustice. In the place of torment there is complete darkness where Satan seduces the soul and metes out the last judgement.

> I said to him, "Christ, those who have known but have turned away, where are their souls?"
> He said to me,
> "They will go to the place where the angels of impoverishment will withdraw, for whom there is no portion of repentance. They will all be preserved for the day on which they will be punished. All who have blasphemed against the Holy Spirit will be tormented in eternal punishment."[105]

There is no quarter for the ignorant; they are to be handed over to the *archons*, seized and cast down into the abyss never to return. There is no reflection of the New Testament teaching of the resurrected Christ descending to hell to convert the departed wicked.[106] But for the spiritual (*pneumatics*) who abide by *gnosis* the assurance is given:

> When we come forth from the labours and sufferings of the body we will obtain rest throughout the Good and reign with the King, and you will be one with him and he one with you from now to (all) eternity.[107]

This teaching is reinforced by Valentinus who wrote of the spiritual being drawn into the "bridal chamber of the Pleroma". As for the hylic (earthly man), however, he will perish with all that is material, and the psychic too will enter the realm of the *demiurge* (the *Hebdomad*). By dealing with the components in this way Valentinus taught the destination of evil, the prospect either of annihilation or of perfect salvation. The release of the soul seems inevitably to involve the discarding of the body, but its punishment is in itself a judgement on those who created it in the first place.

The spiritual survives to share the victory of light over the *demiurge*, "who is impotent to know spiritual beings".[108] The gnostics, furthermore, interpreted belief in resurrection in terms of personal survival. They ruled out the idea of a physical resurrection altogether but developed a doctrine of the resurrection of the soul to those who were gifted with the power of *gnosis*. This is likened to the rekindling of the spark of light and the complete elimination of darkness, which is the state of ignorance. The soul is embraced within an invisible spiritual body which at the resurrection becomes the spiritual resurrection body.

What is the fate of the cosmos when the final apocalyptic events take place? Irenaeus recorded the views of the Valentinian gnostics which specified the end of the world as the time when all that is spiritual reaches perfection through *gnosis*. This will constitute the end of the cosmos and of history. The view of history is of a linear progression leading to a climax. World history is *heilsgeschichte*, a spiritual state created by *gnosis*. (The term *heilsgeschichte* is usually rendered "history of salvation" or "salvation history", but it is used here of that nodal point to which history is directed, in either a linear or other way):

> When this has taken place then the fire that is hidden in the world will blaze forth and burn. When it has consumed all matter it will be consumed with it and pass into non-existence.[109]

When speaking of the end and the restoration of the *pleroma* the gnostics used the concept of the bringing back of all things to their natural state (i.e. *apokatastasis*, a word borrowed from Aristotle). It introduced a cosmological and astrological usage into gnostic thought systems. It is used of the restoration of the spiritual order at the end of time. Valentinians held that Christ was responsible for this restoration when the soul would be at one with the *pleroma*. Basilides, on the other hand, linked the restoration to astral revolutions and the coming of the saviour. There is a movement, he contended, in progress to this end. The Mandaeans wove the idea of restoration into their system and designated the conflagration of the end as a "great year" of twelve thousand years. The gnostic teaching as a whole is consistent with a view of the eschatological restoration as centred on the return of souls to their pure spirituality as in the beginning.[110]

Practices

We come now to consider those key practices that held out for the gnostics the hope of attaining redemption, in anticipation of which they conducted their lives. The context of the gnostics' approach to moral behaviour and ritual and liturgical practices is laid out in *Ptolemaeus' Letter to Flora*:

> Finally, there is the exemplary part, ordained in the image of spiritual and transcendent matters. I mean the part dealing with offerings and circumcision and the Sabbath and fasting and Passover and unleavened bread and other similar matters. Since all these things are images and symbols, when the truth was made manifest they were translated to another meaning. In their phenomenal appearance and their literal application they were

destroyed, but in their spiritual meaning they were restored; the names remained the same but the content was changed.[111]

In the second century the Church engaged in an argument about the formulating of community morals. Irenaeus was among those who would enforce discipline by structured teaching, and deal swiftly with those who dissented. Others adopted a more relaxed view of moral discipline and guided behaviour. Some churchmen wished to operate the transformation in lifestyle and moral discipline which they believed the teaching of Jesus advocated. Others considered that living the life of a Christian was more than a matter of conforming to certain rules and disciplines; it involved abiding by a higher level of moral excellency that was inspired by mature spirituality.

This is exactly what *gnosis* claimed to offer. The spirit within was the source of inspiration and guidance that induced moral behaviour of the highest quality. The experiential knowledge, which has been previously emphasized, modified behaviour which, at best, conforms to the divine will. For example, knowledge of truth is received through revelation and this becomes the stimulus for truthful action:

> As is the case of a person of whom some are ignorant, he wishes to have them know and love him.[112]

This principle of moral behaviour being governed by inner motivation derides the notion of morality as conformity to external law. Gnostics were not averse to disregarding such laws in order to follow the sanctions of conscience and inner impulses. By systematic self-examination and reflection it is possible to discern the strength of inner motivation and act as this directs. The intention behind the act accounts for its moral propriety, *why* the action is performed determines its moral rectitude. Moral behaviour is therefore a matter of personal determination not of conformity to imposed rules. The spur to goodness, gentleness and kindness, as well as to anger, lust or hatred, is inward. This gives freedom to the individual in choosing a way of behaviour. For the Christian gnostic the experience of the continuing presence of Christ becomes the prime motivation of the lifestyle.

Those who opposed the gnostics accused them of overriding the God-given faculty of free will. Valentinus rejected such a charge. He asserted the role of free will but with the proviso that this was not the cause of suffering in the world. Suffering is attributed to the evil inherent in matter and not to the exercise of free will. In this context the alternative interpretation of the biblical story of Adam is relevant. The orthodox Irenaeus surmised that Adam had produced "the ancient law of human liberty"[113] and transmitted the gift of free will to his successors.

The gnostics spoke of Adam's passion for determining his own destiny but that he was the victim of the forces of evil in the material world and from which he and all who came after him yearned to escape. While he was subject to the domination of physical forces he was not wholly free. Only as he was fit to receive the gift of *gnosis* could he be free from the dominion of lesser powers and the obedience they demanded to their command. There is a good deal in the gnostic writings that informs about the lifestyle of the gnostics. The picture is complex as from one point of view popular morality was a matter of obedience to external law, but to show dissent gnostics developed libertine tendencies; whereas from another point of view the tendency was towards asceticism as conscience dictated. There is evidence for both types of behaviour and it is possible to conclude that a combination of both best describes the gnostic lifestyle. Hostility towards the material world bred in some complete revulsion against restrictive laws. They said that to the wholly spiritual all things were permissible for the spiritual could not be harmed by the external laws imposed on the authority of the *demiurge*. The spiritual (*pneumatic*) could not be seduced by the rules of the *archons*, and so gnostics were free to adopt a libertine lifestyle. Being thus minded they practised sexual orgies and indulged in morally devious practices, such as fornication, drunkenness and licentiousness. The *Gospel of Thomas* reports the reputed words of Jesus:

> I stand in the midst of the world and in the flesh was I seen of them. And I found all men drunken, and none found I athirst (for God) among them. And my soul grieveth over the sons of men, because they are blind in their heart, and see not. For empty they came into the world, and empty they seek to leave the world. But for the moment they are intoxicated. When they shake off their wine, then they will repent.[114]

In the gnostic writings attention is given to developing particular patterns of behaviour. The *Gospel of Philip*, for instance, reminds gnostic Christians that they are not exempt from the consequences of evil. The author declares that individuals are responsible for dealing with the evil within, rather than, as the orthodox taught, for abiding by prescribed laws in order to do what is good. He urged:

> As for ourselves, let each one of us dig down after the root of evil which is within one, and let us pluck it out of one's heart from the root. It will

be plucked out if we recognise it. But if we are ignorant of it, it takes root in us and produces its fruit in our heart, it masters us . . . it is powerful because we have not recognised it.[115]

Thus, as was indicated earlier, each person is urged to engage in self-examination and root out such potential sources of evil as lurk in the mind and spirit. What ensures that behaviour is right is the acknowledgement of the evil of the flesh and the continual self-denial of its attraction. In this context the practice of fasting which some gnostics observed needs to be noted. Jesus is reported to have said, "except you fast in the world, you shall in no wise find the Kingdom of God".[116]

The *Gospel of Thomas* also reports how the disciples asked Jesus to tell them how they should act:

His disciples questioned him and said to him, "Do you want us to fast? How shall we pray? Shall we give alms? What diet shall we observe?" Jesus said, "Do not tell lies, and do not do what you hate."[117]

The importance of right motive applies very much to fasting, as to other acts, as Ptolemaeus states in his *Letter to Flora*:

Among us external fasting is also observed, since it can be advantageous to the soul if it is done reasonably, not for imitating others or from habit or because of a special day appointed for this purpose.[118]

Turning now to rites of passage, we may illustrate these from the attitude to celibacy and marriage. The *Gospel of Philip* maintains that those who advocate celibacy are in error. Fornication is also dubbed evil:

The saviour said, Sin as such does not exist, but you make sin when you do what is the nature of fornication, which is called "sin". For this reason the Good came into your midst, to the essence of each nature, to restore it to its rest.[119]

But an alternative view to this is expressed by the Nicolaitans:

The Nicolaitans have as their master Nicolaus, of the seven who were first ordained to the diaconate by the apostles, they lived promiscuously. Who they were is most fully revealed in the Revelation of John; they teach that fornication is a matter of indifference . . . [120]

Marriage is approved as good and by the Valentinians marriage is approved as being preferable to celibacy or the free exercise of the emotions. The *Gospel of Philip* says of the sensitive man that he will not be misled by the physical appearance of anyone, but will regard everyone according to the inner condition of the soul and act accordingly. In general, gnosticism gives a positive answer to the question whether Christians should approve marriage, and gnostics therefore approached the question of the relationship between men and women in a creative way. They did not compose a set of rules for marriage but focused on the internal forces of desire and fulfilment. Man and woman find fulfilment in relationship.

The above gospel sets this in characteristic gnostic mythical form. When Eve, the spirit, separated from Adam, the psyche, it was as though death had happened. Only when the spirit and the psyche came together again in ordinary consciousness did the relationship, that is between Adam and Eve, become complete again. The harmony was restored and fulfilment achieved. The marriage of spirit and psyche makes for wholeness. *Poimandres* elaborated on this idea:

> For all living creatures, previously bisexual, were parted, as was man; they became on the one hand male, and on the other, female. At once God spoke a holy word [*logos*], "Increase and multiply, all creatures and creations . . . "[121]

We now turn our attention to the cultic and liturgical practices of the gnostics. It has already been observed that they did not form a church or a spiritual sect, but alongside their speculative systems of ideas and doctrines they led an active cultic life. Knowledge of their rituals and liturgies is not extensive but is sufficient to give an insight into the way they practised their beliefs in the context of community and ritual.

The gnostics practised a rite of baptism. Baptism by immersion was general, but sprinkling was also permitted. As far as the meaning of the rite goes the gnostics seemed to regard it as a rite of purification or of cleansing in preparation for admission to the *pleroma*. It also had an element of initiation into the mysteries of *gnosis*. The Valentinians viewed baptism as a redemption rite, and both they and the Sethian gnostics regarded baptism as the assurance of immortality. Through baptism the baptized received the spirit of immortality, and thereby the baptized became a *pneumatic* (spiritual being). This was equivalent to receiving the immortal spirit of Christ. Kurt Rudolph quotes a formula used at this ceremony:

> In the name of the unknown Father of all things, unto Truth, the mother of all, unto him who descended on Jesus [i.e. Christ], into union, into redemption (*apolytrosis*), into the communion of powers.[122]

Baptism is considered to be a preparation for the journey of ascent through the spheres as well as introduction to the mysteries of *gnosis*. This was conceived as moving from the servitude of the material to the liberty of the spiritual world. Every sect in all probability had its own baptismal formulae, but certain notions as are referred to here, notably that souls were admitted to the higher world and would be redeemed only by divine intervention, were common to all gnostic systems. Baptism is compared to a "spiritual marriage" with appropriate ritual, as expressed in this account of Marcosian worship:

> Some of them construct a bridal chamber and perform mystical initiation with certain secret expressions for the initiates. They call this rite "spiritual marriage". . . others lead candidates to the water, and in baptising them use this formula: Into the name of the unknown Father of all, into Truth, the mother of all, unto him who came down into Jesus, into Unity and Redemption and fellowship with the powers.[123]

Although the outward rite of baptism was practised the characteristic gnostic belief in the primacy of the spiritual was not ignored. The performance of the rite, no more than the act of confession or martyrdom, could not of itself make a person a Christian. This caused some anxiety as is implied in the words of the *Gospel of Philip*:

> Many people go down into the water and come up without having received anything.[124]

Evidence of spirituality was needed, or of knowing the truth:

> the baptism of truth is something else, it is by renunciation of the world that it is found.[125]

The Christian is not someone who "has passed through the waters" but one who has been initiated into the way of spiritual maturity. The Church is not a physical community of the baptized but an invisible community of the spiritually knowledgeable. Many gnostic texts denounce the futility of formal observances which are void of any perceptible spiritual element or process. The *Gospel of Philip* gives a vivid picture of this futility:

> An ass which turns a millstone did a hundred miles walking, when it was loose it found it was still at the same place. Here are men who make many journeys but make no progress towards any destination. When evening came upon them, they saw neither city nor village, neither human artifact nor natural phenomenon, power nor angel. In vain have the wretches laboured.[126]

Even ascetic practices or good deeds can be spiritually abortive:

> If you fast, you will give rise to sin for yourselves, and if you pray, you
> will be condemned, and if you give alms, you will do harm to your
> spirits.[127]

Such observances may be no more than ego centred and do not
enhance the quality of spirituality. They only create an illusion whereas
in reality they do not bring the performer greater illumination or nearer
to God. True baptism, as all other observances, is spiritual:

> If one go down into the water and come up without having received
> anything and say, "I am a Christian", he has borrowed the name at
> interest. But if he receive the Holy Spirit, he has the name as a gift. He
> who has received a gift never does have to give it back, but of him who
> has borrowed it at interest, payment is demanded.[128]

The gnostics observed the eucharist or the Lord's Supper in a particular way. Some used water not wine at the eucharistic ceremonies, but
wine was also used. Irenaeus has given an account of the practice of the
Marcosians, followers of Marcus, a teacher of the Valentinian school,
which tells how along with a lengthy prayer of invocation cups of mixed
wine were prepared, and then he describes in mythical language how
Grace seems to pour drops of blood into the cup and makes the wine
appear purple and red. Those present show a strong desire to have the
wine so that Grace may be imparted to them. The wine is given to the
women and they are commanded to say the eucharistic prayer, and then
the cup the women have prayed over is taken and the contents poured
into a larger cup as the eucharistic prayer is said:

> May the Grace which is before all, inconceivable and ineffable, fill your
> "inner man" and increase knowledge of her in you, sowing in you the
> mustard seed in good earth.[129]

After this the large cup is filled from the small one so that it over-
flows. There is no record of a common meal as practised by Christians
in apostolic times (*Acts* 2: 44–6) or by the Essenes. The little that is
known about the gnostic cult practice only superficially resembles the
eucharistic practices of the Church. But women were present and they
too partook of the eucharist. How far a sacramental element was
involved is difficult to determine, but the observance was in essence a
spiritual rite when the participants became spiritually incorporated in
the mystical significance of the eucharist.

A final example of the cultic practices is extreme unction. The account comes from Irenaeus. At the point of death the dying is anointed with oil and water, which become incomprehensible and invisible, as the "inner man" ascends invisibly, leaving the body behind in the world. After death takes place those present say:

> I am a Son from the Father, from the Father who was before, a son in him who was before. I have come to see all things which are mine and not mine . . . I trace my origin to the pre-existent One, and I return to my own, whence I came.

The one who says these things evades and escapes from the powers. He says to them about the *demiurge*:

> I am a precious vessel, more precious than the female who made you. Your mother is ignorant of her origin, but I know mine. I know from whence I came, and I invoke the imperishable Sophia who is in the Father, the mother of your mother who has no father or husband.

Those around the *demiurge* recognize their origin and are full of fear, but the gnostic proceeds to his own, casting off his bond, i.e. his soul.[130]

What distinguished gnostic Christians from their contemporaries was their attitude and behaviour in matters of sex, social relations, cultic practices and worship. They believed deeply that their salvation depended on knowledge of their spiritual nature, and this led them to adopt different stances in matters of moral and religious behaviour. Some were extremists who believed they could not be stained by sinful ways; Carpocrates, for instance, allowed his followers freedom in moral behaviour. His son Epiphanes went further and taught that promiscuity was not evil.

The Ophites condoned the action of the serpent in bringing knowledge to Adam and Eve, whilst Cainites respected such a murderer as Cain as well as other Old Testament characters noted for their devious ways. But other gnostics were more conventional and adopted an ascetic attitude to sex and marriage. Those who held the doctrine that humans were originally unisex regarded the creation of women as a source of evil. It resulted in the procreation of children who added to the souls in bondage to the material world. So far as the cult is concerned the gnostics introduced a variety of practices, including the use of pictures, statues, incense and other objects taken over from a variety of sources. There seems to have been a self-conscious attachment to social gatherings as a condition of worship and the development of spirituality. God as divine Father establishes a "communal" relation with himself, fellowship with God whether the "experienced element" is moral, cultic or worshipful in its outcome. The blending of this relationship with God is the touchstone of right moral and cultic action.

Human beings associate with human beings . . . Members of a species usually associate with those of the same species. Just so, spirit unites with spirit . . . and light merges with light. If you are born a human being it is human beings who will love you, if you become a spirit you will unite with their spirit.

The Gospel of Philip

Do not accuse your head (Christ) because it has not made you an eye, but a finger . . . but be thankful that you are not outside the body.

The Interpretation of the Knowledge

The world was not made by the first god, but by a power that was far removed and separated from the sources of being, and did not even know the God who is exalted above all things.

Cerinthus, Hans Jonas, The Gnostic Religion

Jesus was not born of the virgin, but rather he was born of Joseph and Mary just like all other men, but more powerful in righteousness, intelligence and wisdom.

Cerinthus, A.H. i.6

5

Orthodoxy and Heresy

From earliest times the Christian Church has been concerned to define its beliefs in authoritative and orthodox terms. From the beginning it has acknowledged the need to communicate and expound an authentic version of its faith for the sake of instructing its adherents and propagating its message. For this purpose it has aimed to devise the most appropriate language and thought forms such as will make its beliefs intelligible, luminous and meaningful, and at the same time be consistent with the essence of its faith.

But appropriate metaphors for the purpose have never been easy to come by. At times it has seemed as if it is beyond the power of the mind alone and that only the spirit is able to lead into all the truth. Yet truth has to be comprehended and interpreted, and the aim of Christian orthodoxy is to formulate an authentic, creditable and irrefutable version of its beliefs. But the Church has always been plagued by alternative interpretations or competing expositions of its doctrines which have challenged orthodoxy and often led to schism. Heresy is a pejorative term used of alternative formulations of the Church's faith and this was rampant during the second and third centuries. It led Irenaeus to ask:

> How is it that we, for no reason, remain aloof from them, and how is it when they confess the same things and hold the same doctrines, we call them heretics?[1]

Those who Irenaeus denounced as heretics were guilty of devising repulsive and forbidding doctrines and of distorting the true faith. Irenaeus had no alternative but to mobilize the Church in its defence of the apostolic faith, of which he believed it was the appointed guardian, and repel the attack of the gnostics.

Heresy did not suddenly afflict the Church like a bolt out of the blue in the time of Irenaeus for the Church had wrestled with an incipient heresy from the days of the first apostles. But the orthodox–gnostic divide was the most potentially dangerous the Church had faced hitherto. The controversy was broadened and the questions and issues in dispute were sharpened as the controversy became more acute. Questions about the origin and nature of Jesus and the salvation he achieved were redefined and pursued with greater rigour. The temperature of the debate was raised by issues and challenges that arose out of the prevailing culture and the spiritual uncertainty of the times. The Church was under siege and facing a crisis of identity, even of survival. But it reacted forcefully to what Hippolytus, a disciple of Irenaeus, called, "the naked blasphemies of the heretics", and also responded to the variegated social, moral, religious, philosophical and sceptical temper of the time.[2] The gnostics were equally forceful and intent on defending and propagating their doctrines. They had no organizational base but were uninhibited on this account in propounding their beliefs in a forthright and graphic manner. Attack and counter-attack rather than constructive dialogue seemed the order of the day.

The issues of the orthodox–gnostic encounter were basic to the health and survival of Christianity. They went deeper than differences about the meaning of terms like *gnosis* or redemption. The orthodox saw them as lethal, as the heresy faced by the apostle when he wrote about the danger that "some will depart from the faith by giving heed to deceitful doctrines, through pretensions of liars, whose consciences are seared". They looked upon the gnostics "as wrangling among people depraved in mind and bereft of the truth, who indulge in contradictions of what is falsely called knowledge, who swerve from the truth of the resurrection, saying that it is already past and who upset the faith of believers" (*1* and *2 Timothy*).

If heresy sows the seed of "deceitful doctrines", "indulges in contradictions of what is falsely called knowedge" and upsets "the faith of believers", then the gnostics would rebuff the charge by claiming to provide a version of the Christian truth that was mediated directly through the power of God's own gift of knowledge.[3] They responded with their *Gospel of Truth*, which, if we take the title at its face value, is intended to be a true exposition of Christian belief. It was inspired by the spark of divinity within and bore the authority of the divine spirit. Irenaeus, however, implored the faithful to avoid "such an abyss".[4] The essence of truth was at stake in this debate and when the gnostics expounded their insights into the essence of truth in a written gospel the orthodox counteracted with positive action by compiling an authentic collection of Christian books approved by the Church as the canon or rule of true faith. Furthermore, it formulated its faith in the form of a creed which expressed the heart of apostolic doctrine, and it established a hierarchy of bishop, presbyter and deacon as the custodians and official interpreters of the truth. These were powerful measures enacted by the Church as a bulwark against false teaching and to ensure the preservation of the faith delivered once and for all times to the apostles.[5] The gnostics, on the other hand, believed that the revelation they received through the continuing presence of the Holy Spirit absolved them from commitment to an imposed external authority in matters of truth and belief. To the Church this was perversion that had to be resisted.

Although history proves that the strength of the institutional Church prevailed over the uninstitutionalized heretics the embers of the conflict were never completely extinguished and have continued to smoulder even to our own day. Who were the leading contenders in this contest for the heart and soul of believers who made this period so vibrant in the history of Christian thought and culture?

Simon Magus, Father of Heresy

Tradition attributes the origin of Christian gnosticism to Simon Magus. He is mentioned in the *Acts of the Apostles* chapter 8:

> But there was a man named Simon who had previously practised magic ... saying that he himself was somebody great. They all gave heed to him, from the least to the greatest, saying, This man is that power of God which is called Great.
>
> Now when Simon saw that the Spirit was given through the laying on of the apostles' hands, he offered them money, saying:
>
> Give me also this power, that anyone on whom I may lay my hands may receive the Holy Spirit.[6]

The Simon of Acts is of course one of the apostles who had a close association with Philip and Samaria. His contemporaries disdainfully accused him of being a magician (magus = worker of magic). He was believed to possess secrets and wisdom which others did not, and even some special prowess such as flying through the air. Some were awe-struck by this and said, "This man is that power of God which is called Great."[7] Others accused him of being a messenger of Satan, a common charge in those days against mystics and magicians. The Church denounced him as the first author of all heresy.[8] He acquired the reputation of being the ancestor of Christian heresy.

Information about his activities during the apostolic period is extremely fragile and to produce a complete picture of him is difficult. Simon is said to have been converted to Christianity by Philip and to have accepted baptism, but doubt has always been cast on whether this was a genuine conversion. He undoubtedly claimed to be a Christian but his conception of Christianity deviated from that of the apostles, hence he was accused of heresy. Tradition says that he succeeded John the Baptist and that after a while he was usurped from this position by a fellow disciple named Dositheus. This raises the question whether the Simon of these traditions is the Simon of the apostolic age. Hans Jonas has questioned whether this is the case, and Gilles Quispel doubts whether he was a full gnostic. Jonas argues that we should discount the Simon of the *Book of Acts* and concentrate attention on a character of a much later date who bore the same name.[9]

Justin Martyr mentions a Simon amongst a trio of heretics named by him, namely, Simon, Menander and Marcion.[10] Menander is said to have succeeded Simon and Marcion is accused of being a heretic and "the mouth of godlessness". Knowledge of the later Simon comes mainly from the works of the Church Fathers, especially Irenaeus, Justin Martyr, Hippolytus, Tertullian, and the heretic Celsus. The impression gained from these writings is of Simon as a strong and majestic character whom Irenaeus says was regarded by his disciples as "the son of God".[11] His parents were Antony and Rachel and he is said to have had a virgin birth. He lived in Egypt and was educated in Alexandria where he came under the influence of Hellenistic thought, but he ended up in Rome where he met his death. According to one account Simon followed Peter to Rome where he preached heretical doctrines. He boasted that if he were to be buried alive he would rise again the third day. So he commanded his disciples to dig a grave and ordered that he be buried in it. They carried out his instructions but Simon did not reappear, for, said Hippolytus, he was not the messiah.[12] His association with Peter is known from the apocryphal *Acts of Peter* where they are frequently portrayed as engaged in argument.

It is from the many legends that surround Simon that we are able to deduce his gnostic tendencies. He lived and worked in Samaria, the home of many gnostics. He gathered followers who were devoted to him and who are said to have worshipped him as "the first God".[13] These were not only Samaritans but some were from other nations and from Rome in particular. Those who were followers assigned to him a redemptive role and even called him messiah. Legend tells that he descended as the unrecognized redeemer in order to deliver his companion Helen who, according to Justin Martyr, "went about with him in those days".[14]

The focus of the myth and its symbolism is on the attainment of redemption as Simon is portrayed as descending to rescue her from being held in servitude to ever-changing bodies. She had passed through numerous incarnations and suffered greatly before she appeared as "the lost sheep". Simon called her "the mother of all".[15] Helen has been equated with Mary Magdalene and is said to have descended from heaven to be a symbol to the world of true wisdom, but in the eyes of Simon was in need of being rescued from the captivity of matter so that she might be freed to begin her return journey to the celestial realm. Helen therefore is the prototype of a captive soul in search of liberation. And so it is said:

> For this reason he (Simon) came in order to rescue her first and free her from her bonds and then to offer men salvation through his knowledge.[16]

Orthodox Christians rejected such mythology and dismissed it as a stain on their teaching. The myth distorted the spirit of truth and sought to press it into a mould that obscured its substance. So Simon was denounced as being in league with Satan and the orthodox rejected outright his presumptions of being above God, and being worshipped as God, and being awarded Highest Power, or acclaimed as the Mind of all, able to govern everything including men and women. He appropriated to himself terms like "the Standing One", that is, "the Existing One", "the Absolute Sovereign", "the One who is alive and eternal", titles that were applied properly only to Christ.[17] There are elements in his teaching that reflect his gnostic tendencies. He taught that the highest God was not the creator and that the world only had an indirect relation to God. The world is the emanation of the Logos or its source is *ennoia* or *nous*, from this there issued Thought and then the rank of angels by whom the world was made.

Simon regarded himself as spirit possessed (*pneumatic*) and this elevated him above the unredeemed to assume the titles listed above. None of Simon's works have survived and the *Great Annunciation* attributed by tradition to him is disputed, especially as it echoes so much of the thought of Empedocles.[18] As is usual the picture of any heretic in the writings of the Church Fathers is biased and unsympathetic. Hippolytus presents Simon as a wandering prophet babbling about prophecy being fulfilled. The myth of Helen described above shows a degree of contact with Hellenistic thought as well as reflecting the recurrent theme of gnosticism about the descent of the saviour being hampered by hostile forces. From all accounts Simon lived a libertine lifestyle and behaved promiscuously. His system of thought was perpetuated by his pupil Menander and subsequently by the gnostic Saturninus. Simon is an enigmatic character but aspects of his thought relate to the main themes of gnostic teaching. The Helen myth of a striving soul seeking for release into the world beyond and how this is effected through the descent of the saviour on his redemptive mission is consistent with the philosophic stance of gnosticism:

> In every heaven I take a different form, according to the form of the beings in each heaven, that I would remain concealed from the ruling angels and descend to the Ennoia who is called Prunikos and Holy Spirit, through whom I created the angels, who then created the world and men.[19]

Cerinthus, gnostic teacher

Cerinthus was a contemporary of the Apostle John and tradition locates him in Ephesus, the probable place of origin of the *Gospel of John*.[20]

He is reputed to have been skilled in the learning of the Egyptians. Irenaeus portrays him as a dangerous and formidable opponent of traditional apostolic faith and says that John wrote his gospel in response to the heretical teaching of Cerinthus. Irenaeus was so alarmed by the doctrines of Cerinthus that he sought to isolate the faithful from any contact with him – they were not to stay under the same roof. And he reports that some who heard him "relate that John, the Lord's disciple, went to the baths of Ephesus, and rushed out, without taking a bath, when he saw Cerinthus inside, exclaiming, "Let us get away before the baths fall in for Cerinthus is in there, the enemy of the truth."[21]

His teaching is representative of the issues that engaged the gnostics but is also interfused with elements of Judaistic and Ebionite thought. He taught a dualism between God and the world, and between spirit and matter. The creation is the work of angels who are lesser beings than God, of which Cerinthus said:

> the world was made not by the first God, but by a power that was far removed and separated from the source of being and did not even know of the God who is exalted above all things.[22]

Cerinthus identified this power with the God of the Old Testament, and between him and the world there are intermediaries, just as appeared in the later development of gnostic doctrine. He asserted the absolute remoteness of the Supreme God who was immune from all contact with the evil world of matter. The Supreme God is exalted above the creator God and is unassailable and unknowable. With regard to the person of Jesus, Cerinthus taught a wholly docetic view. Of his teaching on this Irenaeus wrote:

> Jesus was not born of the virgin, but rather he was born of Joseph and Mary just like all other men, but more powerful in righteousness, intelligence and wisdom.[23]

At his baptism Christ descended on Jesus from above in the form of a dove, the symbol of purity. Thus he was empowered to proclaim the unknown Father and to perform miracles. In a number of respects the teaching of Cerinthus anticipates aspects of later development in gnostic thought. This applies to his teaching of how Jesus was united with the pre-existent *aeon* who equipped him for his unique mission. The purpose of this mission was to reveal divine knowledge and to prescribe a doctrine of eschatology. On this he taught a highly stylized view:

> There will be a period of a thousand years to be spent in wedding festivities.[24]

This view of the inauguration of the millennium is clothed in materialistic terms. The power of Christ given to Jesus at his baptism remained with him until just before his crucifixion,[25] and then, according to Cerinthus:

> After the resurrection the Kingdom of God will be on earth, and the flesh dwelling at Jerusalem serve lusts and pleasures.[26]

The impact of the teaching of Cerinthus at the end of the first century was considerable, as we gather from the words of Irenaeus. R. McL. Wilson has advanced the view that if it could be proved that Simon Magus' was mainly a pagan system and that the gnostics have read back later developments into Simon's scheme or that he represents a Jewish pagan gnosticism faintly tinted with Christianity, then Cerinthus may be called the first Christian gnostic in the full sense.[27]

Marcion, gnostic reformer

Marcion posed the greatest threat to orthodoxy in the second century. He achieved prominence as an ardent church reformer yet the Church resisted his teaching as causing it immense peril. Marcion was a native of Sinope in Asia Minor but he settled in Rome around 140 where he soon gained a reputation as a formidable controversialist. He was attracted to the views of Cerdo, a Syrian teacher with leanings towards gnosticism, who taught categorically that:

> the God whom Moses and the prophets preached is not the Father of Jesus Christ; the one is knowable and other not, the one merely just, the other good.[28]

Cerdo also rejected belief in the physical resurrection of Jesus and this also attracted Marcion to him. The dualism between the God of the Old Testament and the God of Christianity is a major element in the system of Marcion which he extended to questions of ethics and theology. He set about elaborating this dualism in the belief that he could thereby save the Church from binding itself irrevocably to the legalism and harsh theism of the Old Testament. By doing this he postulated a dualist view of deity, the one just and the other good. The Church was in error in binding itself to the God who was "known", that is, the God of Moses and the prophets, rather than to the God who was "unknown", that is, the God of Christians and the Father of Jesus Christ. The former was the creator God who was a lesser deity; he was responsible for this defective creation and this earned Marcion's disgust and distain for the material world as being evil. He could not deny the existence of the creator God but by clinging to belief in the God of the Old Testament, the "known"God, the Church was creating for itself an intractable problem.[29] How could it reconcile belief in a just and vengeful God with a God of love? Marcion was much exercised by the problem of knowing how to reconcile the dilemma of belief in a divine righteousness and justice with divine love and mercy. This dualism had to be circumscribed and the Jewish Bible ignobly rejected and excluded from the Church's scriptures. Marcion affirmed his adherence to the teaching of the apostles, especially as expounded by his chief mentor and hero the Apostle Paul, and wished to save the Church from apostasy. Paul taught a doctrine of the unmerited and unconditional grace of God and to this Marcion was wholly committed.

Marcion believed in the one true compassionate God who alone is able to rescue humankind from the machinations of the *demiurge*. Whereas the *demiurge* was neither all-powerful or all-merciful the God of the Christians was perfect in all respects and he alone could perfect redemption. Marcion's teaching had a wide appeal and he won many followers and was able to form a rival church. Its cornerstone was the belief in the God of love who was revealed by Jesus Christ. He alone is the true God who is enthroned by Christians. Christianity is not a continuation or fulfilment of the manifestation of the Old Testament God but is a completely new revelation given in Jesus Christ. The way of redemption is through the work of this God of love. Redemption is by faith in him, not knowledge.[30] In asserting this Marcion believed he was consistent with the teaching of the apostles.[31] He demonstrated his commitment to this doctrine by compiling a canon of Christian scriptures whose overriding design was to expound the nature and redemptive actions of this God of love. The canon he compiled consisted of the epistles of the Apostle Paul, with the exception of the pastoral epistles, and an expurgated version of the *Gospel of Luke*, thereby ensuring that the version contained all those qualities of universal love, divine compassion and spirituality that reflected his own presumptions.[32] According to Marcion the *Gospel of Luke* is the one that expounds most effectively the true character of Christian love and Paul's epistles expound truthfully the means of salvation. He made a complete break with the Old Testament and provided the Church with a canon of scripture which, had it prevailed, would have transformed the attitude of the Church to Judaism.

Those who were sympathetic to Marcion's anti-legalism were also prepared to receive his other ideas. The Catholic Church, however, was uncompromisingly opposed to his teaching and accused him of not understanding the truth and, indeed, of degrading it. The distinction he drew between the law and grace, and especially between the "known" and "unknown" God, proved too much for a Church that was irrepressibly devoted to one God and one God only. The Church denounced Marcion's work called *Antithesis* as heretical and rejected outright his view of revelation being restricted solely to Christianity. Yet Marcion insisted in proclaiming his belief that "the stranger" God who had suddenly descended into the world by sending his son to redeem it was the sole redeemer. He did not enter the world as a full human being for he could only enter the physical world if he was immune from its evil. Therefore Jesus only appeared as a human being otherwise he would be linked with the *demiurge*, the God of the Old Testament, and with Cain, the Sodomites and all the Gentiles. On the other hand, those who were considered to be righteous according to Old Testament law were left to remain in the underworld.[33]

Consistent with his own thought Marcion interpreted the doctrine of Chrisian redemption as an act of divine mercy that is only intelligible to those who receive the gift of knowledge. The redemption is an act of ransom, release from the captivity of an unwholesome world for which the redeemer paid a ransom. But the gift of release has to be received by faith. The gift is an extension of the love and mercy of the divine Father, but in expressing this Marcion confessed that he only offered a particle of the Christian gospel and not the whole of it. He trusted his own insights into this and confidently asserted that only souls who had received his doctrine would be saved. No earthly body could participate in salvation for redemption was wholly spiritual.[34] The physical being can have no share in the salvation of the Supreme God for the physical is mortal and tainted; it is the work of the *demiurge* who has no care for the soul. Deliverance only comes about through the mercy of the God of love.

The Catholic Church took a decisive step against the heresy of Marcion in 144 when it excommunicated him. This did not prevent his teaching from living on and his followers continued to teach his doctrines well into the fifth century. Nothing is known of Marcion after his excommunication but in the history of the Church in the second century he is rated as one of the most creative and original Christian thinkers.

Sometimes his relationship with the gnostics has been questioned on account of the highly individualistic nature of his thought, which is difficult to fit into any contemporary pattern. He was committed to the visible and organized church as is seen from the way he organized an alternative church with its own creed, liturgy and constitution. This was not the way with the majority of gnostics, who were averse to forming organized structures.[35] But we see that many of the ideas that Marcion taught were those that appealed also to the gnostics. Like some gnostics he lived an ascetic existence as a mark of his faith commitment.

In stressing the dichotomy between law and grace, and matter and spirit, Marcion entered a debate that engaged Paul and other early theologians. The issue continues to receive attention by Christian theologians to this day. Marcion's involvement in the debate is testimony to his insights into matters of central concern for the understanding of Christian redemption and it has implications for the understanding of the doctrine of good and evil. He also challenged the Church of his day on the question of the relationship between Christianity and Judaism and how far the early Christians had interpreted their faith aright. Had they falsified the gospel by regarding it as a continuation of the revelation to the Jews? Marcion insisted that he stood for the true faith of Christianity and devoted his energies to being what Tertullian called "the first improver" of "the corrupted gospel".[36]

The issues with which he wrestled continued to arouse acute controversy for many years after his departure and this means that he occupies
a unique place in the history of early Christian apologetics. In respect
of his relationship to gnosticism the words of Kurt Rudolph are appo-
site:

> He worked with gnostic ideas available in his time, insofar as they corre-
> sponded to his theological attitude. This links him with the other great
> gnostics of his time who similarly proceeded in an original and inde-
> pendent manner.[37]

Valentinus, gnostic poet and visionary

Valentinus is the most able of the gnostics of the second century. He was
born in Egypt around 110 and educated in the philosophical school of
Alexandria where he is said to have come under the influence of
Theodus, a pupil of the Apostle Paul. He was baptized. In 136 he
removed to Rome where he joined the church congregation and where
his outstanding intellectual gifts soon became known and gained much
respect. He was prominent as a philosopher, a theologian and a gifted
poet, and his reputation was such that by the middle of the century he
was in the running to be appointed bishop. But it is as a distinguished
gnostic teacher that he is best remembered.

Valentinus founded a school of gnosticism in Rome and gathered
around him a group of committed gnostics who shared his views and
spread them to other parts of the empire where they founded communities of Valentinians. These became active and progressive communities
in promoting the teachings of Valentinus so that his influence was far
more wide flung than any of his gnostic predecessors. Valentinus
defined systematically the aims of his school as:

> to set forth the living essence of their religion in the form uncontaminated
> by the Jewish envelope in which they received it and expressed under-
> standing suited (as they might say) to the cosmogony and philosophy of
> their enlightened age.[38]

As a child Valentinus was subject to remarkable visionary experiences and throughout his life he received visions and dreams which he
believed "spoke" to him. Through these visions he received the secrets
and insights of mysterious *gnosis*, which he then taught his disciples.
One such vision was of the *logos*, the energy from which the universe
was formed, and which he took seriously. He was committed to a dualist

view of the universe, and of good and evil controlled by rival gods. His religious system revolved around divine revelation and the mysterious powers of *gnosis*, and at its heart was a firm belief in the Christian hope of redemption. The religious system that he pioneered so efficiently centred around many of the ideas of the Apostle Paul, but there are in it also tinges of oriental thought. In the *Gospel of Truth*, a product of the Valentinian school, we detect a fusion of Pauline theology with gnostic ideas:

> For the rest then, may they know, in their places that it is not fitting for me, having come to the resting place, to speak of anything else. But it is understood that I shall come to be, and (it is fitting) to be concerned at all times with the Father of all and the true brothers, those upon whom the love of the Father is poured out in whose midst there is no lack of him.[39]

The excerpt reflects the teaching of the Epistle to the Hebrews, traditionally attributed to Paul, and the rest that God has promised and prepared for his people.[40]

Valentinus attributed his own spiritual progress to a vision of a new-born infant who announced to him, "I am the Logos". He sought illumination on the meaning of the vision by looking within himself and searching for deeper meaning within the scriptures. He believed that only initiates like himself into the mysterious *gnosis* were equipped to expound the inner meaning of the scriptures.

Valentinus applied himself diligently to the task of exploring the inner meaning of truth and he propounded a system of knowledge that matched the theories and expositions of the orthodox theologians of the Catholic Church. Under him gnosticism achieved a status it had not previously enjoyed. Leaders of orthodox thought took seriously his expositions and system of mystical knowledge. But some were alarmed by his teaching and saw it as competing with the Church's own theologians for the souls of believers. Irenaeus and other Church Fathers viewed his influence as extremely harmful, and Irenaeus, in particular, regarded him as the most threatening to the Church of all the gnostics. Yet in some aspects of his teaching Valentinus was closer to orthodox doctrine than we might at first assume.

It was his genius and teaching that prepared the way for the ancient world to abandon the ways of paganism and to take seriously what he believed to be authentic (intelligible) Christianity. In order to achieve this he was not averse to extracting what was best in faith and ethics from the many creeds and philosophies that prevailed in the open market-place of culture in the world of the time. When he did so he gave them a Christian orientation and thereby advanced a spirit of holism between different belief systems.

Valentinus aimed to bring about a spirit of reconciliation between all who were at variance with the Church in the belief that the Church was the custodian of revealed truth, the manifestation of the divine life of the Spirit and the agent of the divine purpose. He did not therefore set out to establish a rival church or organization. He did, however, stress the divine origin of the Church and advocated that it act according to the true *gnosis* as the only sure way to attaining universal redemption. He had no intention of abandoning the Church but rather wished to ensure that the Church should hold to the knowledge of redemption transmitted to the elect, as it was in the case of the disciples of Jesus who were entrusted with special knowledge ("to you it has been given to know the mystery of the Kingdom of God").[41] This teaching is expanded in other gnostic writings of this school, especially the *Gospel of Mary*, the *Gospel of Thomas* and the *Dialogue of the Saviour*.

Valentinus' exposition of redemption is complex, but the following expresses the essence of his theory:

> Some say (the creator) brought forth Christ, his own Son, but only as psychic . . . This however was the one who passed through Mary . . . and upon him the Saviour formed from the *pleroma* of all (the *aeons*) descended at the baptism (of Jesus) . . . in him also was the spiritual seed of Achamoth.[42]

Valentinus took a docetic view of the nature of Jesus, saying that only someone who was blind would mistake the real Christ as if he were flesh and blood, yet only through the possession of *gnosis* could anyone grasp his purely spiritual nature. His physical form was but an illusion. The *Gospel of Truth* tells how his suffering and crucifixion made Jesus "a fruit of knowledge (*gnosis*) of the Father". Fruit, of course, represents productivity and here the product of the spiritual sacrifice is the gift of knowledge of the divine self within. As divinity resided in Christ so it comes to dwell within the believer, even though Jesus suffered as a human being he also bore within him the divine image and power that is his supreme gift to give. The divine Saviour did not suffer. The seed within that was generated by Sophia was taken from him at his trial before Pontius Pilate so that the divine did not suffer.

The psychic Jesus alone suffered. The divine spirit survived death. From then on he was able to effect salvation. But in order to do this the carnal or non-spiritual had to perish whereas the purely spiritual (the *pneumatic*) was incorporated within the *pleroma*. Christ united with the

Holy Spirit is the *archetype* of the Father and the vehicle of salvation.

The expression "*archetype* of the Father" relates to Valentinus' teaching about the Son and the Spirit who existed with the Father from eternity. Valentinus designated this eternity of being as Silence, as no words are adequate to convey its meaning. Confronted by awesome transcendence Silence alone is appropriate. Within this Silence is comprehended the fullness and harmony of the *pleroma*, and it is from that that the *archetypes* emanated; but this mystery is known only to those who receive the gift of mysterious *gnosis* and experience its power. Those so gifted are assured of salvation, they are truly "the children of God".

Valentinus construed his view of human life as a tripartite compound of body, soul and spirit. Out of the three the world came to be and this accounts also for the evil within it. The creator (*demiurge*) separated from the Father and entrusted to Sophia the process of redemption. The myth is a familiar feature of gnostic thought but takes on a more elaborate form in the system of Valentinus. According to him the All emanated from the Depth called Silence or the womb and then became the progenitor of Christ or Logos on whom depended the thirty *aeons* of the *pleroma*. Through the revelation of Christ, Christians experienced the All whilst the *aeons* formed a union of masculine and feminine, or creative or receptive principles, but when Sophia transgressed in her desire to know the Father or the Deep, a privilege reserved only for *nous*, this led to a separation from Christ. Through this separation there came into being an inferior wisdom, separate from Sophia, and excluded from the *pleroma*. The cause of this separation was a Limit called the cross, and the inferior wisdom received the name Achamoth. In the end Christ and Sophia are reunited as if in the celebration of a mystic marriage.[43] The process of reunion is activated by *gnosis*, which is revealed by Jesus and the spiritual beings who share its mystery and participate in it.

The dualism which is characteristic of gnostic doctrine is implicit in this Valentinian myth, but on some other aspects of the teaching of Valentinus the texts are unclear. He took a balanced and liberal view of the relationship between the sexes and portrayed the union of man and woman as forming a consummated whole.

The identity of maleness within the male is made explicit but it is fused with the identity within of a feminine element.[44] The intercourse enjoyed between male and female is something beautiful and spiritually beneficial. Linked with this is the marriage theme that is prominent in the teaching of Valentinus as in other gnostics. The *Gospel of Philip* speaks of the "mystery of marriage" and of the marriage rituals that culminated in the "sacrament of the bride chamber". It is notable that this is described as a sacrament, and symbolically as the flowing together of masculine and feminine energies in harmony:

> Human beings associate with human beings . . . Members of a species usually associate with those of the same species. Just so, spirit unites with spirit . . . and light merges with light. If you are born a human being it is human beings who will love you, if you become a spirit you will unite with their spirit.[45]

According to the *Gospel of Philip* no act is good or evil in itself; what determines its quality is the inner motive, the degree of self-consciousness with which the act is performed. The existence of pairs of opposites such as good and evil, right and wrong, light and darkness, life and death, implies that choice has to be made between them but at the same time good is good or evil is evil on account of the motivation of the action and not the choice made when performing it.[46] In matters of churchmanship Valentinus and his followers believed that they constituted the true church.

Valentinus rejected the ritual and liturgy of the Catholic Church, its rites and creeds, and only approved baptism when it was performed with a spiritual content. The true church is a community of the elect, the spiritually mature and those who were enlightened by the divine *gnosis*. Both the unity and the authority of the Church are spiritual and are not decided or determined by hierarchical structure or organization. The true church therefore is invisible for only those who have the insights of *gnosis* also have direct access to God, they have knowledge of divine truth through revelation and thus they know that they are destined for salvation.

On the basis of this doctrine some Valentinians in the east took the extreme decision of not recognizing those who did not receive the gift of *gnosis* as being of the Church. Valentinians in the west, however, were more liberal and tolerant as they made a distinction between those who were called by God and those who were chosen. This they believed to be consistent with the teaching of Jesus who had taught that many are called but few are chosen.[47] The "chosen" were those who had received the gift of *gnosis*, but this gift was given for a purpose, namely, that those who were enlightened should be a source of enlightenment to others. Thus they would contribute to creating a truly spiritually united church. Until this was accomplished the more liberal gnostics felt able to co-exist within the Church side by side with those who were not so gifted.

These were regarded as worshippers of the creator God; they were free to observe the rites of the Church even though they did not fully understand them. Their faith was not matched by mature understanding. The author of the gnostic work *The Interpretation of the Knowledge* demonstrates a spirit of tolerance to the unenlightened by addressing an appeal to both groups within the Church, especially to those who felt inadequate because they did not possess the spiritual insight of those endowed with *gnosis*. He wrote:

> Do not accuse your head (Christ) because it has not made you an eye, but a finger . . . but be thankful that you are not outside the body.

and to those who possessed the gift of *gnosis* he wrote:

> Share it without hesitation, Do not approach your brother with jealousy . . . You are ignorant when you [hate them] and are jealous of them.[48]

Undoubtedly Valentinus and the Valentinians had a profound impact on the Church of their time. Their doctrines were spread extensively around the Mediterranean and they brought fresh challenges to those Christians who sought for salvation through the doctrines and observances of the Catholic Church. The Church heresiologists disliked them for their teaching and their practices, so the gulf between orthodoxy and heresy widened as a wider spectrum of Christian beliefs became the subject of intense controversy and dissent.

Basilides, gnostic mythologist

Basilides is another learned second-century gnostic. He was a native of Alexandria and stands second only to Valentinus as a distinguished gnostic teacher. Irenaeus reports that he called himself a Christian, and we gather that he lived and worked as a Christian and had designs on becoming a Christian theologian. Few details of his life are available but he was active in Egypt and the influence of his teaching continued to be felt there until the fourth century. There is a view that he was a disciple of Menander of Antioch but of this we cannot be certain. The industry and intellectual ability of Basilides may be seen from his great work called *Exegetica* (*Interpretations of the Gospels*), written in twenty-four books.

Origen tells that he also composed a gospel but of this there is no trace. We are indebted to Clement of Alexandria for preserving some passages from the *Exegetica* that illumine the thought of Basilides. Some of this conforms to mainstream gnostic teaching. He taught the existence of the lesser God of the Old Testament who created the world. But he also postulated the existence of an unknown God of whom he said:

He not being God, who made a not being world out of nothing.

Within the chaos of the material world the spiritual remains imprisoned waiting to be released. Release was not effected until the appearance of the Father or *nous* in a human form. Knowledge of this rather than faith is the condition of release, but when the restoration is effected it is complete for then the soul is restored to the *pleroma*. The soul entered the body where it became entrapped at the initial chaos of creation. Whilst in this condition the soul suffers and shares in the sin of the world.

Basilides compounded a complex creation myth. Beginning from the figure of "the non-existent", God is then said to produce a threefold sonship which has in every respect the same nature. The sonship is separated into a super-celestial realm (an *Ogdoad* with its great ruler) and the realm where the ruler of this world presides (a *Hebdomad*), and above all the abode of God. Neither the *Ogdoad* or the *Hebdomad* has knowledge of the existence of the Supreme God. This knowledge is only transmitted through the descent of the superior sonship into the material world. His emanation, which proceeds from the unbegotten God, elaborated on the powers within the *pleroma* and defined them as five qualities – the mind of Christ (*nous*), word (*logos*), prudence (*phnesis*), wisdom (*Sophia*), power (*dynameis*). From the couple wisdom and power there originated the three hundred and sixty angelic powers, each of which created a heaven according to the model of the preceding. The purpose of this was twofold, designating the correspondence between the spheres, and the world year or *aeon* of three hundred and sixty-five days. It also symbolizes the great distance between the Supreme God and the creator. The creation of the world and human life is the work of the God of the Jews, who is leader of the lowest class of angels. In this context he is known as Abraxas. It is from him and his works that deliverance is required.

In order to effect this deliverance the Supreme God sent his Christ. As he descended through the *Ogdoad* and the *Hebdomad* he partook of portions from each, each portion having its role, and by following the superior sonship each of the sonships is restored to where it belongs, but at the same time each ruler and realm becomes oblivious to the others.[49]

Basilides also expounded a doctrine of the passion of Jesus. With his passion there began "the distinction of kinds" and just before his crucifixion he changed places with Simon of Cyrene.[50] Simon was crucified out of ignorance, his captors being oblivious to the fact that he had been transformed by Christ so that at the crucifixion he was thought to be Jesus. Jesus then took the form of Simon and observed the crucifixion as a spectator. He watched Simon suffer and die. The power of Jesus to transform Simon into Jesus was the power of the *nous* of the Father and by the same power Jesus was able to ascend again to the Father from whom he had emanated and so mock those who were unable to hold him captive. In fact it was they who were held in servitude to the *demiurge*, whereas Jesus enjoyed the absolute freedom of the divine *nous*. The purpose of his descent was to liberate those who were held in servitude by the *demiurge* and the material world.

It is him (the Christ who possessed the *nous*) whom they called Saviour and not the one who was crucified. When he suffered Jesus fell back into formlessness and that which afterwards rose in the resurrection was the psychic being whose origin is in the *Hebdomad*, and to this it now returned from whence it came. As he ascended Jesus carried all that belonged to the higher spheres and restored them to the *pleroma*. The emphasis on restoration or deliverance from the evil material world is a prime feature of the thought of Basilides. This deliverance is known through the power of *gnosis* but he also comes near to regarding faith as being in a special relationship with knowledge. Faith he conceived of as a state of being. He expounded knowledge as understanding (*noesis*), and this special state of understanding is reached not through reason or intellect, but through election to receive the superior *gnosis*. He explained the possession of this *gnosis* as a state of being which he described as "the eternal beauty of a sudden creation".[51]

It seems that Basilides maintained an association with the Church of Alexandria throughout his life. Even though he taught beliefs that ran counter to the orthodox he was not excommunicated. His teaching had many innovative ideas and he displayed a wide knowledge of gnostic mythology and writings. He is known for his distinctive doctrine of deliverance or salvation. Jesus descended when the time was ripe; he appeared as the prototype of spiritual being; he received the power of enlightenment at the Jordan where he was baptised; he received the gift of *nous* which enabled him to transmit knowledge to humans to make them aware of the Spirit within their innermost being; his power elevated persons to the light of the spiritual realm. This work of revelation Basilides conceived as a work of divine compassion, although Clement of Alexandria reported that:

> The hypothesis of Basilides says that the soul, having sinned before in another life, endures punishment in this.

Yet the message of Basilides is that it was to answer this punishment that the descent of Jesus from the All happened:

> After Jesus came into existence . . . everything took place as it is written in the gospels. These things happened so that Jesus might become the first fruits of the differentiation among confused beings.

Irenaeus, defender of the faith

Irenaeus, Bishop of Lyons (*c.*130–200), took an uncompromising stand against the gnostics and led the defence of the apostolic faith that had been entrusted to the Church as its custodian and exponent. His attack on gnosticism and his interpretation of the faith are a yardstick by which we are able to measure the degree of revulsion felt by orthodox churchmen to the gnostic heterodoxy. Irenaeus is the earliest theologian of note of the sub-apostolic age whose theology was rooted in tradition and apostolic doctrine. He was born in Asia Minor and reared in Smyrna, but moved to Lyons where he became a presbyter and later bishop. His principal work is *Against Heresies*, which is the main source for his theology as well as for his attack on gnosticism.[52]

Irenaeus was fully committed to the Catholic Church and its tradition of apostolic teaching. He expounded the bedrock of this teaching as the work of Christ as Saviour. He affirmed the doctrine of the Church on the Incarnation and the historical revelation of God in Jesus Christ. Christ was the new man or the second Adam. God alone is creator; he created the first man and blessed him with immortality. Through the transgression of Adam, sin entered the world and the hope of immortality was lost.

Therefore the original purpose of creation needed to be restored and this mission was entrusted by the creator to Christ. He was sent by God into the world as his only son in order to complete the work of salvation. He had existed with God from the beginning and appeared in the world as the divine Logos so that Irenaeus was able to state:

> I have shown that the Son of God did not then begin to exist, (i.e. at the birth of Jesus), being with the Father from the beginning.[53]

His incarnation was real, he was fully human, and its purpose was entirely redemptive. He bore the image and likeness of God that had been lost through Adam's transgression and that he now came to restore. Irenaeus presented an exalted view of Christ that he expressed in glowing terms. Christ became man so that man might become what

Christ was. He is the full and perfect revelation of God, his Word or Logos. He is the true teacher and head of the new humanity:

> When he became incarnate and was made man, he commenced afresh the living line of human beings, and furnished us, in a brief comprehensive manner, with salvation, so that what we lost in Adam – namely to be according to the image and likeness of God – that we might receive in Jesus Christ.[54]

Irenaeus also venerated the Virgin Mary and designated her as the great intercessor. There is a suggestion that she was a second Eve and the divine mother of humankind, who had an active role in the work of redemption through the birth of Jesus. Irenaeus found a basis for this idea in the Old Testament, which he accepted as the authoritative word of God, and quoted from the *Book of Isaiah* (7: 14) and the *Book of Daniel* (2: 34) to substantiate his belief. He also held tenaciously to the second coming of Jesus as being imminent and to the complete transformation of the world order at his appearance.

This divine truth, Irenaeus believed, God had entrusted to the Church. The Catholic Church was its guardian and it alone was given authority to expound its meaning and propagate its truth. Irenaeus introduced the term "Catholic" to affirm the Church's belief in one God and one God only. The one and only God had always been invisible until he revealed himself in Jesus Christ. In him he manifested his glory. It was in order to preserve and enact its faith that the Church developed its liturgy and ordinances. Its ritual was meant to undergird the faith of its members. Therefore to take part in the eucharist, as a rite that affirmed the union of the believer with Christ, was a requirement on the part of all who believed. Other observances also, such as rites of passage, at childbirth, anointing, marriage and burial of the dead, were kept as a means of solidarity with the faith of the Church.

Members of the Church were expected to observe and practise the ethical teaching of Jesus in their personal, and family and social life. Irenaeus also affirmed the power and authority of the bishop as the official leader of the Church, who was authorized and empowered to interpret the faith. The bishop also had the authority of ecclesiastical administration. This authority he believed had been directly transmitted from the first apostles through an apostolic succession, so that the Church is both catholic and apostolic.

We have observed earlier how the Church defended and spread its orthodoxy in a period when this was openly and persistently being challenged. The hostile reaction of Irenaeus to the doctrines of the gnostics may be said to be due to his desire to preserve the spiritual health and unity of the Church. Sound doctrine universally believed and practised, and with an authoritative ministry, was the surest bulwark against the acerbities of the gnostic alternative. The test of unity within the Church was orthodox doctrine, authoritative interpretation, obedience to a clerical hierarchy, observance of the sacraments and a Christian ethical lifestyle.[55]

The rigour of Irenaeus' attack on gnosticism has raised the question whether his protest was politically motivated as well. How far was he concerned to stabilize the role and authority of the bishop? Our concern, however, is with his attitude to gnosticism. He opposed all those groups who traced their origins to Simon Magus, but Irenaeus was particularly vehement in his attack on Valentinus and members of his school. We have to bear in mind that his view of gnosticism is highly prejudicial and one-sided. He did succeed in bringing the controversy into the public arena and was fearless in his condemnation as well as industrious in amassing evidence to support his charge against the heretics. Negatively he declared that there is nothing in the Gospels of Matthew, Mark, Luke or John that gives sanction to gnostic doctrine or ideology. Nor is there any justification for their claim to "speak wisdom among the perfect". He saw the gnostics as only bent on division, corruption and heresy. Only the innocent and immature sided with them, and only the dilettanti who wished to discover a god of their own followed them. According to Irenaeus the gnostics had turned their backs on truth, authority and proper behaviour. Gnosticism was an all-out attack on the Christian God and must be eliminated.

Hippolytus, refuter of heresy

Hippolytus was the intellectual disciple of Irenaeus and a Greek-speaking Christian who settled in Rome. He wrote an influential work called *Refutation of all Heresies*. A copy of the work was discovered in 1832 at Mount Athos and is important for its summary of heretical doctrines which Hippolytus rejected outright as blasphemous. The work is in two parts: the first part traces the origins of heresy to pre-Christian Greek philosophy, which he describes as erroneous, and the second part gives an account of thirty-three gnostic systems.

Hippolytus declared that the basis of gnostic doctrine was not Christian and therefore all who believed it were godless. He substantiated this claim by highlighting the false doctrines of Simon Magus, especially what he regarded as his false teaching of the Infinite Force as the original force or the principle of the universe.[56] It was he also who sought to ridicule Simon by telling how he boasted that he would rise after being buried in the earth.[57] A particular emphasis in his teaching is the unsound notion that God's love is unconditional and immeasurable.

There is no forgiveness after baptism and the belief in a loving attitude to sinners is frivolous. The austerity of his teaching marks him out from other Christian teachers of the third century. He was uncompromising in condemning sexual misdemeanour and adultery. For this there was no forgiveness. He believed that the apocalypse was imminent and that Christians should prepare themselves for the return of Christ. This belief had a strong influence on his moral teaching and the strictures he meted to those who did not follow its injunctions.

Hippolytus was a convinced devotee of the Catholic Church and he believed that he must work to preserve its sanctity. Its sanctity depended on the moral calibre of its members in all aspects of their lives. He deplored the sins of the flesh and especially any tolerance of and indulgence in promiscuous behaviour. As the bride of Christ the Church must be pure and spotless. Immoral behaviour threatened to split the Church. But on the attitude to forgiveness there was a division within the Church and Hippolytus was denounced as a schismatic. It seems paradoxical that he who had denounced heresy and immorality so vehemently was forced to separate himself from his fellow churchmen on the issue of forgiveness. He was banished by the Church to Sardinia but was not excommunicated. He was later reconciled to the Church and entered the roll of saints. Of this unusual development Walter Nigg has written:

> A heretic saint is a striking phenomenon, and once again demonstrates how closely the two paths impinge upon one another.[58]

Like his mentor Irenaeus, Hippolytus designated the Church as the sole bearer and guardian of the truth. It must be faithful to the teaching of the apostles and the authority of the bishop. He decried professed Christians who did not abide by the rule of faith and the authority of the Church. The true Church was a divine creation fashioned as a holy community of true spirituality. The rule and authority of the Church was beyond dispute or question and should be prescribed to absolutely by all believers. He harshly denounced those who formed systems of beliefs derived from the philosophies and mythologies of the past. This was the case with the gnostic group of Naassenes. He paraphrased the Naassenes' view of resurrection thus:

The dead shall start forth from the graves, that is, from the earthly bodies being born again spiritual not carnal . . . For this is the resurrection that takes place through the gate of heaven, through which, he says all those who do not enter remain dead. For he says, man becomes a god, when, having risen from the dead, he will enter into heaven through the gate of this time.[59]

Hippolytus was a powerful advocate of the Logos Christology. He also believed strongly in the virgin birth of Jesus, which he linked to the doctrine of the Logos. Jesus was fully human, and so Hippolytus asserted:

Let us believe then, dear brethren, according to the tradition of the apostles, that God, the Lord came down from heaven (and entered) into the holy virgin Mary, assuming also a human, by which I mean a rational soul and becoming then all that man is with the exception of sin, he might save fallen man and confer immortality on men who believe in his name.[60]

The foregoing account of salient features of the orthodox–gnostic encounter and the chief participants illustrates the issues that divided them and with which they wrestled to establish as truth. Neither party was able to isolate itself from the attack of the other; both groups claimed to explicate truth. Gnostics spoke of themselves as people who were despised, pursued and persecuted, whereas the orthodox feared they were being lured away from the truth. The orthodox insisted on the single rule of faith entrusted to the Church to preserve and interpret and so strengthened the institutional appeal of the Church. There was hardly any aspect of the visible or invisible Church that was not invoked and debated, but the strength of the heresiologists was such that the view that there is no salvation outside the Church eventually prevailed.

The Gospel (good news) is according to knowledge (*gnosis*) of the supramundane things in which the great (world) order (*archon*) did not understand.

Basilides, in Grant, Gnosticism: An Anthology

It is you who make sin when you do the things that are like the nature of adultery, which is called sin.

The Gospel of Mary

He who has knowledge of the truth is a free man . . .
Knowledge makes them capable of being free . . .
In fact he who is really free through knowledge is a slave because of love . . .

The Gospel of Philip

Whilst we are in this world it is fitting for us to acquire the resurrection, so that when we strip off the flesh we may be found in rest.

The Gospel of Philip

6

Gospel and the Gnostic Gospels

The foundation documents of Christianity are the four gospels of the New Testament. They were completed and in circulation before the end of the first century. A number of apocryphal gospels were also in being that had a special appeal for church theologians. Along with these the gnostic gospels added their witness to the mounting written documents about the life and mission of Jesus of Nazareth. These are the gospels of the Nag Hammadi Library, three of which have familiar New Testament names – Mary, Philip and Thomas; one has the subject of the gospel as its title; and one names the people to whom it is addressed.

Christians did not invent the word "gospel" but rather they used it as a catchword for works which they composed for a special salvific purpose. It stands for the message and not the book. It translates the Greek word *euangelion*, which means basically "a good announcement" or "good news" or "glad tidings". The term conveys the intention or purpose of compiling a work about Jesus of Nazareth. It was not a biography or chronicle of his life but a presentation or interpretation of its meaning and significance. As such it is a proclamation of what this unique life achieved, conveyed within the framework of a specific historical context and geographical setting. The written gospel pioneered a new kind of literary genre, an account of a life lived in time and space but imbued with an eternal redemptive purpose. The *Gospel of John* summarizes the purpose:

> These things are written that you may believe that Jesus is the Christ, the Son of God, and that believing you may have life in his name.[1]

The opening words of the gnostic *Gospel of Thomas* expresses its purpose in a similar vein in its opening words:

Whoever finds the interpretation of these sayings will not experience death.[2]

Interpreting the gospel

The multiple purpose of composing a gospel about Jesus – theological and apologetic, evangelistic and pedagogic, liturgical and exegetical, to a greater or lesser degree – applies to all the extant gospels of the first Christian centuries, including the gnostic gospels. Their writers' fascination with the work of Jesus as redeemer led them along a number of alternative exploratory and interpretative routes as they aimed to present an appealing version of his mission and achievements. The authors of the gnostic gospels believed they were equipped with superior knowledge and special insights for this task. They also knew the "gospel" needed to be expounded and interpreted in a variety of ways and for a variety of purposes. The meaning of "the good news" had to be extracted from the information about his activities and then made intelligible and explained in meaningful and unambiguous terms. The different possible renderings of its meaning being expounded in many places clearly demonstrated the need for reliable and authentic interpretation if confusion and uncertainty were to be overcome. Those who received the gift of *gnosis* were specially gifted to achieve this and they engaged confidently in the interpretative process.[3]

Even so, the gnostics did not succeed in lowering the temperature of the theological controversies that surrounded discussion and interpretation of the life and achievements of Jesus. These became a feature of the Christian theological landscape of the second and third centuries. As yet, there were no universally approved canons or rules of interpretation, or agreement, about who was best equipped to perform the task.

The gnostic authors were only marginally concerned with the historical details of the life of Jesus; rather they were intent on interpreting his advent into the world as a "revelatory moment", the climactic moment that inaugurated the completion of the redemptive initiative and purpose that God had conceived from the beginning. They interpreted this "revelatory-redemptive" activity as "gospel" or "good news". They assumed a variety of approaches in promoting understanding and elucidating the reason for this pivotal revelation. For this purpose they engaged a variety of literary skills, symbols, images, myths and analogies, as they aimed to outclass the laconic interpretations of those who focused attention mainly on the minutiae of a historical life and external events. The gnostics produced a "spiritual" interpretation which they believed to be the product of incisive *gnosis*.[4]

The methods the gnostics employed varied and there is no obvious correlation between them. The broad spectrum of interpretation aimed to penetrate and come to grips with the infinite depth of meaning of their subject with its main focus on redemption. *Gnosis* made them free to plumb the depths without the sanction of bishop or hierarchical ecclesiastical control. There is progression and development discernible in the gnostic interpretation from the earliest to the latest of the gospels, which can be accounted for by the continuing presence of the Spirit they believed inspired their interpretation and made it adaptable as circumstances required. They broke away from much conservative tradition that characterized so much contemporary theology, with its intention of crystallizing a uniform consensus of interpretation, as alien to the structure of the gnostic mind.

Part of their methodology was selecting well-known biblical narratives and characters or incidents from the life of Jesus, such as his baptism or passion, and either expanding or developing these in their interpretation or, when required, transforming the biblical motif. The interpretation aimed to go deeper than the surface meaning of the text and there are instances when the interpretation can be taken in more than one way.[5] A gnostic reconstruction of a biblical narrative, for instance, if analysed carefully, may be understood from more than one point of view. It is possible to draw different conclusions, for example, from the interpretation of the myth of Adam and Eve or the explanation given of the reception of Christ at Jesus' baptism and his departure from Jesus before his crucifixion. There are discrepancies also between the five gnostic gospels, but at the same time many of the interpretations of the "gospel" are original and subtle, and cannot be matched elsewhere.[6]

The Catholic Church's own theologians were intent on stabilizing a common pattern of interpretation which they believed to have been handed down from the days of the apostles, although in the event this does not mean that the interpretations of the Church theologians are consistent in all respects. Assuming that the apostolic faith was unchanging and eternally relevant they sought to establish static canons of interpretation that would provide the Church with a changeless and authoritative norm. They looked upon the gospel as a seamless and inerrant whole and they aimed to make all interpretation of it likewise.

To study the content of gnostic interpretations against those of the orthodox is a complex undertaking but there are occasions when the former sheds light on the meaning of the canonical text. Does this mean that the gnostic expositors influenced the canonical gospels in any way? The evidence is ambiguous but it has been suggested that the gnostic gospels might be placed on a par with the canonical gospels.[7] The *Gospel of Truth*, for instance, has been termed a fifth gospel. But the gnostic gospels were never given authoritative status by the Church. There was much in the canonical gospels that the gnostics found puzzling but they believed their superior understanding and elucidation of truth was illuminating through the exercise of enlightened *gnosis* that they alone possessed. It extended to every part of their exposition so they conceived of the "good news" as an integrated whole. This *gnosis* was the source and justification of their claim to (spiritual) authority for their interpretation. The sayings (*logia*) of Jesus and other information about him circulated orally initially without having the imprimatur of the Church and so the idea of scriptural authority was fluid, but the gnostics held firmly to the insights of divine *gnosis* as the ground of their authoritative versions of scripture.[8]

With such a degree of fluidity there was bound to be a degree of discrepancy and uncertainty about the exact meaning of every part of the Christian gospels. We cannot tell from this distance what precisely was in the gnostic authors' minds as they compiled their gospels so it is a case of weighing one piece of evidence against another and evaluating the result. We cannot be absolutely certain of the meaning the writer intended to give to a myth or parable. But not to know the author's intention does not mean that we cannot make deductions or inferences on the basis of reliable canons of objective judgement. We can deduce from the text the action of *gnosis* on the mind of the author and how this influenced his exposition. To read the story of the creation literally, for instance, may make little or no sense, but to read it as a spiritual allegory points to a hidden deeper meaning directed by *gnosis* to the redemptive motif of the gnostic exposition.[9] On the level of ordinary consciousness there is mental and cognitive understanding of the myth but there is also the potential of further penetration of meaning. This deeper penetration discerns in the myth of Adam and Eve the kernel of salvific truth that comes to fruition in the action of the Christian gospel. Just as Adam and Eve were given the gift of moral freedom by the Spirit after Adam's transgression and restoration, so some gnostics saw in this a message or prototype of the teaching of Jesus, who conferred on believers the gift of freedom from the consequences of disobedience, passion and lust. This gift explains how Adam and Eve found release from the otherwise irredeemable consequences and anguish of the Fall.

Henceforth the history of humanity developed as the progressive search for freedom from evil, until it is eventually shown the way to complete liberation through the means of reconciliation that was the purpose of God from the beginning and was now made luminous through the revelation of the "good news" (gospel). Naturally the interpreters used the means available to them in their expositions and they often perceived the gospel in a radical new way. The gnostic Basilides said:

> The Gospel (good news) is according to knowedge (*gnosis*) of the supramundane things in which the great (world) order (*archon*) did not understand.[10]

Being directed by this *gnosis* the gnostics used their skills accordingly, although it is difficult to produce from this a schematic methodology. The vagueness that is met with in places is offset by their obvious ingenuity and industry and their individualistic interpretations. They not only made use of biblical characters and incidents in the process but also drew upon other writings then in circulation. They took these seriously, and it has been said of them that:

> although they were not particularly interested in the idea of a fixed canon they eventually treated these texts as having some authority in debate and practice.[11]

The *Gospel of Mary*[12]

This gospel is so named on account of the special revelation given to Mary, who occupies a central place in it. Unfortunately only fragments are available to us and these date from the second century. The setting of the gospel is the secret conversation with the Saviour Christ after his resurrection and before his departure. His final command before his departure is recorded:

> Go, therefore and preach the gospel of the kingdom.

But this caused dismay amongst the disciples who felt that to act on his commission would put their lives in jeopardy, so they asked apprehensively:

> if they did not spare him, how will they spare us?

It fell to Mary to revive their drooping spirits by focusing their attention on his uniqueness and the purpose he had in store for them:

> Let us rather praise his greatness, for he prepared us and made us into men.

These words of encouragement are also a commitment to the continuation of the mission Jesus had in view for them.

One prime topic of the intimate conversations of this gospel is the nature and province of sin. Peter posed the question, "What is the sin of the world?" It may be conjectured whether or not the reputation of Mary may have prompted the question for the answer he received refers to adultery:

> it is you who make sin when you do the things that are like the nature of adultery, which is called sin.

Sin is the failure to practise the moral law and is bound up with the evil of the material world and so has a cosmic dimension. The Saviour was sent into the world so that he could deal with sin in a positive way. The negative consequence of sin is that it is destructive of the relationship with God and this relationship needed to be restored "to its root". This the Saviour accomplished, first by exposing the nature of sin and then by producing a genuine reconciliation with God. The consequence of this action is a source of confidence and reassurance:

> Be of good courage, and if you are discouraged [be] encouraged in the different forms of nature. He who has ears to hear let him hear.

Before his final departure Jesus gave his disciples his blessing of peace and enjoined them to follow the Son of Man (a title Jesus used of himself) who dwelt within them and would continue to do so. This did not relieve the disciples' dismay and it fell to Mary to comfort them. It is in this context that the author reports how Mary made known her transformative vision of Jesus and his comforting words to her.

First she told how she had seen Jesus in a vision. Spiritual vision is the vehicle of divine revelation or instruction. It produces a direct encounter with the divine, introduces a personal visitation from the world beyond and an immediate experience of divine intervention. Such visionary experience created a sense of the numinous presence and a feeling of awesomeness in the presence of divine omnipotence. Mary, however, was commended by Jesus for not being overwhelmed by fear as might be expected when she confronted the resurrected presence in this immediate way. Secondly, he reassured her that he had seen her and served her as a garment even though she did not know him. This was in response to Mary's rebuke that she had not seen him descend, whilst the figure of a garment denotes the protection he provided for her. Thirdly, there is her vision of the soul of Jesus ascended, having fought the seven forms or powers of wrath and whatever else had bound him hitherto.

He had overcome all that held him in servitude and was released "to attain to the rest of the time, of the season, of the *aeon*, in silence". Fourthly, Mary became silent as though in a state of serene tranquillity as she contemplated the implications of the vision. It was the disciple Andrew who broke in on the silence to dispute with Mary that the Saviour had taught these strange things.

Peter concurred with Andrew but went further and raised the contentious matter of whether Jesus did in fact speak with a woman without their knowledge. We can only note here that the intervention of Peter concerns an issue of importance and contention, as the Church had not yet determined the role of women or whether male hierarchy or dominaton was to be a permanent feature.

The reaction of Andrew and Peter and the scepticism expressed grieved Mary and it was Levi who came to her defence with a rebuke for the other disciples and a vindication of Mary:

Surely the Saviour knows her very well. That is why he loved her more than us.

Behind this emphatic reference to the Saviour's knowledge we may see an oblique reference to the character of Mary referred to earlier, but it seems unlikely that we should assume an erotic relationship from the words "he loved her more than us".

The *Gospel of Mary* is a useful reference point also for considering the gnostic presentation of the resurrection. The disciples' sense of dejection after the crucifixion is made very plain, as is also Mary's encouragement on the strength of his words of promise to her:

Do not weep, and do not grieve, and do not doubt, for his grace will be with you completely, and will protect you.

Mary's direct questions to Peter when he and Andrew disbelieved her testimony, and how she confronted them through her tears, are a moving part of the gospel:

My brother Peter, what do you think? Do you think that I thought this up myself in my heart? Do you think that I am lying about the Saviour?

In the end Mary is vindicated in the eyes of the disciples and she joins them as they go out to fulfil Christ's command to preach. In so doing Mary makes claim to the continuing presence of the spiritual Christ. This presence overcomes the seven powers or participants of wrath referred to above – darkness, desire, ignorance, death, flesh, wisdom and wrath. Jesus has manifested himself as the "conqueror of space" and he is free from ignorance and the restrictions of all temporal existence:

> From this time I will reach rest in the time of the moment of the Aeon silence.

The *Gospel of Mary* stands apart from the others on account of it being addressed to a woman who is also the recipient of divine revelation. She is the Mary Magdalene of the canonical gospels but here her relationship with Jesus is more intimate and warmer. Apart from this, some of the prime themes of gnosticism are included, especially redemption through the descent of the Saviour and reconciliation. The Christian commitment of the author is unquestioned but there is an element of antipathy to Peter and his dominance. Does this reflect a struggle between the sexes for equality? Or is it a tilt at the establishment of a male hierarchy of ministry that was being developed at this time? Mary is shown to be the recipient of supernatural visions and the first to have a vision of Jesus after the resurrection, not to soul or spirit but to mind. She is also commended and portrayed as exercising a leadership role in the Christian community as someone who is equipped to reassure the hesitant disciples through the display of superior knowledge. She is commended for her steadfastness and also portrayed as someone gifted to interpret the sayings of Jesus.

The *Gospel of Philip*[13]

This gospel is the most explicitly gnostic of the Nag Hammadi library. It has clear affinities with the school of Valentinians and encompasses the major themes that engaged the gnostics during the latter half of the third century. The work does not read as a continuous whole and it is difficult to reconstruct the plan the author may have had in mind. Many passages are obscure but there are indications that its author may have been influenced by the *Gospel of Thomas* as well as by the apocryphal gospels. Some passages in the gospel can only be understood in the light of Irenaeus' comments, which are mostly prejudicial. A host of miscellaneous sayings are included and some of the assumed acts of Jesus (not recorded in the canonical gospels) are given a mystical interpretation. There are allusions to a number of sacraments but these are not fully developed. There is stress on the possession of *gnosis* as the valid and certain condition of salvation:

> He who has knowledge of the truth is a free man . . .

Knowledge makes them capable of being free . . .
In fact he who is really free through knowledge is a slave because of
love . . .

Revelation is a prime topic of this gospel. Its subject is Jesus, who is
said to have revealed himself in a number of ways but not in a purely
physical form. The purpose of his revelation is made explicit:

Christ came to ransom some, to save others, to redeem others.
He ransomed those who were strangers and made them his son.

This is the culmination of the mission of Jesus. The term "ransom"
(*lutron*) used theologically means the delivering up of a life as a vicarious sacrifice for others. It was used of the pledge paid to release a slave
from slavery, and in the context of the gospel it is the price paid on behalf
of those who were strangers to bring them to freedom. In order to
achieve this, Christ voluntarily laid down his soul:

It was only when he appeared that he voluntarily laid down his life from
the very day the world came into being.

Christ performed this work as "the perfect man", and as "the perfect
man" he brought bread from heaven to nourish the spiritual and to fulfil
a ministry of reconciliation:

Before Christ came from a place they were no longer able to enter, and
they went where they were no longer able to come out. Then Christ came.
Those also who went he brought out, and those who went out he brought
in.

The work of reconciliation conforms to the main thrust of gnostic teaching. The spiritual provision which Christ made and his work of
reconciliation centre on the heavenly Christ who entered him at his baptism, which gnosticism viewed as the source of Christian redemption.

Reconciliation was necessary as a consequence of the Fall in primal
times. Christ was destined to reconcile strangers who were victims of
the Fall ever since the world existed. When he appeared within the world
he laid down his soul as a pledge in order to reconcile those he wished,
both the good and the evil. The consequences of reconciliation are
implicit in many of the sayings of the gospel, especially the freedom it
offers through knowledge ("knowledge is freedom"), the truth it reveals
that is recognized and praised inasmuch "as it is stronger than ignorance
and error", and the union it consummates, as found within are "the
fruits of truth". Those who unite with it will attain fulfilment.

We cannot isolate this view of reconciliation from the doctrine of human life in this gospel. It tells that the world came into being through a transgression but the human being is superior to all else that is created. This superiority is not obvious to the naked eye but it extends to the animal kingdom, with which humans have a kinship even though they have dominion over the animals. Humans also possess the gift of creation given by God so that "he who begets also has the power to create". We note the distinction between the power to "beget" and to "create", for "he who creates works openly . . . he who begets in private". The latter is the role or function of marriage and "it is not fleshly but pure . . . It belongs not to desire but to will." In this connection it is notable how the gospel regards everything that exists as "being in the flesh" and that human beings can be subject to resurrection whilst they are still alive in this world:

> Whilst we are in this world it is fitting for us to acquire the resurrection, so that when we strip off the flesh we may be found in rest.

The meaning of this resurrection is amplified with the statement: that those who say they will die first and then rise are in error. If they do not first receive the resurrection while they live, "when they die they will receive nothing". Such teaching appealed widely as the attraction of experiencing resurrection in the present life postured the possibility of union with Christ now, which therefore issued in the ensuing benefits of reconciliation already referred to. The possibility of present experience of resurrection also held out the hope of transformation, "For this person is no longer a Christian but a Christ." This saying introduces a unique feature of the *Gospel of Philip*, namely, the significance of names.[14]

The gospel states that as truth is revealed it also "brought names into existence in the world because it is not possible to teach it without names". The names Jesus and Christ are specially significant on account of the functions each signifies. The name "speaks" or expresses a special function or performance:

> "Jesus" is a hidden name, "Christ" is a revealed name. For this reason Jesus is not particular to any language, rather he is always called by the name "Jesus". While as for Christ in Syriac it is "Messiah", in Greek it is Christ. Certainly all the others have it according to their own language. The Nazarene reveals what is hidden. Christ has everything in himself, whether man or angel or mystery, and the father.

The name Jesus has no particular religious meaning and none is given by the gnostic author of this gospel. As for Christ (Christos), it means "the anointed" and is a technical term for God's appointed agent or emissary sent to perform messianic functions. In this context Christ is declared as all-sufficient who is endowed with all that he needs and has "everything in himself". As Christ he is the mediator of a new relationship between God and people. In this respect he acts with complete authority and fulfils his role to perfection. In addition to these names the gospel also explicates its notion of the names "father", "son" and "holy spirit". The first two are single names but the third is a double name. With regard to this double name the gospel declares:

> For they are everywhere: they are above, they are below, they are in the concealed, they are in the revealed. The Holy Spirit is in the revealed: it is below: it is in the concealed: it is above.

When the believer receives the name Christian this is a gift, and he "who received the gift does not have to give it back . . . This is the way it happens to one when he experiences a mystery."

Here the gospel draws a distinction between a true and a false Christian. The mystery is within the gift as the essence of knowledge and this has to be known otherwise names can be

> very deceptive, for they divert our thoughts from what is accurate to what is inaccurate. Thus one who hears the word "God" does not perceive what is accurate, but perceives what is inaccurate. So with the Father and the Son and the Holy Spirit and life and light and resurrection, but they perceive what is inaccurate.

Perception of the mystery within the name or the inner meaning it enshrines alone makes it meaningful or "accurate". Turning next to the gospel's doctrine of sacraments a number are mentioned with comments but these are often brief and tantalizing. Baptism is presented as a rite of initiation but the author couples with this a cautionary word of warning to whoever passes through the waters without experiencing transformation. This makes the use of the name "inaccurate"; the person concerned would use the name Christian only in a "borrowed" sense. Baptism that brings about transformation is in the Holy Spirit, which means the baptized receives the name Christian as a reward. This name is afterwards borne forever, for,

> He who has received the gift does not have to give it back . . . This is the way it happens to one when he experiences a mystery.

In amplification of the experience of mystery the gospel tells that those who pass through the waters of baptism do not go down to death but into the Holy Spirit. The Spirit is the agent of transformation, and regeneration takes place through baptism. This gives the baptized renewed access to God and initiation into the divine mysteries. The regeneration brings about a cleansing of the character, which is here described under the image of "the breath of summer".

Baptism is linked with redemption and therefore, as the sacrament of union, it is compared to the ritual of the bridal chamber. Through the perfection of this union the initiated receives the spirit of immortality. This experience of baptism in the Holy Spirit as release into the union of the bridal chamber leads to a comparison of baptism with resurrection:

> Baptism includes the resurrection (and the redemption); the redemption takes place in the bridal chamber.

The spiritual understanding of resurrection in this gospel, referred to earlier, is now compared to awakening from the sleep of death before the final resurrection after death. Spiritual resurrection brings the experience of release when the limitations of the flesh are discarded and the baptized finds a place of rest.

On the eucharist the gospel makes the bold statement "the eucharist is Jesus". The eucharist is a celebratory rite of the passion of Jesus and the statement indicates how it was in the heart and mind of Jesus that the eucharist should be celebrated. On the one hand the saying implicitly relegates the rite into one of mystical union with Jesus through his passion, whilst on the other hand it affirms the real (spiritual) presence of Jesus in the eucharist. The foregoing is an account of the leading ideas of the *Gospel of Philip*. Mary Magdalene figures in it as a symbol of divine wisdom and also as a companion of Jesus. There is an undercurrent of rivalry between her and the male disciples as she makes her appearance obtrusive and receives prominence. The author uses a variety of literary styles – including metaphor, parable, analogy, typology and dialogue – in presenting his gospel. No one who wishes to gain acquaintance with gnostic thought as it developed in the early centuries of the Church can ignore this gospel. Its emphasis on spirituality and the Spirit as both mother and virgin gives insight into the heart of gnosticism from a committed gnostic viewpoint.

The *Gospel of Thomas*[15]

The *Gospel of Thomas* has been acclaimed as the jewel amongst the gnostic texts and the most influential. It consists of one hundred and fourteen sayings, many of which are similar or parallel to the sayings of Jesus known from the New Testament gospels. They were written in Greek and translated into Coptic and one of the Greek fragments is said to come from the first century. The sayings may broadly be divided into four literary groupings: proverbs, parables, prophecies and instructions. The author is given as Thomas the twin, who is named in the *Gospel of John* (14: 5) but was known in the Syrian Church as the brother of Jesus. It is likely that the gospel originated in Syria. As well as sayings paralleled with the canonical gospels some are apocryphal and these contribute primary sources for the study of the tradition underlying the known sayings (*logia*) of Jesus. The opening statement specifies the content and purpose of the gospel:

> These are the secret sayings which the living Thomas spoke and which Didymus Judas Thomas wrote down. And he said, Whoever finds the interpretation of these sayings will not experience death.

The gospel provides a rudimentary gnostic theology through recording words supposedly attributed to Jesus. Knowledge of self that leads on to being known by God is a basic condition of redemption in the gnostic system. On this the *Gospel of Thomas* is explicit:

> When you come to know yourselves, then you will become known.

It assumes the capacity to know the self as being equal to being known by God. In psychological terms it shows how self-knowledge coalesces with divine knowledge. Without this knowledge a person is described as being "completely deficient". The import of this knowledge of oneself is that it carries the potential for good or evil:

> Jesus said, Grapes are not harvested from thorns, nor are figs gathered from thistles, for they do not produce fruit. A good man brings forth good from his storehouse; an evil man brings forth evil things from his evil storehouse, which is in his heart, and says evil things.

An illuminating part of this gospel is the valuable information it sheds on the gnostic approach to the Kingdom of God and the person of Jesus:

> Jesus said to his disciples, "Compare me to someone and tell me whom I am like". Simon Peter said to him, "You are like a righteous angel".

> Matthew said to him, "You are like a wise philosopher". Thomas said to him, "My mouth is wholly incapable of saying whom you are like".

This echoes the conversation between Jesus and his disciples at Caesarea Philippi in the *Gospel of Mark* (chapter 8) although here in an extended (gnostic) form. In Mark, Peter alone is the spokesman and his confession is messianic in style. Here, however, the imagery is that of the intermediaries between God and the world. Elsewhere the gnostic writings tell how God created the angels, and Peter confesses belief in Jesus as righteous, that is, as right with God or fit for the purpose for which he was the intermediary. He was divinely created and sent for a redemptive purpose. The extended account of the conversation includes Matthew's confession of belief in Jesus as philosopher, that is, the arbiter of true knowledge or the fount of revealed wisdom. The conception of him as a philosopher is real enough to identify him with wisdom (*Sophia*), the divine power that pervaded his life. The awesome silence of Thomas gives insight into the reverence the Christian gnostics displayed towards the agent of Christian redemption.

The *Gospel of Thomas* is forthright in its estimate of the kingdom of God as a state of being, rather than a place or location:

> Jesus said, "If those who lead you say to you see the kingdom is in the sky, then the birds of the sky will precede you. If they say to you it is in the sea, then the fish will precede you. Rather the kingdom is inside you, and it is outside you".

We may compare this saying with that of the *Gospel of Luke* (17: 21). There also the Kingdom of God is within and entry to the kingdom is by performing the will of the Father. In the gnostic gospel it is stated that those who so act are Jesus' brothers and mother and it is they who will enter "the Kingdom of my Father". Attention is given to the time of the coming of the kingdom. The disciples put the question to Jesus unambiguously and they received an equally unambiguous reply but not what they expected. Jesus said:

> It will not come by waiting for it. It will not be a matter of saying "here it is" or "there it is".

The time of the coming of the kingdom agitated many in the early church who made it a live issue. Jesus had spoken about the coming of the kingdom but when would it appear?

The imminent advent of the kingdom was a live option among many Christians. It is not unexpected then that the disciples should have questioned Jesus about the time of its coming. But contrary to some expectation Jesus declared that the coming of the kingdom was not an event to be located in time or place but was a matter of inner transformation which was the perfection of spiritual discipline and spiritual development. So the gospel employs a number of familiar images found also in the canonical gospels in explanation of his teaching. The "kingdom of heaven is like a man who has sown good seed" or "the kingdom of heaven is like a merchant who discovered a great pearl and bought the pearl alone for himself". This purchase is a spur to him to "seek the unfailing and enduring treasure where no moth comes near to devour and no acorn destroys". These and many other metaphors of the kingdom have a parallel in the canonical gospels; for instance, the woman with a jar full of meal, and the mustard seed that grows into a great plant. Quite clearly the author of the gnostic gospel drew upon the same tradition of the *logia* (sayings) of Jesus as the authors of the canonical gospels, but to go beyond this in order to establish the relationship of the one to the other requires fuller investigation.

A third aspect of the treatment of the kingdom in the gnostic gospel is its eschatological nature. This is determined by the gnostic view of the end events or the *eschaton*. It will not produce a transformation of the natural world nor will it be the climax of a period of passive expectation. On the contrary it will not come without the active effort of those who receive it within themselves:

> Shall we, then, as children enter the kingdom? Jesus said to them, When you make the two one, and when you make the inside like the outside and the outside like the inside, and the above like the below, and when you make the male and the female one and the same, so that the male be not male nor the female female, and when you fashion eyes in place of an eye, and a hand in place of a hand, and a foot in place of a foot, and a likeness in place of a likeness then you will enter the kingdom.

It is logical therefore for the gospel to follow this with a substantial list of observances that meet this requirement, such as fasting, prayer, alms-giving, love, the renunciation of wealth, and the abandonment of worldliness. These are among the instructions we noted as a feature of this gospel. But they are also integral to gnostic beliefs in the efficacy of spiritual practices, in this instance the power of entry into the kingdom. There is no hint that Jesus forced the issue of the instructions but rather he assumed an acquiescence in concentrated effort in devotion to knowledge and insight on the part of the "solitary" (i.e. the chosen who find the kingdom), who recognize, as the gospel says, "what is in your sight" and then "will find repose for yourselves". It has been claimed that gnostic texts such as the *Gospel of Thomas* project a relatively reliable view of a gnostic community. This serves as a kind of antidote to the one-sided view presented of such a community in the writings of the Church Fathers. On this Kurt Rudolph has said:

> Texts like the *Gospel of Thomas*, which accepts the ethical claims of the Sermon on the Mount and Jesus' parables on the Kingdom of Heaven (indeed making them more demanding in places) and at the same time appeals to the apocalyptic understanding of the initiated to whom the exegesis of the sayings of Jesus is to be imparted, show that the authors of the literature wished to address themselves to all gnostics.[16]

As we observed earlier, a number of the sayings of Jesus have a parallel in the canonical gospels (Jonas reckons there are about twenty such sayings) and we get a flavour of this from the following example. In the *Gospel of Matthew* 23: 13 we read:

> Alas for you lawyers and Pharisees, hypocrites that you are! You shut the door of the kingdom of heaven in men's faces; you do not enter yourselves, and when others are entering you stop them.

The gnostic parallel reads:

> Woe to the Pharisees, for they are like a dog sleeping in the manger of oxen, for neither does he eat or let the oxen eat.[17]

The meaning of the gnostic version is that the Pharisees make no use of what is before them. They are ignorant of what the scripture means, for they are compared to a dog asleep in the manger of oxen. They prevent those who genuinely seek for spiritual nourishment to be fed and so their hunger remains. They are devoid of understanding of truth or the Scriptures, and they confound and hinder those who seek for truth. In both the gnostic and the canonical version of this saying the message is the same, the Pharisees by their action are a barrier to those who would enter the Kingdom of Heaven.

The *Gospel of Thomas* also records a number of the sayings of Jesus in an expanded form, that is, the author has given a gnostic slant on the sayings. These are sayings which depict Jesus as a teacher answering questions or revealing spiritual truths or providing guidance. A number of the sayings are to be treated symbolically, especially those that refer to Mary. She must become male "in order to become a living spirit resembling you males. For every woman who will make herself male will enter the Kingdom of Heaven." What is female (being human) must be transformed into what is divine. We observe how in this context the divine spirit is male. A special characteristic is that women are included among the disciples of Jesus; Salome and Mary are so named, but only after they transcend their human nature and become male, that is, partake of the divine spirit. The gospel contrasts the natural parents of Jesus with the divine Father who is also the Father of Truth, and with the divine Mother the Holy Spirit.

There is a dearth of narrative material in this gospel such as would give a setting or location to the sayings of Jesus. It would seem that the author is single-minded in his purpose of highlighting the sayings of Jesus. In this respect the gospel has provided a series of sayings meant primarily to nurture the inner experience essential for entry to the Kingdom of God. In fact there are many sayings in this collection that dwell on the presence of Jesus as all-pervasive, but the essence of his presence is always within. Consequently, when the individual comes to know this the individual has knowledge of the self and resides in a state of spiritual enlightenment which is tantamount to being one with God. Such a person is immersed in the essence of all that is and therefore "will not experience death".

The *Gospel of Truth*[18]

This gospel has sometimes been attributed to Valentinus, but whether or not this is the case the gospel certainly has affinities with the Valentinian school of gnostic thought. It has a poetic quality and a deep religious sensitivity with a spiritual and evocative appeal. Gilles Quispel has said it is the most important and beautiful document in the Jung Codex.[19] The text was recovered from the Nag Hammadi library but a work bearing the same title was known from the writings of Irenaeus, but little is said there about its contents. The Nag Hammadi text is to be dated around 140–80. The opening statement of the gospel affirms the gift of knowing the Father that is mediated through the power of the Word, who co-exists with his mind and thought. The purpose of the mediation is redemptive. Ignorance of this is compared to a thickening fog which produces a state of error, oblivion and terror.

The main content of the gospel is an exposition of the person and mission of Jesus. Little is said about his activities but there are many insights into the significance of his mission. This is not always as lucid as we might wish and in parts it is elusive. It has been said that in parts we discern:

the elusive character of the discourse, which contains allusions to familiar elements of early Christian tradition, sometimes in unusual associations, with less familiar writings.[20]

This elusiveness makes it difficult in places to grasp the author's purpose and the fact that some concepts or elements are interfused, especially in the case of cosmic, historical and personal factors, makes interpretation hazardous. The gospel may be divided into three main sections: the impact of the Word, the consequences of revelation, and the work of regeneration. The gospel designates Jesus as the Son and identifies him with the Word. He is the first-born Son who has emanated from God and is identified with the Word or with the Name, which has the same significance:

> Now the name of the Father is the Son. It is he who first gave a name to the one (the Son) who came forth from him . . . this is the Name, this is the Son. It is possible for him (the Son) to be seen (in human form). The Name, however, is invisible, because it alone is the mystery of the invisible . . . For indeed the Father's name is not spoken, but is apparent (manifested through a Son).

Jesus is equated with the Word, who is "inscribed in the Book of the living". Those who had experience of the mysterious *gnosis* also carried the Living Book within their hearts. They were the chosen ones who manifested within themselves their personal experience of this mystical Book, as the gospel explains:

> there came the little children also, those to whom belongs the knowledge (*gnosis*) of the Father. They found knowledge (*gnosis*) and were known . . . In their hearts was manifested the Living Book of the Living (the Word) . . . that Book that is written in the Thought and Mind of the Father.

Whilst referring to the gospel's definition of the Book of the Living we note also how it states the Father's prerogative to choose the names of those he wishes to be enrolled in this book. It is those who have superior knowledge that comes to them from above and who do the will of him who chose them. They are the ones with knowledge of their origin and of their destiny. This special knowledge is revealed to the *aeons* for the sake of making the Father known, for

> in this way the Lord goes forth in the totality . . . who chooses them and so receives the *gnosis* of the totality . . . unifying them, bringing them back to the Father to the mother, Jesus of the infinite sweetness.

The sayings provide insight into how Jesus himself conceived the purpose of his mission. It is described as receiving back those who had distanced themselves so that he might anoint them with the ointment of mercy. Then they became perfect according to the will of the Father without whom this would not happen. The Father and the Son are co-existent and through the Son the Father's will is done and his name is spoken. The Son receives this name for he alone saw the Father and so declares his existence:

> the name is therefore that of the Father, as the name of the Father is the Son.

The Son therefore has knowledge to declare the secrets of the Father, to glorify the *pleroma* and the sweetness of the Father. All the emanations of the father are *pleromas* and it is he who has assigned to them their destinies, for the Father is without evil and is impartial. Jesus is shown to act as the bringer of light and through this to give birth to life, thought and understanding, mercy and salvation, and to impart to those who receive it the powerful spirit. Jesus is also portrayed as the shepherd who goes in search of the sheep that have strayed and labours for their recovery even to the extent of "bringing them up from the pit for he gave his life to the sheep" (we note here the association with the parable of the lost sheep in *Luke* 15). The image of the shepherd relates to the work of Jesus as offering forgiveness. The gospel records how "the Eternal One" (Jesus) breaks forth in order to provide forgiveness for sinners. Just as it is in the nature of a physician to seek out for healing those who are sick so it is in the nature of the Spirit to seek those who need the therapy of forgiveness:

> It is for this reason that the Incorruptibility breathed forth; it perused the one who had sinned in order that he (the sinner) might find rest. For nothing else but forgiveness remains for the Light when it comes to the deficiency (the creation) as the Word of All. Just as the physician comes to the place where sickness is, because that is his nature.

As the Father willed that knowledge of himself be shown and known by those who are at present ignorant he decreed that this good news was mediated from himself by Jesus. In this capacity he is also the source of enlightenment to the path of truth. Along with this the Father reveals himself through the Holy Spirit, here called "his bosom" or "the tongue of the Father" or "the manifestations of the Father" or "his revelations to the *aeons*". Those who receive the Holy Spirit greet the Father in truth and are then united with him; they come to knowledge as people who are awakened from sleep or as blind people whose eyes have been opened. As they are enlightened so they wait for the coming of the perfect one without striving or being twisted around the lath, for

> they themselves see the truth, and the Father is within them, being perfect, being undivided in the truly good one, being in no way deficient in anything, but they are set at rest, refreshed in the spirit.

The interpretation of the death of Jesus presents and illustrates the gnostic perspective on this in one or two interesting ways. It tells of Jesus being nailed to a tree and producing the fruit of the tree of knowledge, which is knowledge of life not of death:

> nailed to the tree, he became fruit of the knowledge (*gnosis*) of the Father, which did not, however, become destructive because it was eaten, but gave to those who ate it cause to become glad in the discovery. For he discovered them in himself, and they discovered him in themselves . . .

The gospel expounds the vicarious nature of the passion of Jesus. He was patient in accepting suffering for the sake of others and on the cross he published the edict of the Father. For their sakes "he drew himself down to death though life eternal clothes him". This he did for the sake of teaching the living who are inscribed in the Book of the Living. The same idea is to be found in the New Testament *Book of Revelation*, which tells of those who are redeemed and whose names are written in the Lamb's book of life.[21]

The author sees in the death of Jesus the occasion of discovering the divine self within. This discovery brings about the demise of anguish and horror, of ignorance that causes suffering, oblivion and terror. Existence in such a state is likened to the darkness of a nightmare and those who are caught in it live in confusion, instability, doubt, division and many illusions. Realizing the divine within there comes release from such constraints and the grace of union with the divine:

> The gospel of truth is a joy for those who have received from the Father of truth the grace of knowing him . . . For he discovered them in himself, and they discovered him in themselves, the incomprehensible, inconceivable one, the Father, the perfect one, the one who made all things.

The *Gospel of Truth* ranks high amongst the gnostic writings on account of its depth of thought about the issues of belief and redemption and the range of its interpretation. It was viewed with alarm by Bishop Irenaeus and he denounced it as full of blasphemy and dismissed it as being inconsistent with the truth. He urged the faithful to avoid such an abyss as the heretical gospel represented.[22] Nevertheless for the understanding of gnostic beliefs the gospel is invaluable.

The *Gospel of the Egyptians*[23]

The *Gospel of the Egyptians* identifies itself as "the sacred book of the great invisible spirit". It is the one gospel text from Nag Hammadi that lacks a Christian context. It has been described as offering "a gnostic salvation history".[24] It is a Sethian-type gospel with a mythological content. It tells of the ascetic practices that Christians from a non-Jewish background practised in Egypt, similar to those mentioned by Clement of Alexandria and Origen. The gospel names Seth as its author and he is portrayed as the founder of the gnostics. There are four main parts to the gospel: the origin of the heavenly world, the salvation of the descendents of Seth, a section of hymns, and the transmission of the gospel. In the first the origin of the world is said to derive from the trinity of the Father, Barbelo the Mother and the Son. In the second the origin, preservation and salvation of the race of Seth who descends from heaven and accomplishes salvation for Jews is described. The third section is hymnic in character, whilst the final tells of the Sethian origin and transmission of the gospel. The Sethian character of the gospel is well documented in the portrayal of the origin of his seed and the preservation of his progeny by the heavenly powers. The pinnacle of its presentation of Seth is the portrayal of the mission of salvation he performed through the presentation of the record of the redeemed:

> This is the book which the great Seth wrote and placed in high mountains on which the sun has not risen . . . The great Seth wrote this book with letters of one hundred and thirty years.

As might be anticipated the gospel presents a favourable view of Seth, especially of his role as redeemer and his care of his race on earth. In particular he is portrayed as the champion and the protector of his race from the plans of the devil against them. Naturally the devilish plans are painted in lurid colours to highlight the distain felt and to denounce the evil of his misguided ways. The protection of Seth is matched by practical generosity as he requests water for his seed (water of course being the symbol of life and renewal), and four hundred ethereal angels (the symbols of divine intervention and protection), who came from the *aeons* to watch over the race that was beyond corruption on this account.

The great Seth and his race dwelt in Sodom and Gomorrah to where he brought his seed and sowed it in the *aeons*. The locations are known from the Bible and the reference is either to the pasture found in Sodom for his seed or to the way that Seth took his seed from Gomorrah and planted it in Sodom. The gospel highlights further its exaltation of Seth in a remarkable account of the heavenly Seth being manifested in Jesus, where

> the great incorruptible Seth, the son of an incorruptible man Adamas

is shown on the one side where he is evidently identified with the "great Christ", but on the other side with "Jesus the living", who so nailed

> the powers of the thirteen *aeons* (of the *demiurge*) to the cross.

From the Father there proceed three powers, the first *Ogdoad*, which is thought and the word, the second *Ogdoad*, which is the Mother, and the third *Ogdoad*, which is the Son and the crown and glory of the Father. There also appeared the great light, the Manifestation, who gave birth

> to the great incorruptible Seth, the son of the incorruptible man, Adamas.

Thus the gospel accounts for the greatness of Seth and the endowment he received from the incorruptible Father. Being enriched with this gift he became the Metanoia (repentance) in the world, where he saw the havoc that the devil wrought by his wickedness. The presence of Metanoia shows how great was Seth's care for his race on earth to safeguard and nourish them as they sojourned in Sodom and Gomorrah, notorious cities condemned in the Bible for their wickedness.[25] The message conveyed through this account is the presence of the heavenly Seth who appeared in Jesus and nailed the thirteen *aeons* (of the *demiurge*) to the cross. The Manifestation of the higher being was that of Christ who dwelt with the Father as light and is identified as the Son who came from the Father.

He is the incorruptible man who fulfilled his role as redeemer and light in the world. As in other parts of the gnostic texts, light is a symbol of the salvific work of redemption. The Father from whom he came is also the creator who is described as "the great, invincible, incomprehensible, Virginal Spirit". He was sent by the four lights and the will of the whole *pleroma*, and having passed through the three persons he was then able to serve the race and bring to the world reconciliation. What seems to be an address to the redeemer leads to the close of the gospel:

O living water, O child of the child, O glorious name, really truly, O existing one who sees the *aeons*. Really truly who is eternal, really truly in the heart who exists Son for ever. Thou art what Thou art, Thou art who thou art.

Jesus said to his disciples, "Compare me to someone and tell me whom I am like": Simon Peter replied that he was like "a righteous angel", and Matthew that he was "like a philosopher". But Thomas replied: "Master my mouth is wholly incapable of saying who you are like".

The Gospel of Philip

I am (the word) logos which dwells in the inexpressible light. I alone was inexpressible, undefiled, immeasurable, inconceivable Word.

Trimorphic Protennoia

Do not tire of knocking on the door of Reason (Logos)
and do not cease walking in the way of Christ.

Teachings of Silvanus

Through him he enlightened those who were in darkness, because of oblivion. He enlightened them and indicated a path for them, and that path is the truth that he taught them.

The Gospel of Truth

7

Gnosticism and the Gospel of John

The gnostics probably had access to the *Gospel of John* from the time of its composition, towards the end of the first century. They were attracted to this more than to any other gospel. The gnostic Basilides drew upon it for support of his own ideas and it was a favourite book of Valentinus. According to tradition the gnostic Cerinthus had contact with John in Ephesus, from where the gospel is thought by many to have originated, and it has been conjectured that Cerinthus may have been its author.[1] We know that the gnostics were the first commentators on the gospel and they found its dominant themes reflective of those issues and problems with which they grappled. The gnostic background has been the subject of intense enquiry, and Rudolph Bultmann, the distinguished New Testament scholar, argued in favour of a gnostic origin of the *Gospel of John*.[2] But the current of ideas and concerns that runs through the gospel probably reflects a more diversified background that was a mixture of different aspects of Judaism, Hellenism, Roman and pagan philosophy, as well as gnosticism. According to one authority, "this amalgamation and its fluctuation must be seriously considered in the investigation of the fourth gospel".[3] The author of the gospel seems to have had in mind those Christians who held the Christian faith in a defective way, which needed to be corrected. He was also alive to the questions that gnosticism posed and these also urgently needed to be addressed. An incipient gnosticism seems to pervade many parts of the gospel but in addressing this and other issues the author drew upon his own knowledge and experience and wrote his gospel to confirm apostolic and orthodox faith that "Jesus Christ is the Son of God" and to induce belief in him (*John* 20: 31).

We should avoid reading back into the gospel later gnostic ideas as this would be a mistake; there are traces of nascent gnostic notions that underlie the importance of this study but it has to be kept in perspective.

Issues such as the creation of the world, the humanity of Jesus, understanding his role as redeemer and the nature of salvation, different aspects of the understanding of knowledge and variant views on eschatology, are among those that engaged the gospel writer as well as being prominent aspects of gnostic doctrine. But the style and language of the gospel also would have a special attraction for the gnostics. The wealth of symbolism, imagery, thought forms, analogies and allegories that pervade the gospel are characteristic of the gnostics' own writings and would have a particular appeal.[4] It is not surprising, therefore, that this gospel had a fascination for the gnostics. The Church, however, regarded it as orthodox whatever elements of incipient gnosticism it may contain, and our task is to probe this question.

Interpreting the gospel

Commenting on the text of the Bible is as old as the Bible itself and many commentaries from the biblical period were given special status by those who used them. This is the case with regard to the rabbinical commentaries from the biblical period. They are not all of the same kind. Some, like the rabbinical *midrashim*, are homiletical commentaries that provide an exegesis of the text. Others, like the *pesherim* commentaries, from among the Dead Sea Scrolls, are interpretations with verse by verse commentaries or explanations of events and their contemporary meaning. Such commentaries offered an interpretation of the meaning of the text that penetrates beyond the surface meaning to reveal the truth that is concealed within the text itself.[5] From this they were able to make whatever application suited their purpose. The commentaries that come from the biblical period are mostly of a sectarian character, such as the commentaries from the Dead Sea Scrolls, and we naturally expect any gnostic commentary on the *Gospel of John* or other parts of scripture also to be of this order.

The earliest known gnostic commentary on the gospel is by Heracleon and comes from the second century. A disciple of Valentinus, Heracleon sought in the gospel support for the teaching of his master and his exegesis is the first example of an extensive Christian gnostic commentary on a New Testament gospel.[6] Unfortunately only fragments of his commentary are available to us and these are preserved in the works of Clement of Alexandria, and Origen, who described him as the most distinguished of the school of Valentinus. The tenor of Heracleon's work is distinctly Valentinian; he kept very close to his master's thought, and there is an assumption that Valentinus may have transposed the gospel into a gnostic key. Obviously Heracleon took a high view of the gospel and gave it the status of authentic scripture. He does not name the author of the gospel although his comment on *John* 1: 18 assumes that he was a disciple of Jesus. The parts of the commentary that have been preserved are a careful analytical exposition of the text; in places the text is amplified for the sake of making its meaning clear. Naturally it is gnostic in tone and intention but it does not always come to grips with the profound theological intent of the gospel, and parts of the commentary are obscure and difficult to interpret. There is no doubt about the earnestness of Heracleon's intention or that he shared the gospel author's purpose in aiming to elucidate the meaning and outreach of Christian faith in the most effective way possible. Heracleon's commentary therefore holds an assured place in the history of the exposition of the *Gospel of John*. Whether the gnostics accepted the teaching of the gospel at the time of its composition as authentic and only later did controversy develop on issues that divided gnostics from orthodox believers is an open question. But both the author of the gospel and the commentator probed matters of key importance for presenting and understanding Christian belief. We know that Heracleon composed comments on at least eight chapters of the gospel and these are handed down from the eight books of exposition of the *Gospel of John* by Origen. We can flavour the atmosphere and style of Heracleon's commentary from the following examples.

The prologue

The gospel opens with a prologue as a hymn in praise of the Logos. It has been conjectured whether this reflects an early gnostic hymn on the same subject. We have noticed earlier the occurrence and meaning of the term Logos in the literature and thought of the gnostics, including Valentinus. The term as used in the gospel and in the gnostic writings is not only a name for Christ but it is also rich in theological meaning. In the contemporary religion and philosophy of the time the term Logos had a wide range of meaning. It echoes aspects of the wisdom literature of the Old Testament where *logos* (word) and wisdom are used interchangeably;[7] it has been also associated with the doctrine of Philo of

Alexandria as having Hellenistic speculations. The author of the gospel may have intended not to restrict his use of the term to any one of the current trends but to have adapted it to his own theological purpose. The opening words of the gospel use the term Logos as one that brings together a number of themes in order to assert the status and pre-existence of the divine Word. With this the gospel allies his role in creation – "all things were made through him, and without him was not anything made that was made".[8] In the gnostic *Trimorphic Protennoia* the Logos is said to have existed in eternal light, which establishes in gnostic terms his pre-existence:

> I am (the word) logos which dwells in the inexpressible light. I alone was inexpressible, undefiled, immeasurable, inconceivable Word.

The *Gospel of John* conceived of the Logos as the medium of creation and likewise Valentinus, as we saw earlier, taught that the Word (Logos) was instrumental in bringing humanity into being. The Word emerged from Mind and Truth to perform a creative function. By declaring the Logos to be the agent of creation the gospel asserts that he alone was responsible for the creation – "without him was not anything made" – but this raises the problem of evil in the world. On this there was tension between the gnostics and the orthodox. *How did the gnostics account for evil and how did this differ from the stance of the gospel?* In the commentary of Heracleon the Logos is not expounded as the creator so this then avoids attributing the origin of the material (evil) world to the Logos who was "undefiled". The creation is the work of a "lesser being" and the presence of evil is due to this "lesser being" (the *demiurge*) who functions in opposition to the divine Logos. In this connection two theories of the origin of evil seem to be projected. In the case of gnosticism, which held so strongly to the view of the material world as evil, only a creator who was hostile to the purpose of the Supreme God could be responsible for evil. In the gospel the whole creation is attributed to the Logos, who was with God from the beginning.

It is this hostile being who holds humankind in subjection to the limitations of the material world. But the gospel states categorically that the Logos was the medium of creation. Could this dichotomy be resolved? Valentinus seems to have thought so. His thesis is that the Saviour acted as the *demiurge* and this seems like an attempt to reconcile the two views of Christ, the gospel view of the Logos (creator) and the gnostic alternative view of the "lesser being". Valentinus implies that the *demiurge* operated on the impulse of the divine will of the Supreme God in the act of creation. The theory Valentinus expounded is expressed in mythical form, as is typical of his style. There existed a heavenly hierarchy or *pleroma*, where dwelt the Supreme God (the first Forefather) whose primordial essence was Thought and Grace and Silence, which were invisible to the family of *aeons*. In some way or other Sophia made contact with the first Forefather and desired to have intercourse with him, which was not intended. When she cried out for help to the Father of all the *aeons* he sent to her rescue Horos who separated her from the monster she had conceived and restored her among the *aeons*. That which she conceived was removed from the *pleroma* and became the creator of this material world. In this mythical way Valentinus developed a theory of the origin of the world and of the evil within it.

In the gospel prologue the Logos is also declared to have been manifested in a human life:

And the Word became flesh and dwelt among us, full of grace and truth.[9]

This is unique to the gospel and the only reference anywhere to the Logos appearing in a human form. We have noted earlier the gnostic approaches to the human–divine problem of the person of Jesus,[10] here it is sufficient to note how the gospel unequivocally conveys the complete humanity of Jesus through the use of the word flesh (*sarx*) as the basic component of physical life. We have noted earlier how the gnostics rejected this view of the redeemer in favour of a docetic view of his humanity. Instead they identified Logos with *nous* and *ennoia* as we see from the tract the *Thought of Ennoia*:

Father of All. Ennoia (Thought) of the light
Nous dwelling in the Heights,
above the regions below, Light dwelling in the Heights,
Voice of Truth, upright Nous, untouchable Logos,
and ineffable Voice, incomprehensible Father.[11]

The *Teachings of Silvanus* also identifies the Logos with reason, evidently in a mystical way:

Do not tire of knocking on the door of Reason (Logos)
and do not cease walking in the way of Christ.[12]

This door is the inner mystical door through which the Logos can be contacted. Through this contact with the Logos within, the believer is freed from sin and "the fire of lust", and need no longer submit to barbarism for "it is possible for you through reasoning (meditation, contact with the Logos) to conquer them". Through meditation it is possible to concentrate on the Logos and to establish a relationship with the "holy Logos". In the gnostic writings there is a recurrent attempt to remove the physical reality of Jesus and to dwell more on the possibility of establishing a mystical relationship with him as a wholly spiritual being.

Gnostics seemed intent on protecting the possibility of this union and to separate the human Jesus from the divine Logos. Irenaeus implies that the author of the gospel was aware of this intention for he wrote:

> John seeks to remove the error which by Cerinthus had been disseminated among men that the Son of the Creator was one but the Christ from above another, who also continued impassible, descending upon Jesus, the Son of the Creator, and flew back again into his Pleroma.[13]

Indeed, according to Irenaeus none of the heretics regarded the flesh of Jesus as real. From certain of the comments of Heracleon it is possible to add to the picture of gnostic Christology. He asserts that the Saviour (a title he gives to Jesus) is superior to the *demiurge* but one who is equated with the Logos. He is the lamb of God who is more than a prophet. He is the Christ who is worthy of honour and exaltation. He imparts his Spirit and gives Power. He is the messiah whom the Church had expected and who was believed to know all things. He is the lord who is able to restore all things through his presence. He is the Son of Man who also calls himself the reaper for he sends forth the angels as his reapers who are identified and known through his disciples. Even though he is not present physically he is still able to heal. The revelation of God is made to the *aeons* through *Monogenes*. There is a tendency in the commentary to interpret various aspects in philosophical terms and to present Christ as a separate *aeon* and an intermediary between God and the world. The perfect *aeon*, however, did not come into being through the Logos for he is unbegotten and invisible.

The above comments on various parts of the gospel[14] contribute to our knowledge of the gnostic understanding of the person and work of Jesus Christ. All the titles and expressions have a bearing upon the purpose of his mission and have relevance for the Church's understanding of its role in propagating its faith. It has to be said that Heracleon's commentary is an exposition and not a refutation of the *Gospel of John*, and it is proper to assume that he shared the salvific purpose of its author.

The sacrament of geography

From the amount of space given in the gospel to the journeys of Jesus it is easy to plot the geographical progress of his mission throughout Judaea, Galilee, Samaria and Jerusalem. Heracleon makes reference to the places he visited, but not just as geographical locations or for purposes of territorial identification, which would not be fitting to someone committed to seeking freedom from attachment to the impermanence of the world and its geography. So what then is to be gathered from his explanations of these geographical details in the gospel and other references to particular happenings? They receive a spiritual or a sacramental interpretation and meaning consistent with the gnostic mind. These examples illustrate both the method and style of the gnostic commentary, as well as its intention:

> After this he went down to Capernaum with his mother and his brothers and his disciples . . .
> Heracleon: Capernaum means the end of the world or the material things to which Christ descended . . .

> The passover of the Jews was at hand and Jesus went up to Jerusalem . . .
> Heracleon: the ascent to Jerusalem signifies the ascent from material things to the psychic place, the image of Jerusalem . . .

> It has taken forty years to build this temple, and you will raise it up in three days . . .
> Heracleon: Solomon's temple is an image of the Saviour . . .

> Are you greater than our father who gave us the well . . .
> Heracleon: Jacob's well signified insipid, temporary and deficient life . . .

> Woman believe me the hour is coming when neither on this mountain or in Jerusalem is the place . . .
> Heracleon: the mountain is the creation, the city the worldly way of life
> . . .

> He came again to Cana in Galilee where he made the water wine . . .
> Heracleon: from Judaea to Galilee means from the Judaea above . . .

The journeys were undertaken for a particular purpose and in the gospel they are linked to festivals so that they become part of its structural framework.[15] Worship comprises an essential part of the celebration and in this respect the gnostic comment on the dialogue between Jesus and the woman of Samaria is illuminating.[16] The encounter turned on the traditional place of worship in Jerusalem or on "this mountain", but to the gnostic commentator this represented a complete world of matter and the unwholesome so non-spiritual creation of the *demiurge*. Those who worship here are void of spiritual knowledge of the Father of Truth and worship only a lesser deity. Only those who relate spiritually to the Father worship "in spirit and in truth". The Father belongs uniquely to the realm of the spirit and only those who participate in the reality of the spiritual and are not bound to any material location worship in truth. Worship of this spiritual order is expressed through direct knowledge and immediate experience of the Father of Truth. Those who are void of this knowledge are compared to Levites who worship in the outer temple courtyard,[17] that is, without experiencing the immediate relationship with the object of worship.[18]

Dualism

The language of dualism and dualist thinking are well-known features of the *Gospel of John*. Some immediate parallels between the gospel and the gnostic writings illustrate the prevalence of similar usage here also. In gnosticism the dualism between the material and divine world, between light and darkness, good and evil, spirit and matter, is well documented. These are opposed to each other irreconcilably, not in a physical but in a metaphysical dualism.

The material world, darkness and evil are the seat of hostile powers from which the gnostic sought release to a higher realm. To effect this release is the function of the deliverer and this is expressed in dualist terms:

> Through him he enlightened those who were in darkness, because of oblivion. He enlightened them and indicated a path for them, and that path is the truth that he taught them.[19]

In this context the gnostic text engages light as a metaphor to describe the forces of good as opposed to oblivion and darkness. Here the dualism is absolute, light being of the nature of goodness, and darkness of evil.

In the gospel we read: "I am the light of the world, he who follows me will not walk in darkness, but will have the light of life."[20]

Comparisons with the gnostic notion of enlightenment have to be made with caution especially where the connotation of the imagery is different. The gospel contrasts light and darkness from the perspective of the teaching of the Bible as a whole.[21] There God is declared to be the creator of light *and* darkness and so he is responsible for both within the natural world (*Genesis* 1: 2–3). In the present context, the gospel light is not so much a concept as a function; the gospel uses the term to describe the action of Jesus as the bearer of light. The dualism between light and darkness was widespread in the religious and philosophical connotation of the period of the gospel and it is likely that the author was familiar with its occurrence in Hellenism and in the works of the Qumrân covenanters as well as in orthodox Judaism.

In Judaism good and evil are constantly contrasted as light and darkness. This dualism does raise some interesting questions. The plain verbal similarity is not all that informative, but one difference between the gospel and the gnostic text is that in the former the creator of light *and* darkness is the divine Logos (*John* 1: 3) whereas in gnosticism it is *gnosis* that makes plain the difference between them. To ascertain how far the gospel writer was aware of the existence of gnostic notions would require a thoroughgoing probing of the nature of dualism in each case, but here it is only necessary to note that in gnosticism the divine knowledge is the condition of deliverance whereas in the gospel the dualism faces the individual with a crucial choice, and the decision is linked to the theme of judgement and salvation.[22] The cosmic dimension of the dualism of gnosticism has been noted earlier – it is an integral component of the cosmic order with which everyone has to engage in the struggle for liberation. Those who have within them the spark of divine knowledge are destined to escape the conflict and to progress victoriously to the goal of perpetual light.

The gnostic redeemer

Frequent reference has been made in this study to the myth of the gnostic redeemer. The question that arises in relation to the *Gospel of John* is how far this is independent of the influence of such a work and whether the gospel itself shows traces of gnostic perceptions. The most characteristic feature of the gnostic myth is the descent of the redeemer from the Father and his return to the eternal abode.[23] Around this broad concept are interwoven the distinctive features of the gnostic doctrine. The redeemer descends through the various heavens to undertake his work of redemption. But in the gospel, too, Jesus the redeemer is portrayed as having descended from the Father and will return to be with God:

> I came from the Father and have come into the world; again I am leaving
> the world and going to the Father.[24]

Jesus is portrayed as the descending–ascending redeemer in basically
parallel imagery to that of gnosticism. But it is unnecessary to rush to
conclusions about the association between them.

For one thing, the information about the gnostic conception of the
redeemer who descended and ascended is generally later in time than the
gospel. The main gnostic sources are the Naassene text and the
Mandaean literature, and the citations in the writings of the Church
Fathers from the second century onwards. And there are some texts
from Nag Hammadi that do not specify the redeemer myth in these
terms. This makes it uncertain that the gospel was reflecting gnostic
notions in its portrayal of the redeemer or indeed that the gnostic notion
was influenced by the gospel.

The *Gospel of John* depicts the primary role of the redeemer as essential for salvation; without the redeemer Christ, there is no salvation –
"No one comes to the Father but by me".[25] This is not universally the
case in the gnostic texts. A redeemer myth is not germane or universal
in every part of the gnostic doctrine of redemption. It may also be
observed that the myth of a descending–ascending redeemer was known
extensively in the ancient world in pre-Christian times and later both in
Hellenism and Judaism. The *Odes of Solomon*, for example, describes
the redemptive activity of the redeemer Christ in terms of the
descending–ascending pattern and also speaks of him as the Logos
(Word).[26] Related to this is the relation of the redeemer to the Father,
which appears in both the gospel and the gnostic writings.[27] The question of the redeemer's humanity is relevant to this. In gnosticism the
human body of Jesus is regarded as but a disguise or semblance, whereas
in the gospel his humanity is taken seriously as he came to dwell in the
world as a genuine human being and the bringer of eternal life to
everyone who believes in him. As the life-giver he is associated with light
and truth and grace, and these terms are then designated as titles that are
conferred on him. These have some affinities with later gnostic thought,
but they do not necessarily amount to evidence of interdependence but
are signs rather of the presence of particular ideas and language that
characterized the diversity of culture in which the gospel was produced.

This brief analysis of gnosticism in relation to the *Gospel of John*
highlights the tensions that prevailed as the young church undertook to
express the person and work of Jesus in relation to God's self-conceived
purpose of redemption. It is not enough to use as many of the parallels

as possible between the gospel and gnosticism, arranging them in a theoretically acceptable pattern, without seeking a plausible explanation of how such diverse ideas and notions became current and how they were presumed to have arisen and came to be presented so differently. If any congenial reconstruction of parallels between the gospel and gnosticism is approximately correct it could only be because it arises out of the prevailing environment.

It is only possible, therefore, to highlight those features that can easily be distilled into abstract principles. It is not that such an approach may not be productive but it may disguise the fact that both the gospel and gnosticism have their own distinctive features, both cherishing their own specific beliefs and insights expressed in appropriate thought forms and imagery suited to their purpose at a particular time. Emphasizing parallels excessively may undermine the distinctive character and unity of the gospel as well as the gnostic "alternative". John, being aware of the challenge of gnostic pressures, as he undoubtedly was, also had his own purpose in presenting the Christian message in the style he chose and for this purpose he found and employed his own images, symbols and analogies. He intended his gospel to be congenial and meaningful to the audience to whom it was addressed. It is uncertain in what precise form he encountered the doctrines of gnosticism, but whatever the form was, John did not surrender or compromise the role of Jesus as the Word (Logos) made flesh, who was active in history, or his work as redeemer.

John was committed to expounding the Christian tradition of the redeemer and this brought together the various means he employed in presenting the "good news". He insisted on this as a way through the problems and dilemmas of the gnostic "alternative", whilst faithfully expounding his personal knowledge and experience of the meaning of the life of Jesus in its historical and theological context. Any acceptable portrait of a human being has to be coherent and display an inner unity, and John's portrait of Jesus is of this order. John's portrait of Jesus demonstrates how coherence and unity are impregnated with theological insights essential for others to appreciate and understand who he was. If we accept this as a working hypothesis it helps to clarify those tensions that arose between alternative approaches to the process and agent of redemption. This applies especially to the gnostic understanding of redemption as present experience, with its counterpart in the *Gospel of John* as the experience of eternal life. It also applies to the experience of redemption as a faith commitment, as the gospel maintains, and to the action of mysterious *gnosis* as the arbiter of redemption.

Conclusion

———

The gnostic movement described in this work developed for the most part in relation to the Christian religion. The gnostics embarked on what we can call "a celestial journey" and spread their doctrines mainly in the pale of the Christian Church. Yet gnosticism produced currents of thought whose springs are beyond the confines of orthodoxy and whose influence flowed in wider fields. The gnostic world view, with its affirmation of divine revelation and mysterious *gnosis*, could not easily be accommodated or extinguished. Gnosticism immersed itself in the spiritual quest and intellectual ferment of the age and provided a fresh impetus to more vigorous pursuit of answers to life's profoundest questions.

Gnosticism did not disappear after the first four Christian centuries. Its perceptions have continued in various forms to agitate the human mind and to chart the course of western culture. In the culture of our time, if not in the lifestyle of the majority of people, the search for understanding of the meaning and purpose of human existence goes on unabatedly. This goes also for questions of religion and belief, especially of Christianity. Many who are outside organized religion and its formal practices have an intuition that in religion, or in some form of it, there lies the answer to life's ultimate questions and the road to salvation. They look for the kindling of the inner spark of enlightenment that will constitute the comprehensive knowledge of ultimate truth and how to embrace it. Neither traditional patterns or stereotyped answers are more acceptable today than was the propositional knowledge that the gnostics spurned, and so they turn away from ecclesiastical institutions and hierarchic structures and historical dogmas. They see that these lack reality and stifle the inner yearning to take a grip on life's true meaning and destiny. Such structures only provide the vaguest outline of answers to ultimate questions without penetrating to the root of the matter. They do not provide the new language that speaks intelligently about ultimate reality in an age of spiritual pluralism. The new language of communication can only emerge out of a new spiritual experience kindled by inner perception and knowledge of authentic truth. The search for illuminating truth is still the supreme quest of the human spirit and it is towards the perfection of this experienced spirituality that the modern gnostic is bound. In essence it has to be said that gnosticism remains a living way to explore understanding of the nature of the self, the grandeur and mystery of human life and redemption.

Notes

Chapter 1 *The World of Gnosticism*

1   The *Gospel of Thomas*, in J. M. Robinson, ed., *The Nag Hammadi Library in English* (1988), pp. 124–9. Hereafter NHL. We get a flavour of how the elect cherished this knowledge from the visionary Poimandres who pleads with God, "fill me with power, who implore thee that I may never fall away from the knowledge (gnosis) which is fit for our nature". R. M. Grant, ed., *Gnosticism: An Anthology* (1961), p. 219.

2   According to P. Perkins, *Gnostic Dialogue* (1980), p. 12, the gnostics first appeared as identifiable groups when they were attacked by heresiologists.

3   NHL, pp. 40–51.

4   For further information see R. McL. Wilson, *Gnosis and the New Testament* (1968), pp. 16–17, 23–4; P. Van Beeron, *Towards a Definition of Gnosticism*, in U. Bianchi, ed., *The Origins of Gnosticism* (1967); B. Layton, ed., *The Discovery of Gnosticism* (1978); G. Quispel, *Gnostic Studies* (1974, 1975).

5   K. Rudolph, *Gnosis* (1983), pp. 56–7.

6   Perkins, *Gnostic Dialogue*, p. 15.

7   *The Book of Thomas the Contender*, NHL, pp. 198–207. *All* refers to everything that is.

8   Quoted by W. R. Inge, *Faith and its Psychology* (1911), p. 27.

9   NHL, pp. 232–43.

10 Ibid., pp. 449–59.

11 *1 Timothy* 6: 20, NEB.

12 To have "shot wide of the truth" is tantamount to sin in the biblical sense of "missing the mark" or "failing to reach the target".

13 *Stromateis*, Clement of Alexandria, quoted in H. M. Gwatkin, *Selections from Early Christian Writers* (1937), p. 109.

14 *The Epistle to the Hebrews*, chapter 11.

15 Inge, *Faith and its Psychology*, p. 21.

16 NHL, p. 451.

17 Ibid., pp. 30–7.

18 Gwatkin, *Selections from Early Christian Writers*, p. 107.

19   *Stromateis* v1.13. See excerpts in H. Bettenson, *The Early Christian Fathers* (1969), pp. 168–84, and *The Writings of Clement of Alexandria* by W. Wilson (1867–9).

20   Ibid., 1.1.

21   Elaine Pagels, *The Gnostic Gospels* (1979), pp. 134ff.

22   For further discussion on this see Bertrand Russell, *Our Knowledge of the External World* (1916).

23   NHL, pp. 40–51.

24   Irenaeus, *Against Heresies* 1.1. Hereafter A.H. See excerpts in Bettenson, *The Early Christian Fathers*, pp. 65–102, and the edition of the works of Irenaeus by W. W. Hardy (1897, reprint 1965).

25   *Basilides' System*, in Grant, *Gnosticism: An Anthology*, pp. 125–34.

26   *The Gospel of Truth*, NHL, pp. 32–52.

27   Perkins, *Gnostic Dialogue*, p. 10.

28   Cf. *The Gospel of Truth*, in Grant, *Gnosticism: An Anthology*, pp. 150–1. "While his wisdom meditates on the logos (and) since his teaching expresses it, his knowledge has been revealed ... it has revealed his image. Thus the logos of the Father goes forth into the all."

29   See further, *The Apocalypse of Peter*, NHL, pp. 372–8, 523–7. For an account of Gnostic revelation dialogues, see Perkins, *Gnostic Dialogue*, p. 60.

30   See *The Origin of the World*, NHL, p. 185.

31   *The Apocalypse of Adam*, NHL, pp. 279–86.

32   Quoted from Rudolph, *Gnosis*, p. 53.

33   On the other hand, there is a certain ambivalence on this score, for there is a view that after the primal revelation, the inner power of the revelation did not withdraw, but remained in the world as a guide to the goal of redemption.

34   NHL, pp. 40–51. Also Basilides 24.3–6, in Grant, *Gnosticism: An Anthology*, p. 153.

35   The *Gospel of Philip*, NHL, pp. 139–61.

36   *The Discourse on the Eighth and Ninth*, NHL, pp. 321–8.

37   The *Book of Thomas the Contender*, NHL, p. 193.

38   See The *Gospel of Truth*, NHL, pp. 40–51.

39   *The Teaching of Silvanus*, NHL, pp. 381–95.

40   Basilides 24.3–6; Grant, *Gnosticism: An Anthology*, pp. 31–2.

41   Basilides, ibid.

42   The *Gospel of Thomas*, NHL, pp. 124–39.

43   G. Quispel, *Gnosticism*, in *Encyclopedia of Religion*, vol. 5, ed. Mircea Eliade (1987), pp. 566ff.

44   The *Gospel of Thomas*, NHL, pp. 124–39.

45   The *Gospel of Truth*, NHL, pp. 40–57.

46   For discussion on this see Hans Jonas, *The Gnostic Religion* (1988), pp. 194ff.

47   The *Gospel of Thomas*, NHL, pp. 124–39.
48   *Dialogue of the Saviour*, NHL, pp. 244–56.
49   The *Gospel of Philip*, NHL, pp. 141–60.
50   *Trimorphic Protennoia*, NHL, pp. 461–7.
51   Irenaeus, *Praefectio* 2.3 15.1–2. See also Bettenson, *The Early Christian Fathers*, pp. 65–102.
52   NHL, pp. 40–57.
53   Grant, *Gnosticism: An Anthology*, p. 113.
54   Ibid.
55   Ibid.
56   For discussion of how this concept of mystery differs from the Dead Sea Scrolls where mystery is of a theological kind, see G. R. Driver, *The Judaean Scrolls* (1965), p. 564.
57   NHL, pp. 372–8.
58   *Tractate 1 Poimandres*, in Grant, *Gnosticism: An Anthology*, p. 217.
59   *The Tripartite Treatise*, NHL, pp. 60–104.
60   A.H. 21.1–5. Also Bettenson, *The Early Christian Fathers*, pp. 65–102.
61   The *Gospel of Truth*, NHL, pp. 38–51.
62   *Treatise on Resurrection*, NHL, pp. 52–3.
63   NHL, pp. 487–9.
64   NHL, p. 150. Compare with this the description of the five ineffable seals given for the salvation of the initiate in the *Trimorphic Protennoia* 48, C. W. Hedrick, ed., *Nag Hammadi Studies, xxviii* (1990), p. 429.
65   *Apocryphon of John*, NHL, pp. 104ff.
66   Quoted in T. Churton, *The Gnostics* (1987), pp. 57–8.
67   NHL, pp. 139–61.
68   *The Pleroma* in the *Valentinian System of Ptolemaeus*, in Grant, *Gnosticism: An Anthology*, p. 163.
69   The *Gospel of John* 10.1–16; 15.1–10.
70   *The Apocryphon of John*, NHL, pp. 104ff.
71   NHL, pp. 139–61.
72   Ibid.
73   See Pagels, *The Gnostic Gospels*, p. 36.
74   Ibid., p. 24.
75   NHL, pp. 104ff.
76   Jonas, *The Gnostic Religion*, p. 256.
77   *The Ophite Diagrams*, in Grant, *Gnosticism: An Anthology*, p. 89.
78   Ibid., p. 158.
79   NHL, pp. 139–61.
80   Ibid.

Chapter 2   *Gnostic Communities: Origins and History*

1   For further discussion of origins, see Rudolph, *Gnosis*, p. 225. For indi-

vidual opinions the following are informative: R. M. Grant, *Gnosticism and Early Christianity* (1966); G. Quispel, *Gnosticism: From its Origins to the Middle Ages*, in *Encyclopedia of Religion*, ed. M. Eliade; E. R. Dodds, *Pagan and Christian in an Age of Anxiety* (1965); H. Jonas, *The Gnostic Religion*.

2 Jonas, *The Gnostic Religion*, p. 16.

3 Hans Kung, *Eternal Life* (1982), p. 81.

4 E. Hennecke, *The New Testament Apocrypha*, ET R. McL. Wilson (1963–1964). Cf. J. N. Farqhar, *The Apostle Thomas in North India and in South India* (1926, 1927).

5 Pagels, *The Gnostic Gospels*, p. xix.

6 Ibid., p. xxi.

7 Rudolph, *Gnosis*, p. 132.

8 Compare with this the various stages of the gnostic initiation ceremonies, pp. 15ff.

9 For full discussion of Jnana see B. K. Matilal, *Jnana*, in *Encyclopedia of Religion*, vol. 8, pp. 94–5.

10 See J. Fowler, *Hinduism* (1997), p. 120.

11 Ibid., pp. 10ff.

12 Ibid., pp. 120–1.

13 Ibid., p. 106.

14 Ibid., pp.16ff.

15 Cf. p. 15.

16 H. Saddhatissa, *The Buddha's Way* (1988), pp. 81–7.

17 See W. Bousset, *Kyrios Christos*, E.T. (1970), p. 145, who sought to relate the beginnings of gnosticism to Babylonian and Persian sources and to the religious concepts and dualist views of the cosmos in the religion of Babylon and Persia.

18 "The hypothesis once supported by Richard Reitzenstein, Geo Widengren, and Rudolph Bultmann, that gnosticism is of Iranian origin has been abandoned: the alleged Iranian mystery of the 'saved saviour' has been disproved." G. Quispel, *Gnosticism: From its Origins to the Middle Ages*, in *Encyclopedia of Religion*, ed. M. Eliade.

19 Rudolph, *Gnosis*, p. 236, is ready to concede that "A whole series of Gnostic ideas, therefore, must be conceived as having arisen against the Iranian background." Whilst R. McL. Wilson seems not to abandon the connection he sounds a more cautious note, "Something may be due to Zoroastrianism or other oriental systems of thought, but how much is extremely doubtful, certainly whenever oriental elements are present they have been worked over in the light of Platonic and other doctrines." R. McL. Wilson, *The Gnostic Problem* (1958), p. 108.

20 From the *Gatha*, Zoroastrian scriptures.

21 T. Ling, *A History of Religion: East and West* (1974), p. 78.

22 Wilson, *The Gnostic Problem*, p. 225.

23　Rudolph, *Gnosis*, p. 283.

24　For the text of the *Song of the Pearl*, see Grant, *Gnosticism: An Anthology*, pp. 116ff.

25　Jonas, *The Gnostic Religion*, p. 123.

26　Rudolph, *Gnosis*, p. 358.

27　With this we may compare the accounts of the heavenly journey of Zoroaster through the ether, the seven pillars of the *archons*, the place of repentance, and finally the levels of the *aeons* of light. The ascent represents the liberation from the bondage of the world and initiation into knowledge of God. See *Zostrianos* viii, NHL, pp. 404–31.

28　Jonas, *The Gnostic Religion*, p. 230.

29　A. H. Armstrong, *Gnosis and Greek Philosophy* (1978).

30　Rudolph, *Gnosis*, p. 284.

31　Quispel, *Gnosticism: From its Origins to the Middle Ages*.

32　N. Smart, *The World's Religions* (1993), p. 232.

33　Timaeus 28 B, *Plato: Collected Dialogues*, ed. E. Hamilton and H. H. Cairns (1961).

34　Ibid., 29 B.

35　Ibid., 38D. Compare this with the Supreme God of gnostic mythology, p. 95.

36　Quoted in Rudolph, *Gnosis*, pp. 60–1.

37　Timaeus 28B.

38　We note how this differs from the gnostic concept, see pp. 103ff.

39　Clement of Alexandria was deeply steeped in Hellenistic philosophy and is credited with having brought this into orthodox Christianity.

40　Quoted in J. Campbell, *Occidental Mythology* (1976), p. 251.

41　Rudolph, *Gnosis*, p. 6.

42　See Churton, *The Gnostics*, p. 45.

43　The evidence for the existence of Jewish communities throughout Asia Minor, Egypt, Syria and Rome during the pre-Christian and early Christian periods is well documented, for example, in the Elephantine Papyri.

44　For example, the Books of Proverbs and Ecclesiastes form part of the same movement of the human mind as is characteristic of the Greeks.

45　See Chapter 7.

46　Philo, *On Dreams*, in *Philo* vols i–x, tr. F. H. Colson and G. H. Whitaker (1941), vol. v, pp. 369–73.

47　Cf. Ezekiel 1: 26.

48　For further information on the Kabbalists, see A. Unterman, *The Jews: Their Religious Beliefs and Practices* (1996).

49　For an account of the awakening of Adam, see Rudolph, *Gnosis*, pp. 94ff.

50　Wilson, *The Gnostic Problem*, p. 175.

51　The Book of Wisdom 9; Proverbs 8: 22–31.

52　Pagels, *The Gnostic Gospels*, pp. 51ff.

53 Grant, *Gnosticism: An Anthology*, pp. 213–14.
54 See further, H. H. Rowley, *The Relevance of Apocalyptic* (1944); James Barr, *Jewish Apocalyptic in Recent Study* (1975).
55 I. Gruenwald, *Knowledge and Vision*, in *Israel Oriental Studies* (1973).
56 *The Teachings of Silvanus*, NHL, pp. 381–95.
57 The New English Bible: *Apocrypha* (1970), pp. 134ff.
58 NHL, pp. 141–60.
59 See p. 66.
60 *The Wisdom of Solomon*, 6.12f.
61 Ibid., 6.19.
62 Ibid., 6.18.
63 NHL, pp. 83ff.
64 *The Wisdom of Solomon*, 2.21–2.
65 See pp. 111–14.
66 See further, A. Dupont–Sommer, ET G. Vermes, *The Essene Writings from Qumrân* (1961); G. Vermes, *The Dead Sea Scrolls in English* (1988).
67 *The Manual of Discipline*, x–xi; T. H. Gaster, *The Scriptures of the Dead Sea Sect* (1957), pp. 285–8.
68 Vermes, *The Dead Sea Scrolls in English*, p. 750.
69 Gaster, *The Scriptures of the Dead Sea Sect*, pp. 257–84.
70 Ibid.
71 Ibid., pp. 53ff.
72 F. Legg, *Forerunners and Rivals of Christianity* (1915).
73 M. Burrows, *The Dead Sea Scrolls* (1955), pp. 252ff.
74 Ibid.
75 G. R. Driver, *The Judaean Scrolls* (1965), pp. 562ff.
76 For further information on the gnostic communities, see Rudolph, *Gnosis*, pp. 206ff.
77 On the powerful appeal of *gnosis*, see *Second Treatise of the Great Seth*, NHL, pp. 49–70.
78 A.H. iv.3. Gwatkin, *Selections from Early Christan Writers*, pp. 99ff.
79 The *Gospel of Mark* 1: 14.
80 See Paul's Letter to the Galatians.
81 Rudolph, *Gnosis*, p. 171ff.
82 The *Gospel of Mark* 13.
83 Grant, *Gnosticism: An Anthology*, p. 176.
84 Pagels, *The Gnostic Gospels*, p. 115.
85 See further, the section on Christology, pp. 95–103.
86 See further, H. Chadwick, *The Early Christian Community*, in *The Oxford History of Christianity*, ed. J. McManners (1993), pp. 63–9. Also NHL, pp. 40–57.
87 Pagels, *The Gnostic Gospels*, p. 150.
88 The Greek form of the name is Theophilus. Bogomil in Bulgarian means "loved of God".

89 Churton, *The Gnostics*, p. 72.
90 See further, Colin Morris, *Christian Civilization (1040–1400)*, in *The Oxford History of Christianity*, ed. J. McManners (1993), p. 223.
91 See also the article on Jacob Boehme by P. C. Erb in *Encyclopedia of Religion*, vol. 2, pp. 275–6.
92 Ibid.
93 Ibid.
94 Grant, *Gnosticism: An Anthology*, p. 214.
95 Jonas, *The Gnostic Religion*, p. 111.
96 Ibid.
97 Churton, *The Gnostics*, p. 142.
98 W. H. Stevenson, ed., *The Poems of William Blake* (1971).
99 Ibid.
100 Ibid.
101 Ibid.
102 Ibid.
103 Pagels, *The Gnostic Gospels*, p. xi.
104 C. G. Jung, *Psychology of the Unconscious* (1916).
105 C. G. Jung, *Psychology of Types* (1920).
106 Ibid.

Chapter 3 *Gnosticism and its Literature*

1   C. H. Dodd, *Interpretation of the Fourth Gospel* (1953), p. 97.
2   Rudolph, *Gnosis*, p. 28.
3   A.H. xxxiii.1.7. Also Bettenson, *The Early Christian Fathers*, pp. 65–102.
4   *Stromateis* 1.1 (15.1), ibid., pp. 168–82.
5   Ibid., pp. 18–22.
6   *De Anima* 21, ibid., pp. 104–65. Also *The Writings of Tertullian*, ET Holmes (1869–70).
7   J. H. Charlesworthy, *Odes of Solomon* (1973).
8   Ibid.
9   See Rudolph, *Gnosis*, p. 122.
10   M. R. James, ed., J. K. Elliott, *The Apocryphal New Testament* (1993).
11   Ibid., p. 401.
12   Ibid., pp. 251–2.
13   Ibid., pp. 97–104.
14   Pagels, *The Gnostic Gospels*, p. 73.
15   See J. Davidson, *The Gospel of Jesus* (1995), pp. 629–31.
16   Quoted by Rudolph, *Gnosis*, p. 179. See also pp. 357ff for Mandaean teaching.
17   Davidson, *The Gospel of Jesus*, p. 674.
18   Rudolph, *Gnosis*, p. 363.
19   Davidson, *The Gospel of Jesus*, p. 598.
20   For further accounts of the Hermetic literature, see Rudolph, *Gnosis*, pp.

25–6; G. Quispel, *Gnosticism in Religions of Antiquity*, ed. R. M. Seltzer (1989), pp. 259–71; G. Quispel, *Gnosticism*, in *Encyclopedia of Religion*; Grant, *Gnosticism: An Anthology*, pp. 211–26.

21   A. D. Nock, *Corpus Hermeticum* (1960), p. 121.

22   V. MacDermot, *The Books of Jeu and the United Text in the Bruce Codex* (1978), p. 119.

23   Ibid., pp. 229–48.

24   E.g. the survey of the tractates in Rudolph, *Gnosis*, pp. 42–8.

25   Athanasius was one who complained, 39th Festal Letter.

26   See Burrows, *The Dead Sea Scrolls*, pp. 252ff.

27   For an account of the discovery and the fate of the books, see Churton, *The Gnostics*, pp. 16–17. Also R. McL. Wilson, *Nag Hammadi: Progress Report*, ET (1974), pp. 196–201.

28   Jonas, *The Gnostic Religion*, p. 290.

29   As Athanasius declared. Cf. his 39th Festal Letter.

30   Burrows, *The Dead Sea Scrolls*, pp. 81ff.

31   Rudolph, *Gnosis*, p. 43.

32   See for example the image of the Church in Galatians 4: 21–31, which is also found in the gnostic texts.

33   NHL, p. 4.

34   Cf. Jonas, *The Gnostic Religion*, p. 293.

35   See J. Gray, in T. W. Manson, ed., *A Companion to the Bible* (1963), p. 279.

36   NHL, pp. 124–39.

37   Jonas, *The Gnostic Religion*, p. 215.

38   Perkins, *Gnostic Dialogue*, p. 191.

39   J. N. D. Kelly, *The Athanasian Creed* (1964).

40   B. M. Metzger, *The Canon of the New Testament* (1988).

41   Gwatkin, *Selections from Early Christian Writers*, p. 58.

42   Ibid., p. 131.

43   C. H. Dodd, *Interpretation of the Fourth Gospel*, p. 98.

Chapter 4   *Beliefs and Practices*

1   NHL, pp. 381–95.

2   Wilson, *The Gnostic Problem*, p. 69.

3   NHL, pp. 40–51.

4   See pp. 73–4.

5   Grant, *Gnosticism: An Anthology*, p. 211.

6   Rudolph, *Gnosis*, pp. 309–12.

7   A.H. 1.1.

8   *Allogenes* x1.3. NHL, pp. 491–500.

9   NHL, pp. 40–51.

10   A.H. 112.

11   This was the view of the Valentinian school of gnostics. See further, Rudolph, *Gnosis*, p. 320.

12   NHL, pp. 60–103.

13   *The Thought of Norea*, NHL, pp. 446–7.

14   Ibid.

15   *The Tripartite Tractate*, NHL, pp. 51–140.

16   NHL, pp. 581–95. Cf. the work by J. Zandee under the same title (1991).

17   NHL, pp. 104.

18   Churton, *The Gnostics*, p. 45. Cf. *The Teachings of Silvanus*, NHL, pp. 381–95.

19   NHL, pp. 127–37.

20   NHL, pp. 141–60.

21   Quoted in Davidson, *The Gospel of Jesus*, p. 265. Cf. Churton, *The Gnostics*, p. 45.

22   Cf. *Wisdom of Solomon* 12.1.

23   *Paidagogos* 1.6. Also Bettenson, *The Early Christian Fathers*, pp. 168–82.

24   Grant, *Gnosticism: An Anthology*, p. 65.

25   NHL, pp. 40–51.

26   Ibid.

27   NHL, pp. 141–60.

28   See Grant, *Gnosticism: An Anthology*, p. 51. NHL, pp. 141–60.

29   *Apocryphon of John*, NHL, pp. 104ff.

30   NHL, pp. 90–119.

31   Grant, *Gnosticism: An Anthology*, p. 51.

32   NHL, pp. 141–60.

33   *Saturninus*, in Grant, *Gnosticism: An Anthology*, pp. 31–3. Rudolph, *Gnosis*, p. 328.

34   In this context the view of R. McL. Wilson may be noted, namely, that the Valentinians thought of three Christs, the first as Logos descending from God, *The Gnostic Problem*, p. 191.

35   Grant, *Gnosticism: An Anthology*, pp. 36–41. See also Rudolph, *Gnosis*, pp. 247, 286, 301.

36   Grant, *Gnosticism: An Anthology*, pp. 36ff.

37   Hippolytus, *Refutation of All Heresies*, pp. 347, 386. See F. Legg, *Forerunners and Rivals of Christianity* (1921).

38   Grant, *Gnosticism: An Anthology*, p. 31. NHL, pp. 124–39.

39   Ibid.

40   See pp. 111–14.

41   NHL, pp. 381–95.

42   NHL, pp. 124–39.

43   Grant, *Gnosticism: An Anthology*, p. 31.

44   Ibid., p. 38.

45   Ibid., p. 102.

46   Ibid., p. 212.

47   NHL, pp. 40–57.

48   See pp. 111–14.

49 NHL, p. 352.
50 NHL, pp. 40–57.
51 *Tripartite Tractate*, NHL, p. 87.
52 The *Gospel of John* 20.
53 The *Gospel of Luke* 24.
54 The *Gospel of John* 21.
55 The *Gospel of John* 20.
56 The *Gospel of Luke* 24.
57 The *Gospel of John* 21.
58 The *Gospel of Philip*, NHL, pp. 141–60.
59 Ibid.
60 Ibid.
61 NHL, pp. 132–40. See also on Christmas Light, Rudolph, *Gnosis*, p. 339.
62 M. R. James (1993), ed. J. K. Elliott, *The Apocryphal New Testament*.
63 Cf. Rudolph, *Gnosis*, pp. 25f.
64 Ibid.
65 *The Gospel of Philip*, NHL, pp. 141–60.
66 Jonas, *The Gnostic Religion*, p. 277.
67 Rudolph, *Gnosis*, pp. 60f.
68 NHL, pp. 381–95.
69 See further Jonas, *The Gnostic Religion*, p. 217.
70 See also A. D. Nock, *Gnosticism*, in *Essays in Religion in the Ancient World*, ed. J. S. Steward (1972).
71 *Saturninus 4*, in Grant, *Gnosticism: An Anthology*, p. 31. Quispel, *Gnosticism*, p. 566.
72 See also Rudolph, *Gnosis*, p. 73.
73 Grant, *Gnosticism: An Anthology*, p. 41.
74 See pp. 108–14.
75 Wilson, *The Gnostic Problem*, pp. 45–7. Cf. Jonas, *The Gnostic Religion*, p. 217.
76 Grant, *Gnosticism: An Anthology*, pp. 146f. Also Rudolph, *Gnosis*, pp. 91f, 186.
77 A.H. 1.5. Cf. Bettenson, *The Early Christian Fathers*, pp. 65–102.
78 *The Secret Discourse on the Mount Delivered by Hermes Trismegistos to his Son*, in Grant, *Gnosticism: An Anthology*, p. 208.
79 *The Apocryphon of John*, NHL, pp. 104ff.
80 Grant, *Gnosticism: An Anthology*, p. 172.
81 Celsus' Description, in Grant, *Gnosticism: An Anthology*, p. 90; see also the Diagram of the Ophites in Rudolph, *Gnosis*, p. 68.
82 *The Gospel of Truth*, NHL, pp. 40–57.
83 Wilson, *The Gnostic Problem*, pp. 120ff.
84 NHL, pp. 141–60. See Heracleon's *Exegesis of John* for a view of how the world and what is in it came to be through God. Grant, *Gnosticism: An Anthology*, p. 146.

85 Jonas, *The Gnostic Religion*, p. 328.

86 A.H. 1.54. Also Bettenson, *The Early Christian Fathers*, pp. 65–102.

87 Ibid.

88 NHL, pp. 104ff. See also the account of how Ialdabaoth came to be, in Grant, *Gnosticism: An Anthology*, pp. 74–8.

89 NHL, pp. 40–51.

90 See pp. 8–12.

91 *The Gospel of Philip*, NHL, pp. 141–60.

92 *The Gospel of Truth*, NHL, pp. 40–57.

93 Grant, *Gnosticism: An Anthology*, p. 175.

94 Ibid., p. 176. For a similar thought, see *The Gospel of Philip*, NHL, pp. 141–60.

95 Grant, *Gnosticism: An Anthology*, p. 230.

96 Ibid., p. 59.

97 Ibid. See also Rudolph, *Gnosis*, p. 323.

98 Grant, *Gnosticism: An Anthology*, p. 116.

99 Ibid., p. 35.

100 Ibid., pp. 146ff.

101 The *Apocryphon of John*, NHL, pp. 104ff.

102 See Rudolph, *Gnosis*, pp. 111ff, 175ff.

103 Ibid., pp. 86f, 104f, 177ff.

104 Grant, *Gnosticism: An Anthology*, p. 173.

105 Ibid., p. 175.

106 1 Peter 3.

107 Grant, *Gnosticism: An Anthology*, p. 188. Cf. R. Turton, *Apocatastasis* (1987), ET D. C. Dyges, in *Encyclopedia of Religion*, vol. 1, pp. 344ff.

108 *The Gospel of Truth*, in Grant, *Gnosticism: An Anthology*, pp. 146ff.

109 A.H. 4.37. Also Bettenson, *The Early Christian Fathers*, pp. 65–102.

110 See Rudolph, *Gnosis*, p. 245.

111 Ibid., pp. 259ff, 323.

112 *The Gospel of Thomas*, NHL, pp. 124–39.

113 See Bettenson, *The Early Christian Fathers*, pp. 65–102.

114 NHL, pp. 124–39.

115 NHL, pp. 141–60.

116 *The Gospel of Mary*; Grant, *Gnosticism: An Anthology*, p. 65.

117 NHL, pp. 124–39.

118 Rudolph, *Gnosis*, p. 260.

119 NHL, pp. 141–60.

120 *The Gospel of Truth*, NHL, pp. 40–57. See also Rudolph, *Gnosis*, pp. 304f.

121 Grant, *Gnosticism: An Anthology*, p. 193.

122 Rudolph, *Gnosis*, p. 226.

123 *Marcosian Worship*, in Grant, *Gnosticism: An Anthology*, p. 193.

124 NHL, pp. 141–60.

125 *The Gospel of Thomas*, NHL, pp. 124–39.

126 NHL, pp. 141–60.
127 Ibid.
128 Grant, *Gnosticism: An Anthology*, p. 65.
129 *The Gospel of Philip*, NHL, pp. 141–60.
130 See pp. 104ff.

Chapter 5   *Orthodoxy and Heresy*

1 Quoted in Pagel, *The Gnostic Gospels*, p. 33.
2 Ibid., p. xviii.
3 Cf. Marcus Wiles, *Orthodoxy and Heresy in Early Christianity*, ed. I. Hazlett (1975), p. 201.
4 Preface to A.H. (1.180). Also Bettenson, *The Early Christian Fathers*, pp. 65–102.
5 H. Chadwick, *The Early Christan Community*, in *Oxford History of the Christian Church*, ed. J. McManners, p. 28.
6 Acts 8: 5.
7 Acts 8: 10.
8 Eusebius, *The Ecclesiastical History* 11 (xiii), in Loeb Classical Library (1928), 1.139.
9 Jonas, *The Gnostic Religion*, pp. 103–11; cf. Wilson, *The Gnostic Problem*, p. 99.
10 Rudolph, *Gnosis*, p. 10.
11 A.H. xviii. Also Bettenson, *The Early Christian Fathers*, pp. 65–102.
12 Hippolytus, *Refutation of Heresies*, vi, xx.
13 Justin Martyr, *Apology*. Rudolph, *Gnosis*, pp. 294.
14 *Apology* l.xxvi. Also Bettenson, *The Early Christian Fathers*, pp. 58–64.
15 A.H. 1.xxiii.
16 Grant, *Gnosticism: An Anthology*, p. 25.
17 *Clementine Recognitions* 11.viii. See also Rudolph, *Gnosis*, pp. 294–6.
18 *Clementine Recognitions* vi.19.6.
19 Jonas, *The Gnostic Religion*, p. 108.
20 Gaius, a notable orthodox Christian from Rome, went so far as to attribute the *Gospel of John* and the *Book of Revelation* to the gnostic Cerinthus (see Davidson, *The Gospel of Jesus*, p. 115).
21 A.H. iii.3, 4. Also Bettenson, *The Early Christian Fathers*, pp. 65–102.
22 Quoted in Jonas, *The Gnostic Religion*, p. 156. The powers distinct from the Supreme God are identified as the God of the Jews and the giver of the law.
23 A.H. i.26. Also Bettenson, *The Early Christian Fathers*, pp. 65–102.
24 Grant, *Gnosticism: An Anthology*, p. 41.
25 Wilson, *The Gnostic Problem*, p. 102.
26 Grant, *Gnosticism: An Anthology*, p. 41.
27 Wilson, *The Gnostic Problem*, pp. 99–100.
28 A.H. 1.27. ii. According to Marcion the God of the Old Testament was the

alien, a *demiurge* and a lower divinity, a judgemental God rather than a God of love, a God of justice not of mercy.

29 Associated with this is Marcion's view of the world as an enclosed cell into which or out of which life may move. See Jonas, *The Gnostic Religion*, p. 55.

30 Christ descended into hell in order to redeem all those souls who had not yielded to the God of the Old Testament. This view borders on the atoning work of Christ and the ransom he paid for their redemption. Marcion clearly took seriously the redemptive significance of the passion of Jesus. See Grant, *Gnosticism: An Anthology*, p. 46.

31 "Until Augustine no-one understood Paul as well as Marcion, yet Marcion, the one genuine pupil, misunderstood as well. Notwithstanding his dialectics Paul never regarded the created world, sexuality or the people of Israel, as did Marcion." Quispel, *Gnostic Studies*, vol. 1 (1974), p. 24.

32 "Furthermore Marcion circumcises the gospel according to Luke and takes out everything written about the generation of the Lord (Luke 1–2.52), as well as many items about the teaching of the Lord's words in which the Lord is most plainly described as acknowledging the creator as his father. Marcion 1.27–2.3, in Grant, *Gnosticism: An Anthology*, p. 45.

33 A.H. 1.2. Also Bettenson, *The Early Christian Fathers*, pp. 65–102.

34 Grant, *Gnosticism: An Anthology*, pp. 45–6.

35 Tertullian, *Against Marcion*. See Bettenson, *The Early Christian Fathers*, pp. 104–65.

36 Rudolph, *Gnosis*, p. 316. For a view of Marcion's position in the history of gnostic thought, see Jonas, *The Gnostic Religion*, pp. 137–46.

37 Rudolph, *Gnosis*, p. 316.

38 R. M. Grant, *Gnosticism and Early Christianity* (1966).

39 Valentinus is reported to have composed a *Gospel of Truth*, but whether it is the one in NHL is disputed; however, the identification of the thought is clear. See Grant, *Gnosticism: An Anthology*, p. 146.

40 *Epistle to the Hebrews* 4.

41 The *Gospel of Mark* 4.

42 Rudolph, *Gnosis*, p. 166.

43 The Greek word *syzygy* occurs frequently in the gnostic texts (Latin equivalent *contininatio*). For discussion of this, see E. C. Stead, *The Valentine Myth of Sophia*, in *Journal of Theological Studies* 20 (1969), pp. 75–104.

44 *The Gospel of Philip*, NHL, pp. 141–61.

45 Ibid.

46 Ibid.

47 The *Gospel of Matthew* 20: 16.

48 NHL, p. 433. Cf. Pagel, *The Gnostic Gospels*, pp. 116–17.

49 Rudolph, *Gnosis*, p. 311. Cf. Grant, *Gnosticism: An Anthology*, pp. 33–5.

50 Ibid., p. 134.

51 See Rudolph, *Gnosis*, pp. 309–12.

52 The full work is in five volumes written in refutation of heresy and called *The Refutation and Overthrow of Falsely So Called Knowledge of Gnosis*. It is also a source of history of religious sects in the second century. Cf. Henry Chadwick, *The Early Church* (1967), p. 50.

53 A.H. iii.18.

54 H. Koester, *The Structure of Early Christian Beliefs*, in *Trajectories through Early Christianity* (1971), p. 231. See Bettenson, *The Early Christian Fathers*, pp. 65–102.

55 See pp. 147.

56 Hippolytus, *Refutation of all Heresies*.

57 Ibid.

58 Walter Nigg, *The Heretics: Heresy Through the Ages*, ET R. and C. Watson (1990), p. 109.

59 Ibid.

60 Hippolytus, *Refutation of all Heresies*.

Chapter 6   *Gospel and the Gnostic Gospels*

1   The *Gospel of John* 20.

2   NHL, pp. 141–60.

3   G. Quispel, *The Jung Codex: A Newly Discovered Gnostic Papyrus* (1955), p. 48.

4   Cf. the arch allegorist Philo whose method received considerable currency in the period of the early church, and is one example of this varied interpretation.

5   See Rudolph, *Gnosis*, p. 152.

6   Rowan Williams, in Hazlett, *Early Christianity*, p. 85.

7   NHL, pp. 523–7.

8   Cf. Grant, *Gnosticism: An Anthology*, pp. 65–9.

9   Ibid.

10 Ibid.

11 Rowan Williams, in Hazlett, *Early Christianity*, p. 85.

12 Grant, *Gnosticism: An Anthology*, pp. 66ff.

13 NHL, pp. 141–60. See further Rudolph, *Gnosis*, p. 62.

14 The gospel has been called the jewel of the Nag Hammadi library by Churton, who has given an account of its discovery, *The Gnostics*, pp. 12, 14, 16. See also the negative estimate on p. 30. Quispel proposed a date of around 140 for the gospel, but it has been conjectured it represents a tradition as early as 50. See Pagels, *The Gnostic Gospels*, p. xvii.

15 NHL, pp. 124–39.

16 Rudolph, *Gnosis*, p. 260.

17 NHL, p. 134.

18 NHL, pp. 40–57; Grant, *Gnosticism: An Anthology*, pp. 146ff.

19 NHL, p. 38. G. Quispel, *Gnostic Studies* (1974–1975).

20 H. W. Attridge and G. W. MacRae, NHL, p. 38.

21   *The Book of Revelation* 21.
22   A.H. iv.1.7.
23   NHL, pp. 40–69.
24   A. Bohlig and F. Wise, NHL, p. 39.
25   Genesis 13.

Chapter 7   *Gnosticism and the Gospel of John*

1   Rudolph, *Gnosis*, p. 298.
2   C. K. Barrett, *The Gospel According to St. John* (1995); R. Bultmann, *The Gospel of John*, ET, 1971.
3   Barrett, *The Gospel According to St. John*.
4   See pp. 18–25.
5   On the *pesher* technique, see B. Thirering, *Jesus the Man* (1993), pp. 28–35.
6   A. E. Brooke, *The Fragments of Heracleon* (1891); cf. E. Pagels, *The Johannine Gospel in Gnostic Exegesis* (1973); Rudolph, *Gnosis*, pp. 323–4.
7   *Wisdom of Solomon* 9.1, 2.
8   The *Gospel of John* 1: 3.
9   Ibid. 1: 14.
10   Pp. 95–102.
11   For an account of *ennoia*, see Rudolph, *Gnosis*, p. 77.
12   NHL, pp. 381–95.
13   See Bettenson, *The Early Christian Fathers*, pp. 65–102.
14   The *Gospel of John* 1: 23, 27, 29; 4: 22, 36, 37.
15   Passover 2: 23; Feast of the Jews 5: 1; Tabernacles 7: 2; Passover 6: 4, 12: 9, 13: 1.
16   The *Gospel of John* 4.
17   Cf. Pagels, *The Gnostic Gospels*, p. 116.
18   Ibid.
19   *The Gospel of Truth*, NHL, pp. 40–57.
20   The *Gospel of John* 8: 20.
21   Ibid. 16: 28.
22   Ibid. 14: 6.
23   *The Gospel of Truth*, NHL, pp. 40–57.
24   The *Gospel of John* 17: 11.
25   Ibid. 14: 6.
26   *Odes* 12, 16.29.
27   The *Gospel of John* 5: 19–29.

Pre Nag Hammadi Texts/Codex
Index of the Texts

Pre Nag Hammadi Texts*

Codex 1769

The Gospel of Mary
The Apocryphon of John
Sophia of Jesus Christ
Acts of Peter

Patristic Writings

Justin Martyr
Irenaeus
Clement of Alexandria
Hippolytus
Epiphanius
Origen
Eusebius

The Apocryphal *Acts of Thomas*
Acts of John

Song of the Pearl

Mandaean Literature

The Great Book
Book of John
Book of the Zodiac

Odes of Solomon

Manichaean Literature

Hermetic Literature

Asclepius
Poimandres

Bruce Codex

Two Books of Jeu

* Texts known before the discovery of the Nag Hammadi Codices.

Codex Askew

Pistis Sophia
Extracts from the Books
of the Saviour
The Book of the
Great Logos

Codex Index of the Nag Hammadi Texts

Codex 1 (the Jung Codex)
The *Prayer of the Apostle Paul*
The Apocryphon of James
The *Gospel of Truth*
The Treatise on the Resurrection
The Tripartite Tractate

Codex 2
The *Apocryphon of John*
The *Gospel of Thomas*
The *Gospel of Philip*
The Hypostasis of the Archons
The Origin of the World
The Exegesis on the Soul
The Book of Thomas the Contender

Codex 3
The *Apocryphon of John*
The Gospel of the Egyptians
Eugnostos the Blessed
The Sophia of Jesus Christ
The Dialogue of the Saviour

Codex 4
The *Apocryphon of John* (long version)
The Gospel of the Egyptians (second verson)

Codex 5
Eugnostos the Blessed (second version)
The Apocalypse of Paul
The Apocalypse of James (first)
The Apocalypse of James (second)
The Apocalypse of Adam

Codex 6
The Acts of Peter and the Twelve Apostles

Glossary

Abraxas	Deity above the God of the world and the devil.
Achamoth	Inferior wisdom, identified with *Ogdoad*.
Adam Qadmon	The eternal man, reflection of the true God.
Adamas	The hidden heavenly Adam.
Adonaios	One of the seven planetary angels.
Aeon	Age; also space or spiritual being who governs space either here or below.
Apolytrosis	Redemption.
Apokatastasis	To bring back to the natural state, restoration.
Aporia	Roadlessness, loss.
Archon	Ruler, a governor of an *aeon*.
Authentia	The supreme power above, absolute sovereignty.
Barbela	Perfect power or seminal thought of the Highest God.
Boule	Will, female divine principle.
Daueithe	The third light appointed over the third *aeon*.
Demiurge	Creator God, subordinate God, subservient to the Supreme God.
Dyad	Duality.
Echamoth	Wisdom of death, the little wisdom.
Eleieth	The fourth light over the fourth *aeon*.
Ennead	The sphere beyond the eighth.
Ennoia	First thought, first emanation, insight.
Epinoia	Insight of light or spirit of truth.
Harmozel	The first light, angel of light in the first *aeon*.
Hebdomad	Sphere of the universe, including the seven planets equivalent to the spiritual world.
Heimarmené	Destiny.
Hieron	Holy place.
Hyle	Matter.
Ialdabaoth	Name of God, often applied to the *demiurge*.
Kakia	What is bad.
Logos	Word.
Manda dehaiji	Knowledge of life.

Mandaya	Having knowledge.
Masiqta	Ascent of the soul.
Monad	Monarchy with nothing above.
Monogenes	Supreme being.
Naas	Serpent, power aiding or opposing the Highest God.
Nasiruthe	Cultic wisdom.
Noema	Concept of great power.
Nous	Mind.
Ogdoad	Inferior heaven.
Ophis	Serpent.
Ororael	Second light appointed over the second *aeon*.
Phóstér	Light bearer.
Pleroma	The totality of the *aeons*.
Pneuma	Spirit.
Prunicon	Desire.
Prunicos	Name given to Sophia.
Rhema	Word of God.
Ruha	Wicked spirit.
Sophia	Wisdom, first female principle emanating from the Supreme God or from a succession of *aeons*.
Surd	Irrational element, rebellion against God.
Syzygy	Couple or pairs of *aeons*, consort.
Tetrad	Group of four primary *aeons* or four great lights from which emanation originated.
Uthra	Being of light.
Zozezé	Name of seal.

Select Bibliography

Armstrong, A. H. (1978) *Gnosis and Greek Philosophy*, in *Gnosis: Festschrift für Hans Jonas*, Gottingen.

Asmussen, J. P. (1975) *Manichaean Literature*, New York.

Barr, J. (1975) *Jewish Apocalyptic in Recent Study*, Manchester.

Barrett, C. K. (1955) *The Gospel According to St. John*, SPCK.

Baur W. (1971) *Orthodoxy and Heresy in Earliest Christianity*, SCM.

Bettenson, H. (1969) *The Early Christian Fathers*, Oxford University Press.

Bianchi, U., ed. (1967) *The Origins of Gnosticism*, Leiden.

Boehme, J. (1612) *The Aurora*, London.

Boehme, J. (1620) *The Great Mystery*, London.

Bousset, W. (ET 1970) *Kyrios Christos*, Stuttgart.

Brock, R. van Den, ed. (1981) *Studies in Gnosticism and Hellenistic Religions*, Cambridge University Press.

Bronowski, J., ed. (1958) *William Blake*, London.

Brooke, A. E. (1891) *The Fragments of Heracleon*, Cambridge University Press.

Bultmann, R. (ET 1971) *The Gospel of John*, Oxford University Press.

Bultmann, R. (ET 1963) *History and Eschatology*, London.

Burkitt, F. C. (1932) *Church and Gnosis*, Cambridge University Press.

Burrows, M. (1955) *The Dead Sea Scrolls*, New York.

Campbell, F. C. (1976) *Occidental Mythology*, London: Penguin.

Chadwick, H. (1963) *The Early Church*, London: Penguin.

Chadwick, H. (1993) *The Early Christian Community*, in *Oxford Dictionary of Christianity*, ed. J. Manners, Oxford.

Charlesworth, J. H. (1973) *The Odes of Solomon*, Oxford University Press.

Churton, T. (1987) *The Gnostics*, London: Weidenfeld and Nicolson.

Clement of Alexandria, *Stromateis*, London.

Clement of Alexandria, *Miscellanies*, London.

Colson, F. H. and Whitaker, G. H. (1941) *Philo*, London.

Davidson, J. (1995) *The Gospel of Jesus*, Dorset: Element Books.

Dodd, C. H. (1953) *Interpretation of the Fourth Gospel*, Cambridge.

Dodds, E. R. (1965) *Pagan and Christian in an Age of Anxiety*, London.

Doresse, J. (1966) *The Secret Books of the Egyptian Gnostic: An Introduction to the Gnostic Coptic Manuscripts Discovered at Chernoboskion*, Vermont.

Driver, E. S. (1937) *The Mandaeans of Iran and Iraq*, Oxford.

Driver, G. R. (1965) *The Judaean Scrolls,* Oxford: Blackwell.

Duport/Sommer, A. (1969) ET G. Vermes, *The Essene Writings from Qumrân,* Oxford: Blackwell.

Erb, P. C. (1987) Boehme, Jacob, in *Encyclopedia of Religion,* ed. M. Eliade, vol. 2, New York.

Eusebius (1928) *The Ecclesiastical History,* Loeb Classical Library, London.

Farqhar, J. N. (1926, 1927) *The Apostle Thomas in North India and in South India,* London.

Filorama, G. (1990) *A History of Gnosticism,* Oxford University Press.

Foerster, W., ed. (1974) *A Selection of Gnostic Texts,* Oxford University Press.

Fowler, J. (1997) *Hinduism,* Brighton: Sussex Academic Press.

Gaster, T. H. (1957) *The Scriptures of the Dead Sea Sect,* London: Secker and Warburg.

Grant, R. M., ed. (1961) *Gnosticism: An Anthology,* Harper and Row.

Grant, R. M. (1966) *Gnosticism and Early Christianity,* New York.

Greenless, D. (1958) *The Gospel of the Gnostics,* Madras.

Greenless, D. (1958) *The Gospel of the Prophet Mani,* Madras.

Grobel, K. (1960) *The Gospel of Truth,* A&C Black.

Gruenwald, I. (1973) *Knowledge and Vision,* London.

Guirdham, A. (1977) *The Great Heresy,* Jersey.

Gwatkin, H. M. (1937) *Selections from Early Christian Writers,* Macmillan.

Hazlett, I., ed. (1995) *Early Christianity,* SPCK.

Hedrick, C. W. and Hodgson, R., eds (1986) *Nag Hammadi Gnosticism and Early Christianity,* Massachusetts.

Hoeller, S. A. (1989) *Jung and the Lost Gospels,* Illinois.

Inge, W. R. (1911) *Faith and its Psychology,* Duckwell.

Irenaeus, *Against Heresies,* Oxford.

Irenaeus, *Praefectio,* Oxford.

James, M. R. (1993) *The Apocryphal New Testament,* ed. J. K. Elliott, Oxford.

Jonas, Hans (1988) *The Gnostic Religion,* Boston.

Jung, C. G. (1916) *Psychology of the Unconscious,* London.

Jung, C. G. (1920) *Psychology of Types,* London.

Kelly, J. N. D. (1964) *The Athanasian Creed,* A&C Black.

Kelly, J. N. D. (1972) *Early Christian Creeds,* Longman.

Keynes, G., ed. (1967) *Blake's Song of Innocence and Experience,* London.

King, C. W. (1982) *The Gnostics and their Remains, Ancient and Medieval,* San Diego.

Koester, H. (1971) *The Structure of Early Christian Beliefs,* Oxford.

Krause, M., ed. (1979) *Gnosis and Gnosticism,* Leiden.

Kung, Hans (1982) *Eternal Life,* Collins.

Lawson, J. (1948) *The Biblical Theology of Saint Irenaeus,* London.

Layton, B. (1978) *The Discovery of Gnosticism,* New Haven.

Layton, B. (1987) *The Gnostic Scriptures,* SCM.

Legg, F. (1915) *Forerunners and Rivals of Christianity,* Oxford.

Ling, T. (1974) *A History of Religion: East and West*, Methuen.

Logan, A. H. B. and Wedderburn, A. M. (1983) *New Testament Gnosis*, London.

MacDermot, V. (1978) *The Books of Jeu and the United Text in the Bruce Codex*, Leiden.

Manson, T. W., ed. (1963) *A Companion to the Bible*, Edinburgh.

Matilal, B. K. (1987) *Jnáná*, in *Encyclopedia of Religion*, vol. 8, New York.

Mead, G. R. S. (1997) *Pistis Sophia: A Gnostic Miscellany*, New York.

Metzger, B. M. (1985) The Canon of the New Testament, London.

Meyer, M. (1988) *The Gospel of Thomas: The Hidden Sayings of Jesus*, San Francisco.

Morris, C. (1993) *Christian Civilization (1040–1400)*, in *Oxford Dictionary of Christianity*, Oxford.

Martyr, Justin (1956) *Apology*, in *The Early Christian Fathers*, Oxford.

Nigg, W. (ET 1990) Rad C. Watson, *The Heretics: Heresy Throughout the Ages*, New York.

Nock, A. D. (1960) *Corpus Hermeticum*, London.

Nock, A. D. (1964) *Early Gentile Christianity and its Hellenistic Background*, London.

Nock, A. D. (1972) *Gnosticism*, ed. J. S. Steward, *Essays in Religion in the Ancient World*, London.

O'Grady, J. (1985) *Heresy: Heretical Truth or Orthodox Error?* Element.

Pagels, E. (1973) *The Johannine Gospel in Gnostic Exegesis: Heracleon's Commentary on John*, New York.

Pagels, E. (1979) *The Gnostic Gospels*, London: Penguin.

Pagels, E. (1988) *Adam, Eve and the Serpent*, New York.

Pearson, B. A. (1990) *Gnosticism, Judaism and Egyptian Christianity*, London.

Perkins, P. (1980) *Gnostic Dialogue*, New York.

Petrement, S. (1970) *A Separate God: The Christian Origins of Gnosticism*, San Francisco.

Philo, *On Dreams, vols I–X* (1941), ET Colson, F. H. and Whitaker, G.H., London.

Plato, *Timaeus* (1961) *Collected Dialogues*, ed. E. Hamilton, Princetown.

Quispel, G. (1950) *The Jung Codex: A Newly Discovered Gnostic Papyrus*, Macmillan.

Quispel, G. (1974, 1975) *Gnostic Studies*, Leiden.

Quispel, G. (1987) *Gnosticism: From its Origins to the Middle Ages*, in *Encyclopedia of Religion*, ed. M. Eliade, New York.

Quispel, G. (1989) *Gnosticism in Religions of Antiquity*, ed. R. M. Seltzer, London.

Raine, K. (1979) *Blake and Antiquity*, Oxford.

Robinson, J. M., ed. (1988) *The Nag Hammadi Library in English*, Leiden.

Rocquebert (1985) *Cathar Castles*, London.

Rowley, H. H. (1944) *The Relevance of Apocalyptic*, London.

Rudolph, K. (1983) *Gnosis*, Edinburgh.

Russell, B. (1916) *Our Knowledge of the External World*, London.

Saddhatissa, H. (1988) *The Buddha's Way*, Hodder.

Schmidt, C. (1978) *The Book of Jeu and the United Text in the Bruce Codex*, Leiden.

Segal, R. A., ed. (1985) *Allure of Gnosticism: Gnostic Experience in Jungian Psychology and Contemporary Culture*, London.

Smart, N. (1993) *The World's Religions*, Cambridge.

Smith, M. S. (1996) *Gnosticism: The Path of Inner Knowledge*, London.

Sparks, H. E. D. (1985) *The Apocryphal Old Testament*, Oxford University Press.

Stead, E. C. (1969) *The Valentine Myth of Sophia*, London.

Stevenson, W. H., ed. (1971) *The Poems of William Blake*, Longman.

Tertullian, *De Anima*, in H. Bettenson (1956) *The Early Christian Fathers*, Oxford.

Tertullian, *Against Marcion*, in H. Bettenson (1956) *The Early Christian Fathers*, Oxford.

Thirering, B. (1993) *Jesus the Man*, Corgi Books.

Turner, H. E. W. (1954) *The Pattern of Christian Truth: A Study in the Relations between Orthodoxy and Heresy in the Early Church*, Oxford.

Turton, R. (1987) *Apocatastasis*, ET P.C. Dyges, in *Encyclopedia of Religion*, ed. M. Eliade, vol. 1, New York.

Unterman, A. (1996) *The Jews: Their Religious Beliefs and Practices*, Brighton: Sussex Academic Press.

Van Beeron, P. (1967) *Towards a Definition of Gnosticism*, in *The Origins of Gnosticism*, ed. U. Bianchi, Leiden.

Vermes, G. (1988) *The Dead Sea Scrolls in English*, Pelican Books.

Walker, B. (1983) *Gnosticism: Its History and Influence*, Wellingborough.

Widengren, G. (1961) *Mani and Manichaeism*, London.

Wiles, M. (1993) *Orthodoxy and Heresy in Early Christianity*, in *Oxford History of the Christian Church*, Oxford.

Williams, J. A. (1988) *Biblical Interpretation in the Gospel of Truth from Nag Hammadi*, Georgia.

Williams, M. A. (1996) *Rethinking Gnosticism*, London.

Williams, R. (1991) *The Bible in Early Christianity*, SPCK.

Wilson, R. McL. (1958) *The Gnostic Problem*, London.

Wilson, R. McL. (1968) *Gnosis and the New Testament*, Oxford.

Wilson, R. McL. (1974) *Nag Hammadi: Progress Report. Expository Times*, Edinburgh.

Wilson, R. S. (1933) *Marcion: A Study of a Second Century Heretic*, James Clarke.

Yamouchi, E. (1973) *Pre Christian Gnosticism*, SCM.

Zandee, J. (1991) *The Teachings of Silvanus*, Leiden.

Index